Dominique Jacquin-Berdal is a PhD student and Tutorial Fellow in the Department of International Relations at the London School of Economics, London.

Andrew Oros is a PhD student and Fellow of the Faculty in the Department of Political Science at Columbia University.

Marco Verweij is a researcher and PhD student in the Department of Social and Political Sciences, European University Institute, Florence.

CULTURE IN WORLD POLITICS

In association with *Millennium: Journal of International Studies*

Titles include

Hugh C. Dyer and Leon Mangasarian (*editors*)
THE STUDY OF INTERNATIONAL RELATIONS: The State of the Art

Lorraine Eden and Evan Potter (*editors*)
MULTINATIONALS IN THE GLOBAL POLITICAL ECONOMY

Rick Fawn and Jeremy Larkins (*editors*)
INTERNATIONAL SOCIETY AFTER THE COLD WAR

Dominique Jacquin-Berdal, Andrew Oros and Marco Verweij (*editors*)
CULTURE IN WORLD POLITICS

Kathleen Newland (*editor*)
THE INTERNATIONAL RELATIONS OF JAPAN

Ian H. Rowlands and Malory Greene (*editors*)
GLOBAL ENVIRONMENTAL CHANGE AND INTERNATIONAL RELATIONS

Culture in World Politics

Edited by

Dominique Jacquin-Berdal
Department of International Relations
London School of Economics and Political Science

Andrew Oros
Department of Political Science
Columbia University

and

Marco Verweij
Department of Social and Political Science
European University Institute

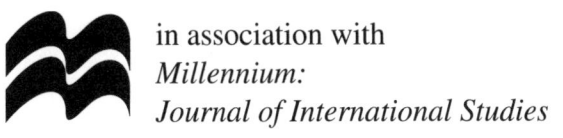 in association with
Millennium:
Journal of International Studies

First published in Great Britain 1998 by
MACMILLAN PRESS LTD
Houndmills, Basingstoke, Hampshire RG21 6XS and London
Companies and representatives throughout the world

A catalogue record for this book is available from the British Library.

ISBN 0–333–69380–9 hardcover
ISBN 0–333–69379–5 paperback

 First published in the United States of America 1998 by
ST. MARTIN'S PRESS, INC.,
Scholarly and Reference Division,
175 Fifth Avenue, New York, N.Y. 10010

ISBN 0–312–21546–0

Library of Congress Cataloging-in-Publication Data
Culture in world politics / edited by Dominique Jacquin-Berdal, Andrew Oros and Marco Verweij.
  p. cm.
Includes bibliographical references and index.
ISBN 0–312–21546–0 (cloth)
1. International relations and culture.   I. Jacquin-Berdal, Dominique.   II. Oros, Andrew.   III. Verweij, Marco.
JZ1251.C85   1998
306.2—dc21   98–17284
                                                              CIP

© *Millennium* Publishing Group 1998

All rights reserved. No reproduction, copy or transmission of this publication may be made without written permission.

No paragraph of this publication may be reproduced, copied or transmitted save with written permission or in accordance with the provisions of the Copyright, Designs and Patents Act 1988, or under the terms of any licence permitting limited copying issued by the Copyright Licensing Agency, 90 Tottenham Court Road, London W1P 9HE.

Any person who does any unauthorised act in relation to this publication may be liable to criminal prosecution and civil claims for damages.

The authors have asserted their rights to be identified as the authors of this work in accordance with the Copyright, Designs and Patents Act 1988.

This book is printed on paper suitable for recycling and made from fully managed and sustained forest sources.

10 9 8 7 6 5 4 3 2 1
07 06 05 04 03 02 01 00 99 98

Printed and bound in Great Britain by
Antony Rowe Ltd, Chippenham, Wiltshire

Contents

List of Contributors vii

1. Culture in World Politics: an Introduction 1
   Marco Verweij, Andrew Oros and Dominique Jacquin-Berdal

2. Looking Backwards at Contemporary Polities 11
   Yale Ferguson

3. Culture, Power and International Negotiations: Understanding Palau–US Status Negotiations 34
   Peter Black and Kevin Avruch

4. International Political Economy as a Culture of Competition 61
   David Blaney and Naeem Inayatullah

5. Neorealist Claims in Light of Ancient Chinese Philosophy: the Cultural Dimension of International Theory 89
   Roland Bleiker

6. Conflict Resolution across Cultures: Bridging the Gap 116
   Raymond Cohen

7. The Bounds of 'Race' in International Relations 134
   Roxanne Lynn Doty

8. The Cultural Dynamics of Ethnic Conflict 156
   Marc H. Ross

9. Cultural Aspects of Peacekeeping: Notes on the Substance of Symbols 187
   Robert A. Rubinstein

10. Towards an International Theory of State–Non-state Actors: a Grid–Group Cultural Approach 206
    Veronica Ward

Index 245

List of Contributors

Kevin Avruch is Professor in the Department of Anthropology and Sociology at George Mason University.

Peter Black is Professor in the Department of Anthropology and Sociology at George Mason University.

David Blaney is Associate Professor in the Department of Political Science at Macalaster College.

Roland Bleiker is a PhD Student in the Department of Political Science at the Australian National University.

Raymond Cohen is Associate Professor in the Department of International Relations at the Hebrew University of Jerusalem.

Roxanne Lynn Doty is Associate Professor in the Department of Poltical Science at Arizona State University.

Yale Ferguson is Professor of Political Science at Rutgers University.

Naeem Inayatullah is Assistant Professor in the Maxwell School of Citizenship and Public Affairs at Syracuse University.

Dominique Jacquin-Berdal is a PhD student and Tutorial Fellow in the Department of International Relations at the London School of Economics.

Andrew Oros is a PhD Student and Fellow of the Faculty in the Department of Political Science at Columbia University.

Marc H. Ross is William Rand Kenan, Jr., Professor in the Department of Political Science at Bryn Mawr College.

Robert A. Rubinstein is Director of the Program on the Analysis and Resolution of Conflicts in the Maxwell School of Citizenship and Public Affairs and Associate Professor of Anthropology at Syracuse University.

Marco Verweij is a Researcher in the Department of Social and Political Sciences at the European University Institute.

Veronica Ward is Associate Professor in the Department of Political Science at Utah State University.

1 Culture in World Politics: an Introduction
Marco Verweij, Andrew Oros and Dominique Jacquin-Berdal

The purpose of this book is to discuss and show the importance of applying a variety of cultural theories to the study of world politics. The general case for this can be made in at least two ways. First, it can be argued that existing theories of international relations (IR) overlook important explanations and aspects of world events by not focusing on cultural phenomena. A powerful argument along these lines is made by Yale Ferguson in chapter 2. The importance of the adoption of cultural studies within IR can also be highlighted by pointing to the proliferation of cultural analyses within other branches of the social sciences during recent decades.[1] Perhaps it has never been a wise move to exclude cultural issues from international theory. However, the argument can be built that with the increased use, variety and sophistication of cultural studies within sociology, political science and literary studies in recent times, IR's neglect of the issues of culture and identity has become even more untenable.

This argument has motivated us to collect essays that show or discuss the applicability of a different cultural approach in the study of world politics. Our volume does not aim to be an exhaustive overview of the numerous alternative cultural theories that have been developed. The growth of cultural analysis within the social sciences has been too extensive and rich for this to be possible within one volume. Rather, we want to present some of these theories and hope thereby to stimulate further adoption of these approaches as well as consideration of other cultural views.

In this chapter we outline some of the main differences among the theoretical perspectives adopted by our contributors: their concepts of culture; their views of cultural and social change; and their understandings of how international processes and cultural issues are interrelated. In the process, we attempt to relate the perspectives taken up in these essays to wider currents that have emerged in cultural analysis.[2] We conclude this introduction by reference to a number of contributions that cultural approaches can make to the understanding of world politics.

First, we must ask: What is a culture? Similarly, what are cultural concerns? These are questions we put to all the contributors to this volume. We proposed as a working definition that a culture could be conceived as any interpersonally shared system of meanings, perceptions and values. Although this definition appropriately left much room to the contributors to develop their own views of culture, it did exclude behavioural definitions of the concept.[3] We feel that cultural analysis cannot but directly address perceptions, meanings and values,[4] even if this may perhaps be methodologically awkward, as people's predispositions can often only be inferred from their behaviour and language and not directly observed.[5] In addition to the above question, we asked the contributors to address the following questions: (1) By which factors and processes are cultures formed and transformed? and (2) How do cultures influence the practice and/or theory of international relations? Below, we will use these three questions to highlight some important differences and similarities of the perspectives offered by the authors in this book, as well as outline the contributions that these perspectives have to offer to the study of IR.

WHAT IS A CULTURE? WHICH CULTURES CAN BE DISTINGUISHED?

Cultures can be distinguished at (the intersection of) several levels of analysis. Most often, it seems, systems of meanings, values and perceptions have been perceived at the national or society-wide level. Such cultural studies may, for instance, differentiate between American, Dutch and French culture. At a certain point in social theory, such national cultures were thought to be incomparably different.[6] However with the emergence of Talcott Parsons' 'general theory of action' within sociology and the rise of Gabriel Almond and Sydney Verba's 'civic culture' approach in political science, possibilities were created for systematically comparing and classifying whole societies and polities.[7] In political science, the development of sample survey techniques in the 1950s – such as those conducted by Almond to research domestic public opinion on foreign policy issues – provided a potential breakthrough for the political culture approach. Almond and Verba were the first to employ this technique cross-culturally in *The Civic Culture*, and, moreover, used these surveys not simply to gather information from the public about a current issue, but to uncover underlying beliefs. In the 1960s, following the intellectual wave of the behavioural revolution, studies moved away from macro-cultural questions focusing on entire societies and into specific aspects of political culture, particularly the issue of political participation.[8]

In this volume, the contributions by Peter Black and Kevin Avruch, Raymond Cohen and Marc Ross distinguish between cultures at the national or ethnic level. Cohen hereby bases himself partly on the classificatory scheme offered by Geert Hofstede,[9] whereas Ross has built his own classifications of ethnic communities.[10]

Cultures have also been conceived of at the sub-society level. For instance, the grid–group theory that has been developed by Mary Douglas, Michael Thompson, Aaron Wildavsky and others[11] posits that within each society four distinct and opposing ways of life exist: fatalism, individualism, hierarchy and egalitarianism. According to these authors, cultural theory will only be able to explain social change if it distinguishes between alternative systems of perceptions, meanings and values within a society. Social transformation can then be seen as the rise of one (sub)culture at the cost of other (sub)cultures. The complaint that cultural analysis is unable to account for social change has often been made.[12] In this collection of essays, Veronica Ward shows how grid–group theory can be used to clarify the relationship between state and nonstate actors in the international political economy. Another important, and not dissimilar, cultural study is the work of the French sociologist Pierre Bourdieu, whose ideas have thus far not really been taken up in the field of IR.[13]

Cultures can also be seen at the transnational or supranational level. For instance, an unending number of cultural analyses have been offered of the consequences of the worldwide spread of modern and postmodern economic and political practices, of the social impact of the development of the natural sciences, and of the global influence of religions (to name but a few transnational cultural phenomena).[14] In this volume, David Blaney and Naeem Inayatullah discuss and criticize what they view as the constitutive principles of the international political economy. Also, Roland Bleiker illuminates the cultural bias underlying neo-realist IR theory by comparing this perspective with ancient Chinese philosophy of peace and war.

Although alternative perspectives conceive systems of meanings at different units of analysis, it is important to note that cultural studies have often been at the forefront of attempts to analyse the links between the individual, society, regional and global units of analysis.[15] In some studies, for instance, the interplay is analysed between local and national or global cultures.[16] In the present volume, Rubinstein analyses how the symbols provided by an international organization, the UN peacekeeping forces, influence the perceptions of warring nations. Moreover, in other cultural studies, systems of meanings and perceptions are said to have a profound impact on the shaping of the boundaries between the individual, societal and international levels. It is often argued that different cultures have alternative conceptions of, and preferences for, the self, the proper organization of society and the state, and the international system. By trying to effectuate their conceptions and preferences, the members of a culture then contribute to the (re)shaping of the boundaries between these levels. In the present volume, Roxanne Lynn Doty looks at how the concept of 'race' can be used to differentiate between various groups of people or nations. Lastly, cultural studies have often considered the degree to which individual people are able to make up their own minds versus the degree to which their mindsets are influenced by the various cultures and social settings in which they take part.

Another major difference between alternative concepts of culture is the coherency and content of the perceived systems of meanings, perceptions and values. The coherency of a culture stands for the logical links between the meanings, values and perceptions that the members of a culture hold.[17] These links will be especially extensive when the meanings, perceptions and values that make up a culture support a certain way of organizing society and politics. For instance, in the grid–group theory of Mary Douglas it is assumed that people's policy preferences with regard to all kinds of issues as well as their perceptions of human nature, the environment, risk, etc. are all compatible with one of four ways of organizing social relations (i.e. the fatalistic, individualistic, egalitarian and hierarchical ways of life).[18] Also, in Bourdieu's perspective (roughly speaking), the views that individuals have with regard to all kinds of issues (their habitus) lead them to favour, strive for and act out certain kinds of social structures. Furthermore, in 'civic culture' studies, cultures are defined in terms of values that directly support a way of organizing social and political life.[19] Ronald Inglehart's analysis of the rise of the post-materialist values has also emphasized the reciprocal linkages among political culture, economic development and stable democracy.[20] We do not imply here that only a few differences exist between the cultural approaches offered by Douglas, Bourdieu, Inglehart and the civic culture approach. We merely want to highlight one characteristic that is common to all of these frameworks: the assumption that people's preferences, meanings and perceptions lead them to prefer, act out or strive for certain kinds of social structures. This assumption makes the cultures that are distinguished by the approaches mentioned above more coherent than the systems of meanings in other frameworks.

Cultural analyses that try to uncover the preferences for social order that may underlie certain constructions of reality, policy views, etc., have an important normative contribution to make. By showing how different kinds of social organization are privileged by certain views and perceptions, they may highlight the way in which the existing social order is sustained by (widespread) beliefs and ideas. In other words, these cultural studies may illuminate the social consequences of widespread adherence to certain beliefs, ideas and myths, and thus broaden and clarify the social and political choices that people face.[21] In this volume, David Blaney and Naeem Inayatullah argue that the present-day world economy is partly based on a culture of competition between people and between states. Realizing this, they suggest, may be a first step towards a fuller judgement of the organization of the current world economy and of alternative orders.

The meanings, perceptions and values on which other cultural theories focus are not so much related to the whole organization of domestic and international social life, but relate to the boundaries between groups of people. Such theories concentrate on the ways in which distinctions between groups of people (such as ethnic communities, nations, races, etc.) are created and effectuated. Iver B. Neumann has recently advocated the use of such approaches in the study of world politics.[22] In our volume, as indicated above, Roxanne Doty explains how the concept of 'race' can be used as a marker of group boundaries.

This by no means exhausts the possibilities for cultural analysis. For instance, many studies have taken 'identity' as a starting point. The identity of a group of people may encompass not only their preferred form of social organization and external boundaries, but also their imagined and shared history, idea of time, language, conflict resolution mechanisms, etc.[23] This is the approach adopted by Raymond Cohen, Marc Ross and Robert Rubinstein in this volume. Yet other cultural studies assume that people's meanings, perceptions and values can best be described in terms of binary principles (such as good/evil, dark/light, sane/mad, reasonable/hysterical).[24] A last example of an alternative cultural approach captures cultures in terms of narratives; this approach portrays systems of thought and perception as ironical, tragical, romantic, heroic, realistic, and so on.[25]

HOW ARE CULTURES FORMED AND TRANSFORMED?

The question of cultural change has often been seen as problematic. A number of cultural approaches stress the importance of early socialization, that is the adoption by children of the meanings, perceptions and values of the social environments in which they live. If adults have learned their predispositions early in life, how can cultural and social change then be accounted for?[26] The issue of change of perceptions, meanings and values is vitally important, not only for analytical reasons, but also because cultural change and accommodation seems often a prerequisite for the resolution of international violence.[27] There are several ways in which to account for cultural adaptation. The three contributions in this book that address international conflict resolution (by Cohen, Ross and Rubinstein) all analyse the effects of third-party mediation on warring parties with different cultural backgrounds. Each of these authors contends that such mediation will have a much higher chance of success when it attempts to accommodate or adapt the meaning systems of the antagonistic parties.[28] Other developments through which cultural change and adaptation may be caused include military and economic change (e.g. conquest, technological advances), creative intellectual efforts and perceived changes of reality that contradict expectations that are central to a certain cultural system.

HOW DO CULTURES INFLUENCE INTERNATIONAL RELATIONS (THEORY)?

This question can be reformulated as: what are the contributions that cultural approaches can make to a richer understanding of international relations? Several such contributions can be outlined. Most existing models of world politics analyse how the interests and power resources of groups of people influence the international system. Cultural approaches try to surpass these analyses, as cultural approaches not only try to demonstrate how group perceptions of interests and power shape the international system, but also seek to clarify to which groups individuals feel they belong, as well as how shared perceptions of interests and power themselves are shaped. These perspectives attempt to show that the perceptions of interests, power and group identities that international actors have are tied to their preferred way of organizing social relations, their conceptions of time and space, their systems of allocating honour and blame, their favoured way of dealing with conflicts, and so on. In doing this, cultural perspectives also stress and highlight the immense variety (both in time and in space) of the ways in which people can think and perceive. Thus, they also hope to highlight the possibilities for miscommunication between people from different cultural backgrounds, and the adverse social consequences thereof. For instance, in this volume, the articles by Black and Avruch, and Cohen address the negative social effects of cultural blindness on the part of states that are military and economically superior.

Another reason for promoting cultural approaches is that some of them are applicable to theories of international relations, and thus may be able to clarify the implicit assumptions of, and differences between, these theories. In other words, when applied to theories of world politics, cultural perspectives may enhance the 'reflexivity' of IR theorists. This may help IR specialists in more fully examining the normative and other biases that underlie their research. In this publication, Roland Bleiker provides an example of such reflexivity.

To conclude, cultures influence world politics in numerous ways. Cultures partly constitute the international system: they make up people's ethnic, national and political identities. Also, often ingrained within different cultures are alternative visions of how the world system should be regulated. Within the international system, the goals that actors seek to achieve, as well as the means with which they try to do so, are informed by the cultures to which these actors belong. Therefore, we believe that a full understanding of world politics would not only include the effects of institutional structures and power configurations, but would also incorporate a focus on cultural issues. Since the end of the Second World War, the field of IR has largely ignored culture.[29] We have organized the present volume in an attempt to help to redress this imbalance.

ACKNOWLEDGEMENT

We are grateful to Klaus Eder, Iver B. Neumann and James Walsh for their helpful comments on an earlier version of this introduction.

NOTES

1. An overview of the emergence of a variety of cultural analyses within sociology is Robert Wuthnow and Marsha Witten, 'New Directions in

the Study of Culture', *Annual Review of Sociology* (Vol. 14, 1988), pp. 49–67. An introduction to this field of study is Wendy Griswold, *Culture and Societies in a Changing World* (Thousand Oaks, CA: Pine Forge Press, 1994).

2. We will focus mainly on cultural studies that have been undertaken in sociology and political science, and less on cultural analyses that have been undertaken by anthropologists. For a discussion of the use of anthropological concepts and methods within IR, see Thomas Hylland Eriksen and Iver B. Neumann, 'International Relations as a Cultural System: an Agenda for Research', *Cooperation and Conflict* (Vol. 28, No. 3, 1993), pp. 233–64.

3. For instance, Robert Wuthnow, James Davidson Hunter, Albert Bergesen and Edith Kurzweil advocate the understanding of culture as 'the symbolic-expressive dimension of behavior in their *Cultural Analysis: The Work of Peter L. Berger, Mary Douglas, Jürgen Habermas and Michel Foucault* (London: Routledge and Kegan Paul, 1984), p. 255. Wuthnow elaborates this definition further in his book *Meaning and Moral Order: Explorations in Cultural Analysis* (Berkeley, CA: University of California Press, 1987).

4. Anton Zijderveld, *De Culturele Factor* (Culemborg, The Netherlands: Lemma, 1988), chapter 1; Wendy Griswold, 'A Methodological Framework for the Sociology of Culture', *Sociological Methodology* (Vol. 17, 1987), pp. 3–4.

5. Gary King, Robert O. Keohane and Sydney Verba have emphasized the methodological difficulties of using concepts that are often not directly observable (such as meanings and perceptions) in causal reasoning. See their *Designing Social Inquiry: Scientific Inference in Qualitative Research* (Princeton, NJ: Princeton University Press, 1994), pp. 109–112 and 191–3. Albert Yee, however, has highlighted the importance of focusing on intersubjective meanings and discursive practices in empirical studies by problematizing the concept of 'causality' that is used by King, Keohane and Verba (and many others). According to Yee, a causal explanation of an action is methodologically incomplete without a specification of the intentions (and therefore understandings and meanings) of the actor(s). See Albert S. Yee, 'The Causal Effects of Ideas on Policies', *International Organization* (Vol. 50, No. 1, 1996), pp. 69–108.

6. As exemplified by Ruth Benedict, *The Chrysanthemum and the Sword: Patterns of Japanese Culture* (Boston, MA: Houghton Mifflin, 1946); and Margaret Mead, *And Keep Your Powder Dry: an Anthropologist Looks at America* (New York: Morrow, 1942).

7. See especially Talcott Parsons and Edward A. Shils (eds), *Toward a General Theory of Action: Theoretical Foundations for the Social Sciences* (Cambridge, MA: Harvard University Press, 1951); and Gabriel Almond and Sydney Verba, *The Civic Culture: Political Attitudes and Democracy in Five Nations* (Princeton, NJ: Princeton University Press, 1963).

8. The best example of such a study is Sydney Verba, Norman H. Nie and Jae-on Kim, *Participation and Political Equality: a Seven Nation Comparison* (Cambridge: Cambridge University Press, 1978).

9. See Geert Hofstede, *Culture's Consequences: International Differences in Work-Related Values* (London: Sage, 1984).
10. See Marc H. Ross, *The Culture of Conflict: Interests, Interpretations and Disputing in Comparative Perspective* (New Haven: Yale University Press, 1993). To be accurate, it must be noted that although Ross has thus far mainly analysed cultures of ethnic groups that make up a whole society, he has also maintained that within present-day industrial societies, multiple ethnic groups and cultures interact. See in particular the last chapter of his book.
11. For further reference, see Mary Douglas and Aaron Wildavsky, *Risk and Culture: an Essay on the Selection of Technological and Environmental Dangers* (Berkeley, CA: University of California Press, 1982); Michael Thompson, Richard Ellis and Aaron Wildavsky, *Cultural Theory* (Boulder, CO: Westview Press, 1990).
12. Harry Eckstein has also tried to answer this criticism in his essay 'A Cultural Theory of Political Change', *American Political Science Review* (Vol. 82, No. 3, 1988), pp. 789–804. See also his subsequent 'controversy' with Herbert Werlin over the degree to which he has been able to answer this criticism: 'Political Culture and Political Change', *American Political Science Review* (Vol. 84, No. 1, 1990), pp. 249–59.
13. Key works by Bourdieu are: *La Distinction: Critique Sociale du Jugement* (Paris: Editions de Minuit, 1979); and *Le Sens Pratique* (Paris: Editions de Minuit, 1980).
14. For applications of such studies within the study of IR, see Martha Finnemore, 'Norms, Culture and World Politics: Insights from Sociology's Institutionalism', *International Organization* (Vol. 50, No. 2, 1996), pp. 325–47; John Meyers *et al.*, 'A World Environmental Regime, 1870–1990', *International Organization* (Vol. 51, No. 4, 1997), pp. 623–52.
15. A similar point is made in R.B.J. Walker, 'The Concept of Culture in the Theory of International Relations', in Jonsuk Chay (ed.), *Culture and International Relations* (New York: Praeger, 1990). pp. 3–17.
16. Roland Robertson, *Globalization: Social Theory and Global Culture* (London: Sage, 1992); Hugh C. Dyer, 'EcoCultures: Globalisation in the Age of Ecology', *Millennium* (Vol. 22, No. 3, 1993), pp. 483–504.
17. Neil J. Smelser, 'Culture: Coherent or Incoherent', in Richard Munch and Neil J. Smelser (eds), *Theory of Culture* (Berkeley, CA: University of California Press, 1992), pp. 3–28.
18. For an elaboration of this, see Marco Verweij, 'Cultural Theory and the Study of International Relations', *Millennium* (Vol. 24, No. 1, 1995), pp. 87–111.
19. The *locus classicus* of this research tradition is Gabriel Almond and Sidney Verba, *op. cit.*, in note 7. An outstanding recent contribution to this research tradition is Robert D. Putnam, with Roberto Leonardi and Raffaella Y. Nanetti, *Making Democracy Work: Civic Traditions in Modern Italy* (Princeton, NJ: Princeton University Press, 1993). A forceful attack on this research tradition is Margaret R. Somers, 'What's Political or Cultural about Political Culture and the Public Sphere? Toward an Historical Sociology of Concept Formation', *Sociological Theory* (Vol. 13, No. 2, 1995), pp. 113–44. Other criticisms are

contained in Gabriel Almond and Sydney Verba (eds), *The Civic Culture Revisited* (London: Sage, 1989).
20. Ronald Inglehart, 'The Renaissance of Political Culture', *American Political Science Review* (Vol. 82, No. 4, 1988), pp. 1203–30; *Culture Shift in Advanced Industrial Society* (Princeton, NJ: Princeton University Press, 1990).
21. This is why Bourdieu insists that competent sociology always works emancipatory. See the excellent introduction to his work, Pierre Bourdieu and Loïc J.D. Wacquant, *An Invitation to Reflexive Sociology* (Cambridge: Polity Press, 1992), pp. 194–5.
22. Iver B. Neumann, 'Collective Identity Formation: Self and Other in International Relations', *European Journal of International Relations* (Vol. 2, No. 1, 1996), pp. 139–74.
23. An influential example is Benedict Anderson, *Imagined Communities: Reflections on the Origin and Spread of Nationalism* (London: Verso, 1991).
24. See Jeffrey C. Alexander, 'The Discourse of American Civil Society: A New Proposal for Cultural Studies', *Theory and Society* (Vol. 22, 1993), pp. 151–207.
25. In 'Modern, Anti, Post and Neo: How Social Theories Have Tried to Understand the "New World" of Our Time', *Zeitschrift für Soziologie* (Vol. 23, No. 3, 1994), pp. 165–97; Jeffrey C. Alexander combines this approach with the analysis advocated in his other essay, *op. cit.*, in note 24. For an application of this approach in the field of international relations, see Isabelle Grunberg, 'Exploring the "Myth" of Hegemomic Stability Theory', *International Organization* (Vol. 44, No. 4, 1990), pp. 431–77.
26. Harry Eckstein, *op. cit.*, in note 12.
27. For this reason Beate Jahn has advocated a dynamic conception of culture, see her essay 'Globale Kulturkämpfe oder Einheitliche Weltkultur: Zur Relevanz von Kultur in den Internationale Beziehungen', *Zeitschrift für Internationale Beziehungen* (Vol. 2, No. 1, 1995), pp. 213–36.
28. Samuel Huntington has offered a bleak view of the possibilities for such cultural accommodation: 'The Clash of Civilizations', *Foreign Affairs* (Vol. 72, No. 3, 1993), pp. 27–49. A more optimistic view is offered in Richard Shapcott, 'Conversation and Coexistence: Gadamer and the Interpretation of International Society', *Millennium* (Vol. 23, No. 1, 1994), pp. 57–83.
29. Although the tide may now be turning. See: Friedrich Kratochwil and Yosef Lapid (eds), *The Return of Culture and Identity in IR Theory* (Boulder, CO: Lynn Riener, 1995); Thomas Biersteker and Cynthia Weber (eds), *State Sovereignty as Social Construct* (Cambridge: Cambridge University Press, 1998); and Peter Katzenstein (ed.), *The Culture of National Security* (New York: Columbia University Press, 1996).

2 Looking Backwards at Contemporary Polities
Yale Ferguson

In T.H. White's *The Once and Future King*, Merlin turns the young Arthur into a bird so that he can take to the skies and gain a more accurate vision of the world below.[1] A key lesson was the relative insignificance of boundaries seen from above:

> [Arthur] saw the problem as plain as a map.... Frontiers were imaginary lines. The imaginary lines on the earth's surface only needed to be unimagined. The airborne birds skipped them by nature. How mad the frontiers ... seemed ... and would to Man if he could fly.[2]

Merlin's objective was to plant in Arthur's mind the vision of a universalistic regime based on 'right' principles emanating from the Round Table in Camelot. The Camelot experiment seemed to prosper for a while but, like all universalistic ambitions, eventually foundered on the shoals of inevitable human divisions. 'Mad' as they might be, 'unimagined' or not, 'lines' of one sort or another kept reappearing.

Surely, the young Arthur could not help but have observed in his flight that some lines were not imaginary at all, but rather are quite visible and substantial. Hedgerows demarcated fields; moats and walls protected castles; and some towns, too, were walled. Indeed, an older and wiser King Arthur sadly acknowledged that even imaginary lines might prove to be formidable and dangerous. He observed: 'There was no visible line between Scotland and England, although Flodden and Bannockburn had been fought about it. It was geography which was the cause – political geography. It was nothing else.' Political divisions were inevitable and regularly overlapped. The key to peace, therefore, was finding the proper relationship between and among overlapping identities and polities:

> Nations did not need to have the same kind of civilization, nor the same kind of leader ... They could keep their own civilizations, like Esquimaux and Hottentots, if they would give each other freedom of trade and free passage and access to the world. Countries would have to become counties – but counties which could keep their own culture and local laws.[3]

Idealistic? Only in its goal of completely eliminating conflict and violence. Arthur's vision is actually quite close to those arrangements prevailing, not only under some of the more successful ancient and modern empires, but also at numerous levels by all sorts of political entities since time immemorial. Fuzzy in terms of the authoritative domains of particular units? To be sure, and therein precisely lies the vision's past and present relevance and utility. Fuzziness is a vital characteristic of politics as it has always been practised and continues to be practised everywhere in the late twentieth century. As Richard W. Mansbach and I have argued in a series of recent works,[4] actual control or effective influence over the allocation of values has always been divided and has regularly overlapped as well. Different polities have shared some of the same political space, often at least part of the same territory but also persons, loyalties and resources in the context of particular issues.

THE DISTORTED VISION AFFLICTING CONTEMPORARY INTERNATIONAL THEORY

Arthur's vision offers a much less distorted picture of the complex relationships that normally prevail in political life than the blinkered views of contemporary self-styled Realists and Neorealists. Soaring aloft from the countryside in modern Britain, they would entirely miss the hedgerows, local authorities, variations in legal systems between England and Scotland, and cultural differences among English, Scots, Welsh, Irish – not to mention the religious and class distinctions that have fuelled violence in Northern Ireland. Most Realists and Neorealists see the world simplistically as one of state boxes, into which are neatly gathered and managed practically everything that is significant politically. They are the true idealist scholars and macho-romantic 'statesmen' (the word itself is revealing), who revel in the perennial struggle for power among discrete units in a supposedly anarchic political universe. Neorealists would only add into consideration the 'structure' of the 'international system', conceived narrowly as the balance of power or distribution of capabilities among states. The mote in the eyes of both Realists and Neorealists is the state.

Different though they are from Realists and Neorealists and from one another in many respects, the same fatal eye disease even infects self-styled Institutionalists and Constructivists. A recent exchange between prominent proponents of the various schools in *International Security*[5] is helpful in clarifying this point.

Robert O. Keohane and Lisa L. Martin write:

> [L]iberal institutionalists treat states as rational egoists operating in a world in which agreements cannot be hierarchically enforced [and] only expect interstate cooperation to occur if states have significant common interests. Like realism, institutionalist theory is utilitarian and rationalistic.... [I]nternational institutions are created in response to state interests, and ... their character is structured by the prevailing distribution of capabilities.

States create institutions because they expect that they will affect behaviour; and institutions therefore do 'matter'. States create them with that purpose in mind and may become sufficiently convinced of their utility to extend their functions over time.[6]

Alexander Wendt maintains that 'constructivists' like himself share with various 'critical' theorists 'two basic claims: that the fundamental structures of international politics are social rather than strictly material ... and that these structures shape actors' identities and interests, rather than just their behaviour...'[7] By contrast to Neorealists who emphasize 'the distribution of material capabilities', Constructivists argue: '[S]ocial structures exist, not in actors' heads nor in material capabilities, but in practices. Social structure exists only in process. The Cold War was a structure of shared knowledge[8] that governed great power relations over forty years, but once they stopped acting on this basis, it was "over".' Significantly, however, Wendt also declares:

> I share all five of [John J.] Mearsheimer's 'realist' assumptions ... that international politics is anarchic, and that states have offensive capabilities, cannot be 100 percent certain about others' intentions, wish to survive, and are rational. We share two more: a commitment to states as units of analysis, and to the importance of systemic, or 'third image' theorizing.[9]

Much of the actual debate between Mearsheimer, Keohane/Martin, Wendt and others concerns the extent to which their respective claims are empirically verifiable. Keohane/Martin and Wendt declare themselves unequivocally to be proponents of 'science'. Keohane/Martin: 'The point of a new theory is to generate testable hypotheses: liberal institutionalism, like any other theory, has value insofar as it generates propositions that can be tested against real evidence.'[10]

Wendt: 'Constructivists... are modernists who fully endorse the scientific project of falsifying theories against evidence.'[11] All insist that their approaches are bearing substantial empirical fruit, while admitting some limitations. Keohane/Martin: 'The real empirical issue is how to distinguish the effects of underlying conditions from those of the institutions themselves.... Rarely, if ever, will institutions vary while the 'rest of the world' is held constant. Thus finding the ideal quasi-experimental station to test the impact of institutions is not possible.'[12] Wendt: 'All observation is theory-*laden* in the sense that what we see is mediated by our existing theories, and to that extent knowledge is inherently problematic.' However, neither 'observation' nor 'reality' is 'theory-*determined*': 'The world is still out there constraining our beliefs, and may punish us for incorrect ones.... We do not have unmediated access to the world, but this does not preclude understanding how it works.'[13]

Agreed! Nevertheless, especially insofar as all observation is, indeed, theory-laden, it behoves us to start our quest for understanding of the world 'out there' with the best theory we can generate – and Institutionalism and Constructivism are only slight improvements over Realism and Neorealism in that regard. All these theories boast of their present contributions and empirical research promise; however, at one level, they tell us very little that the proverbial person on the street would find especially interesting or surprising. Mearsheimer comments on the 'academic flavour' of some of these debates,[14] and he is absolutely correct. There is no world government; we do have sovereign states; policy-makers attempt to formulate conceptions of interests and often do not act altruistically; the way material capabilities is distributed in the world has considerable effect; structures of knowledge, including rules, also have an impact; institutions are founded for a purpose and are not unimportant; and so on. One is tempted to shout: 'Of course! Now please tell us something we do not already know.'

In other respects, unfortunately, all these theories are pernicious because much of what they have to suggest is plainly false or seriously misleading, and also because they do not begin to address much that we need to know. To be sure, 'states' exist and (like other institutions) 'matter' to a degree. However, an exaggerated focus on states fails to give adequate attention to 'governance' by numerous other authorities and their relationship to a wide range of human identities and loyalties. There are various sources of this statist 'blind spot', and it is worthwhile examining a few of the main ones:

Eurocentricity and Ahistoricism

History for most statists began with Westphalia, with a possible gesture of acknowledgement (for pedigree) back to Thucydides. Multicultural they are most decidedly not. The term 'the state' has a continental European ring, and today is not widely used by many live persons apart from social scientists and surviving Marxists. We should pause to consider what different connotations the word would hold for a Texan, a Bosnian, a Sikh, a Colombian, a Sendero Luminoso (Shining Path) rebel, a Chechen, a Buddhist monk, an Islamic fundamentalist, a Haitian, a Kurd, and so on. Pre-Westphalia, the state is an even more dubious concept. Poor Thucydides keeps getting quoted, but his was a political universe of empire (Athens), hegemonial alliance (Sparta) and cities – not a 'state' in sight. We use the term 'city-state' just to make things more comprehensible to our concept-impoverished contemporaries.

Legalistic Bias

Statist theorists have traditionally placed much too much stress on law and 'rules' as defining and legitimating political 'authority'. International law says we have a world of sovereign states, *ergo*, sovereignty is an actual condition and states continue to be the primary actors in global politics. International lawyers might be forgiven for being legalistic in this regard, and some have been; although others have been far more ready than many political scientists to credit the important role of international institutions and norms affecting matters from human rights to fishing.

Constructivists have been a particular disappointment. Some like Wendt started out by inquiring into the relationship between 'agents' and 'structures',[15] which should have been healthily subversive, opening up consideration of many polities and domains. Unfortunately, the answer has too often been cast in familiar – and tautological – terms: states are the main actors in global society, and their practices create the social structures that influence themselves. This line of reasoning is neatly summed up in the title of one of Wendt's articles, 'Anarchy is What States Make of it: The Social Construction of Power Politics'.[16] To the contrary, as I later observe, states are not unitary and rational agents, and definitely are not the only agents; moreover, describing the world as 'anarchic' fails to reflect, not only the cooperative choices of states (as Wendt implies), but also the routine 'governance' exercised within their respective domains by numerous other polities.

Constructivists seem bound by their own emphasis on rules to continue to insist upon the primacy of the state. Rules are inevitably associated with the status quo but cannot necessarily sustain it. Rules like sovereignty are cold comfort to states when their effective control and influence is being steadily drained away, and institutions and ideas in the real world move on. Not surprisingly, there is often a serious lag between the time that changes in material conditions occur and ideology and (last of all) law catch up. Thus, Grotius and others described the rules of a European system of sovereign states that had already substantially appeared, and that mind-set persists to some degree in our own time, although the world of Westphalia is now as dead as (or, I should say, no more alive than) that of the ancient Greeks. Indeed, the ancient world offers a better guide for deciphering contemporary global politics than the 'Westphalian moment' and, as I shall argue, the uniqueness of the Westphalian transformation, too, has been exaggerated.

Underestimation of the Importance of 'Nonstate Actors'

For many theorists, nonstate actors exist only at the margin. International organizations or 'regimes' are fundamentally created and controlled by their member states; or, at most, may influence the perceptions of member states and bargain with them in the top half of a two-level game. 'Domestic' interest groups come into play only insofar as they influence governments in the bottom half of the two-level game. 'Outlaws' like terrorist organizations or 'tribes' are noteworthy only because they are responsible for occasional outbreaks of violence. Business firms, religious denominations and other civil society actors hardly count at all. The vast 'private sector' exists because the governments of capitalist states allow it to exist and is largely irrelevant for students of IR, except perhaps for those focusing on issues of international political economy. As the increasing popularity of that subfield suggests, traditional theorists might concede, there are some interesting subcurrents in today's world; but, not to worry, it remains and will continue to be overwhelmingly state-centric.

Bloated Estimates of the Extent of State Resources and Control

Weber warped everybody's thinking by stressing the state's presumed monopoly of the legitimate exercise of violence. Should the main issues in this respect not be, rather: (a) how much violence perpetrated by governments is effective, whether or not it is widely regarded as a legitimate or an illegitimate exercise? and (b) How much outlaw violence occurs and is effectively suppressed? Violence exercised by the USSR's KGB or various Latin American dictatorships was regarded by many, perhaps most, citizens in those societies as illegitimate, yet it was usually extremely effective. By contrast, many governments of states around the world, with varying degrees of popular legitimacy, have to deal with almost continual civil unrest or violence in some significant quarters. We have to ponder the implications of the fact that for innumerable persons across the globe, warlords, revolutionary bands, terrorists, drug dealers, Mafia-style criminal organizations, street gangs or even individual violent acts are far more legitimate than governments. Any talk, therefore, of a state monopoly on the legitimate exercise of violence is nonsense.

Much the same sort of legerdemain occurs in discussions of the resources presumed to be at the ready disposal of the state. Once again, the Eurocentric bias of many IR theorists is all too evident. They learned their European history about the growth of the state (i.e. king) in the early modern period in successful competition with the varied elements of segmentary society that had predominated during the Middle Ages. Kings had an army, a large and secure tax base, and an ideological foundation. Divine right monarchy evolved into secular sovereignty with the rise of national identity. The state became ever more secure with greater democracy and popular participation, or when buttressed by totalitarian ideologies like National Socialism or Marxism.

All largely correct as far as it goes – which isn't nearly far enough. The problems with this line of reasoning are two. First, we need to ask ourselves, seriously, how many governments of states around the world today actually do have a large and secure tax base, a national army that is both effective and trustworthy, and an ideology that inspires citizens' loyalty? In fact, many, if not most, governments are gravely deficient in one, more or all these respects.

A second and more profound problem is that the argument conveniently overlooks the so-called private sector, or what others prefer to label civil society. Governments have no more monopoly of 'governance' than they do of violence or legitimacy. Other entities have enormous resources that make those available to most governments seem paltry by comparison. It is often observed, but nonetheless significant, that many of the largest corporations have annual profits much greater than the GDP of many countries. And while we are counting, how many governments of the world have a full grasp of what is happening in their own national economy, who is producing what, what taxes are owed – let alone the capacity to collect them and keep the national treasury from being deposited by corrupt officials in foreign banks? For example, in the cradle of the state, Italy, most of private sector – the most dynamic part, composed mainly of small enterprises – is largely undocumented and virtually untaxed, with the result that it is almost impossible accurately to rank the productivity of leading European economies.

Financial institutions and individual investors themselves have influence greatly exceeding that of governments and central banks, even when they (rarely) manage to act in concert. As a consequence, one major national currency after another has fallen victim to speculators' sporadic feeding frenzies. Central banks typically have a remarkable degree of autonomy and jealously guard their independence from politicians; yet a central bank's manipulation of national interest rates, so often in the past a major tool of state economic policy, is now a literal drop in the bucket of transnational flows occasioned by inter-firm trade, private investment and computerized currency speculation. The planet has become a cyberspace marketplace in which governments are doing little more than counting sheep. They are held accountable by their citizens for numerous matters they do not remotely understand and therefore cannot even gather adequate data about, let alone design effective policies to control. All of this, of course, assumes that one can meaningfully speak of 'their' in any context referring to 'governments', which brings us to still another point.

Reification of the State

In only one limited sense can the state be considered a unified actor, and it is never an independent one. If an analyst wishes arbitrarily to confine the study of international relations to the interplay of official government policies in the global arena, then the state may be seen as a unified actor in that narrow context. At the moment of output, from the vantage point of its state peers, one may perhaps usefully speak of France's policy regarding nuclear testing, Japan's position on tuna fishing, China's statement on a new electoral law in Hong Kong, and so on. Still, one needs to be exceedingly cautious, for what a 'state's' policy actually is often very much depends on which official or government agency is explaining or implementing that policy. In any event, such a reified state perspective will be of little utility if our objective is to explain where policies come from in the first instance or how likely they are to change. The most hidebound IR scholars regard these sorts of things as being out of their purview, in the province of foreign policy analysts, but we have little choice but to explore them. Confining international relations to pronouncements emanating from various quarters in government is only a little less sterile than looking to international law for an understanding of what is really happening in world affairs.

A closer look inside the black boxes of even those states that have reasonably stable and highly institutionalized governments reveals that they are anything but unified actors. The less unified states are in their decision-making, the further away we get from any but the most rarefied academic definitions of 'rational' behaviour. Where is the 'mind' at work in the victory of one bureaucracy or political faction over another? As writers on bureaucratic politics have long reminded us, what 'the national interest' is often depends on where one sits in the executive bureaucracy or national legislature. In the United States, building consensus within the executive branch proves a major task before nearly every important foreign policy initiative. That consensus tends to unravel almost as soon as a policy is announced and implemented. It is, of course, virtually certain that a Republican-controlled Congress will seek to distance its own position from a Democratic President's whenever it can – not that there is any consensus within the Republican (or Democratic) Party either. Cabinet governments like that in the United Kingdom desperately seek to maintain a façade of unity, but any reader of the British press knows that on key matters like Europe, there are profound arguments going on, not only between the various parties but also within them. Yet London is calm compared with Moscow, where a debilitated President Yeltsin must deal with a national legislature whose fractiousness makes the US Congress seem tame by comparison. And so on.

Much of the internal pulling and hauling that almost always characterizes the policy-making process, and from time to time brings it to a virtual impasse, derives not from particular personalities or bureaucratic turf battles, *per se*, but from the fact that the perceived interests of those whom they represent diverge. The state is not an autonomous actor any more than it is a unified one and, indeed, is not unified partly because it is not autonomous. Statist theorists like to suggest that the state is strong precisely because its various divisions represent and reflect the genuine divisions in civil society. Government supposedly remains strong because everyone recognizes that formulating 'the public interest' and implementing policy for the good of society as a whole is a necessary function. A less idealistic view, however, is that most of what government is doing is protecting its own interests as an institution or making policy for the selfish benefit of powerful interests in society at large, those who have the most financial clout, friends in high places or capacity to deliver votes at the ballot box.

We are back to the public/private sector division criticized earlier. Students of international relations need to be aware not only of the important autonomous activities of private sector actors, but also the considerable extent to which the state itself is merely an extension of civil society. At one level, for example, US military spending reflects government revenues and relatively objective bureaucratic assessments of the military forces required to support US foreign policy objectives in the post-Cold War world. However, one would have to be naive not to recognize that the military establishment is also fighting to preserve itself from too rapid a dismantling, that those industries servicing the military have stepped up their lobbying, that local communities with military bases are seeking to keep them open, and that politicians in Washington are keenly aware that voters demand a reduction in federal taxes or the deficit (preferably both). Likewise, US policy regarding Chinese violations of human rights reflects contradictory pressures from human rights groups and businesses seeking to take advantage of expanding markets. In modern Japan so close has been the relationship between government and business that the label Japan Inc. has seemed highly appropriate, at least until the recent scandals that exposed widespread links to organized crime. Whose interests does the government of Colombia serve? or Sadam Hussein's regime?

A Misleading and Increasingly Untenable Distinction between Inside/ Outside the Legal Boundaries of the State

As has been noted, IR theorists tend to be ahistorical and this even includes a failure to draw the appropriate lessons from the processes through which territorial boundaries emerged with the Westphalian state in Europe.

As Peter Sahlins explains, the process was gradual and not entirely unidirectional. He observes that linear boundaries were not unknown to the Greeks and Romans and that many feudal jurisdictions were also territorially well defined. In the eleventh and twelfth centuries kingdoms were essentially feudal fiefdoms, and not until the later thirteenth century did 'a new insistence on royal territory give to the boundary a political, fiscal, and military significance different from its internal limits'. Yet the French monarchy, which is usually regarded as the model, 'continued to envision its sovereignty in terms of its jurisdiction over subjects, not over a delimited territory, relying on inherited notions of "jurisdiction" and "dependency" instead of basing its administration on firmly delineated territorial circumscriptions'. Thus the Pyrenees boundary between France and Spain was not laid out by means of boundary stones until 1868. The French state made its presence felt in the selfsame area only later, during the Third Republic (1870–1914), when it created 'the road and railway networks, policies of compulsory primary education, and the universal military conscription by which peasants became French'. Sahlins demonstrates that French identity formed on the periphery actually earlier than it did in the centre, because the cultural distinction between French and Spanish was more obvious on the frontier. The emergence of sovereign territory at the level of France 'was matched and shaped by the territorialization of the village communities', and local identity and perceived interests persisted.[17]

Like the supposed French 'model' state, other icons in the statist temple have non-state implications that are often ignored. The Peace of Westphalia explicitly sought to defuse the religious controversies that had triggered communal strife *within* as well as *among* polities during the Thirty Years' War. The Concert of Europe was established in 1815 in part to suppress the sort of *domestic* revolutionary activity that statesmen believed to have been responsible for the wars that had ravaged Europe for more than two decades. The 1919 Versailles Treaty attempted to establish the rights of national minorities *within* the countries of Central Europe, even as Wilsonian ideology equated democracy at home with international peace. In more recent years, the United Nations has grown bolder in ignoring its Charter prohibition against intervention in the 'domestic jurisdiction of any state', when a particular situation is deemed to be a threat to 'international peace and security'.

Boundaries still have some meaning. The response of most governments to Sadam Hussein's invasion of Kuwait reaffirms that state boundaries do matter when someone marshals an army and marches across them in the stance of a naked aggressor. Moreover, most states do have some control over the movement of persons and goods across their boundaries. However, boundaries are being rearranged from the inside today in many parts of the world and the extent of control exercised by states over transnationalism is often not nearly as much as they would like.

In the long stretch of human history, change has been endemic, and one can thus argue about how unprecedented present conditions are. Be that as it may, change in the world at many levels has appeared to be speeding up over the past few decades, and we are experiencing more and more of what James M. Rosenau terms general 'turbulence' and 'fragmegration'.[18] The world has obviously gained in other ways from the end of the Cold War, but we have lost whatever stability emanated from the two blocs. Information and transaction flows generated by worldwide revolutions in technology and communications ignore state boundaries. Although ill-defined and unlikely to be realized to any great degree in very many places, 'democracy' and 'free markets' have become global ideological watchwords. From Japan to Russia to Europe and the Western Hemisphere, escalating citizen demands overwhelm the capacity of governments – hampered by traditional political culture and institutions, bureaucratic intransigence and legislative gridlock – to react. 'Foreign' and 'domestic' policies overlap one another with greater frequency and complexity. Markets have shifted from an emphasis on national capitalism to alliances between and among firms, which appear to be light years ahead of most governments in thinking globally.

International organizations, less formal regimes and NGOs are taking on more and more vital functions that were formerly in the domain of states. Institutionalists would have us preserve the fiction of sovereignty by envisaging regimes as mere institutional creations of state interests, but how much choice do states actually have: how inevitably and irrevocably is their authority being drained away? Regimes and NGOs can impose a measure of order over turbulence in the larger world that states cannot adequately affect through other means. Not for nothing has the number of lobbyists in Brussels doubled since 1990, now some 10,000, representing no less than 3000 separate groups. Civil society, too, is increasingly organizing itself transnationally.

One of the trends in the contemporary world (that has actually been going on since time immemorial) is the creation of larger and larger units – e.g. firms, regimes, NGOs – even while we have increasing political fragmentation. The two trends are going on simultaneously and are related. For example, the very existence of larger entities like the European Union, NAFTA and globalized business and finance – as well as some older organizations like the UN and NATO – seems to make smallness a more viable alternative for breakaway mini-nationalisms like the Croatians or Estonians, or separatist Québecois. They think they may have new affiliations to fill some of the gaps left by the ties they chose to sever. Preserving and enhancing one's small group may provide a last refuge for the familiar in the midst of global change. Yet small is often vulnerable, and a radical decline in living standards – not to mention death at the hands of ethnic cleansers – may well be too high a price to pay for reaffirming small group identity.

Neglect of Other Identities than the State

From the R/N perspective the state is the highest and noblest identity of all. Unfortunately for state enthusiasts and maybe fortunately for the rest of us, this notion appears to be getting harder than ever to sell to ordinary citizens.

The state is only one of many group symbols with which persons identify, and it is a profound error to overestimate the extent to which loyalty to the state, anywhere, always or often comes first (or much farther down the list). All of us humans have multiple identities and loyalties, most of which coexist without serious conflict most of the time, but which under certain conditions can be the source of cross-cutting pressures or prove entirely irreconcilable. Loyalties to self and such extensions of self as family, clan, village, city, ethnicity, religion, profession, firm, political party, faction or ideology regularly undermine the political stability of states and everywhere limit support for government policies.

An essential puzzle is not whether individuals have many identities – of course they do – but why some identities and loyalties come to the fore at certain times and not others. Why were most Yugoslavians reasonably content to be Yugoslavians one year, and the next year were violently divided into Serbs, Bosnians, Croatians, Slovenes and so on? Elsewhere, why were Ukrainians reasonably content one year to be part of the Soviet empire, the next in open revolt, and another year electing a leader pledged to closer ties with Russia? It appears that multiple identities and loyalties can coexist for long stretches of time, but then situations or issues arise that force individuals and groups to make invidious choices. The political change that results from such choices is continuous, although in some periods it proceeds so slowly that it is almost imperceptible.

CULTURE, IDENTITIES AND POLITIES

History is increasingly difficult for anyone to ignore. Opposite to Fukuyama's controversial assertion a few years ago,[19] history has not 'ended' in the present post-Cold War period; rather, historical memories – hatreds as well as age-old affinities (like the Russians' for 'Slavs') – are being resurrected and reconstructed around the world, often with explosive consequences. Historical memories relevant to places like the former Yugoslavia are many centuries, even millennia, old. Serbs have been at war with Moslems much longer than they have been at peace, and the very name of Macedonia (unfortunately for its present non-Greek inhabitants) still connotes the homeland and glorious conquests of Philip and Alexander.

It is important to think carefully about the terms we use, because they convey our images of the world – or, more often, betray the fact that we are struggling to describe something important that is only vaguely understood. 'Multiculturalism', which is currently so fashionable and controversial, is just such a word. In the United States, multiculturalism and its connections with such things as bilingual education, for some, implies a threat to national unity, while proponents suggest that acceptance of a multicultural 'mosaic' actually offers the best means of preserving national unity in the midst of growing diversity. Use of the term multiculturalism seems to presuppose that we know what we mean by 'culture', and that is uncertain as well. Aren't most of the so-called cultures that we can identify already amalgams of sorts? Similar conceptual problems beset Huntington's recent thesis that the future of world politics will be a 'clash of civilizations'.[20] His critics[21] took him to task on various points, not least pointing out that virtually any 'civilization' we might name has serious internal faultlines. For instance, can we ignore the perennial conflict between secular and religious authorities in Islam, different branches of the Islamic faith (e.g. Sunni, Shi'ite), and residual family/clan/tribal identities?

Huntington replied to his critics by asking, 'If Not Civilizations, What?'[22] What, indeed? How are cultures and civilizations related, and what do they, in turn, have to do with other familiar concepts like race, ethnicity, 'minorities' in the 1919–39 sense, national self-determination, nationality, nationalism and international relations? All concepts of this sort, I argue, must be considered in a broader context that includes human identities and their relationship to political authorities.

The American humourist Will Rogers once said, 'All I know is just what I read in the [news]papers'. In truth, one would do better to try to learn from them than from most textbooks on international relations, which purport to offer eternal verities but are really only carriers of the R/N eye disease. Certainly, today's print and broadcast media are replete with stories about identities. Allow me to highlight three of many such stories that appeared in the *The New York Times* in the same week that I wrote the first draft of this chapter, which, although all American in source and two from commencement addresses at universities, nevertheless help to illustrate how broad and pervasive the problem of identities is.

US Vice-President Al Gore expressed his mixed-metaphored shock at Vladimir Zhirinovsky's comment in an interview that what he disliked most about President Clinton's foreign policy was that Gore 'is a Jew'. Gore commented: 'What a week it has been! In the same seven-day period I have been bestowed an honorary degree of humane letters by this great institution [the Jewish Theological Seminary] and I have been given the honorary title of Jew by a hatemonger.... In Zhirinovsky's crude words we hear ugly reminders ... that the evil of ethnic hatred still pockmarks many corners of our globe. An Ebola virus of vicious hatred of the other lurks coiled in many societies.'[23]

Henry Louis Gates Jr, Chairman of Harvard University's African-American Studies Department, remarked:

> Too often we consider race as something only blacks have, sex orientation as something only guys have, gender as something only women have. If we don't fall into any of those categories, then we don't have to worry.... In the 21st century the problem is ethnic identity as 48 countries are ravaged by ethnic violence. Who would have thought 20 years ago when you mentioned ethnic violence in Georgia in 1995, you'd be talking about the Soviet Union rather than the United States? ... The stronger a sense you nurture of the contingent nature of all such identities, the less likely you will be harmed by them, or in their name inflict harm on others.[24]

Lastly, for a different slant on the politics of identity, the US Supreme Court by narrow 5–4 rulings has lately been wrestling with constitutional issues of crucial importance to the power of the Federal government in Washington. It would be misleading to view these cases as the Federal government deciding on the limits of its own authority, for the Court's membership (because of presidential appointment) currently reflects a challenge to that very authority mounted in recent years by conservative states' rights advocates. In one case, the Court (barely) decided against the capacity of states to enact term limits on Congress; in another, against Washington's extending its power to regulate 'interstate commerce' so far as to make it a Federal crime to possess a gun near a school. Yale Law School professor Paul Gewirtz observed that

Justice Clarence Thomas's dissent in the term limits case actually embodied 'the first principles of those who opposed ratification of the Constitution'. Gewirtz recalled that the American patriot ('Give me liberty or give me death!') Patrick Henry had declared in 1788: 'I am not really an American, I am a Virginian', and complained that the authors of the Constitution had no authority 'to speak the language of "we the people" instead of "we the states" '. Justice John Paul Stevans, for the majority in the term limits case, pointed out that the Preamble to the Constitution goes on to mention a 'more perfect union'. However, Justice Thomas countered that the original formulation of the Preamble was: 'We the people of the states of New Hampshire, Massachusetts' and so on, and that the phrase 'the United States' is used consistently throughout the Constitution 'as a plural noun'.[25] State-centric IR theorists and others should not fail to notice that 'state' has a special meaning in the US context.

Identities are continually being shaped, reshaped and labelled; and their political implications debated. Mansbach and I maintain that 'international relations' is inseparable from politics at all levels. The subject, we insist, is *politics*. Our primary concerns are the connections among patterns of authority (which we define as effective control), identities, loyalties and ideology; and what such connections have to tell us about why political entities prosper, expand or decay. In our view, the political universe is not exclusively or even primarily made up of 'states', rather, many types of polities – layered, overlapping, nested and interacting – coexist, cooperate and conflict. A 'polity' as we define it is any entity that has a measure of identity, a degree of institutionalization and hierarchy, and the capacity to mobilize persons for political purposes (that is, for value satisfaction or relief from value deprivation). 'The state' in our framework is just one type of polity, distinguished only by its particular legal status.

Concepts, like all theoretical constructs, oversimplify 'reality' and tell us what is important and what we can safely ignore. Some suggest that 'the state' is a concept that we who study international relations would have to invent if it did not already exist. I should put it differently: it's the invention part that is dangerous. As I have said, the question is not whether 'the state' is observable and matters, but to what extent does it explain the things we need to understand. Sovereign states exist as legal/normative entities, but, Mansbach and I suggest, that tells us not much more about the 'real world' than does a cinema set. In the Western movie, everything in town is façade and the rest is nothing but desert hot air.

So it is in global politics. Precious few sovereign states are genuine nation-states. Many of them do not have effective governments, and even the best of them are beset by bureaucratic battles and inter- and intra-party strife. What exactly, then, do we *mean* by 'the state'? Who or what is the state, and what practical impact does each of its identifiable dimensions have? The state is a variable – highly contingent and subject to prevailing conditions. Its degree of coherence, resources and control over civil society and the external universe vary significantly by place, time and the political issue at hand. Make-believe aside, there is a great deal more to the world than states. Ethnic and religious conflicts and worsening income inequalities (have/have not divisions) are having such profound effects that they are more difficult than ever to ignore. Dramatic change is the order of the day around the globe, and petrified as they are like Jurassic Park mosquitoes in their Westphalian amber, state-centric international theorists simply do not have the conceptual tools to account for change.

Nevertheless, it is encouraging to recognize how far we have come from the attitudes of, say, the mid-1970s, when I participated in a panel on 'Nonstate Actors in World Politics' at a meeting of the International Studies Association. A few of the panelists then privately expressed their amusement that one of the papers was about the Kurds. Who, indeed, were the Kurds? Who could possibly care? Political scientists then regarded ethnic groups as quaint residues of benighted 'tribal' times, amorphous identities that the political socialization campaigns of modern governments were inexorably erasing. Since the 'nation-state' was ascendant almost everywhere, we could safely leave the Kurds and other such exotica to anthropologists or ethnomusicologists.

Not long ago 'nationalism', too, was strictly a phenomenon associated with states. The 'new nations' were insisting on their 'right' to 'national self-determination'; colonial empires were crumbling; and new nation-states were emerging with boundaries that normally reflected former-colonial administrative divisions. In a broader sense, nationalism was seen as the characteristic assertive behaviour of all old and new states in international politics. R/Ns confidently assured us that we now had a world of billiard ball states – with no 'insides' worth considering except for power capabilities – and what we mainly needed to worry about was ameliorating interstate conflicts.

In retrospect, IR theories were far more 'primitive' and benighted than ethnicity! We did not fully appreciate, first, how different most of the states in much of the rest of the world were from their European progenitors. Nor did we understand that the relative quietude of ethnic strife even in the heart of Europe reflected not so much the triumph of the state as an institution, as it did the dampening effect of bipolar postwar *empires*. Fukuyama got it reversed: It was the Cold War rivalry, not its demise, that temporarily made 'history' *seem* to 'end'. Now that the Soviet Union and its empire has 'deconstructed' no one is laughing about the likes of the Kurds anymore.

Yet ethnicity, too, is obviously an exceedingly troublesome concept, not much of an improvement over the hoary nonsense of 'race'. Those who study these things assure us that any two individuals who happen to share, for example, skin colour typically have many more things in common with other individuals who may or may not have the same skin colour. However, skin colour, of course, has often provided a highly visible basis for 'racial' discrimination, just as in many societies it has been ignored when particular individuals have been sufficiently wealthy or influential. Gender and caste have been equally powerful general predictors of discrimination. It is as hard to pinpoint what constitutes an 'ethnicity' or a 'people' as it is a 'race'. For every common history, there are aspects of history that are not shared; for every language, dialects; for every religion, different versions of the one true faith. Given their continuing internecine conflicts, it is still appropriate to wonder: who *are* 'the Kurds'? Is 'Slavic' a meaningful category? and so on. Ethnicity, like race and caste, is more a state of mind – identity assumed and/or imposed – than anything else. The jury is still out on gender.

At this juncture, we need to turn to another fuzzy concept, the 'nation' that the UN Charter proclaims has a right to national self-determination. This nation is distinct from, although often related to, the legal 'nationality' recognized by states as well as the more restrictive category of 'citizen'. The only wholly secure definition of 'nation' is 'a people who think they are one'. That is actually about all one can say with certainty, but the question remains: *why* do they think they are one? There is considerable literature on this subject,[26] which boils down to those writers like Anthony D. Smith who stress the ancient 'primordial' and/or 'perennial' historical roots of 'nation' and those like Ernest Gellner who determinedly argue that nations are the essentially artificial creations of the modern state.

This intellectual controversy seems to me to be much ado about little. To be sure, nearly all governments – as well as many elites who oppose them – are hard at work, for their own ends and with greater or lesser success, trying to socialize persons politically. The US government over time did an impressive job convincing an ethnic 'melting-pot' of citizens that they were 'American' and nonetheless could maintain some of their ethnic heritage, a compromise symbolized today by hyphenated Italian-Americans, African-Americans, Mexican-Americans, and others. By contrast, Rwandan government political socialization efforts utterly failed, even as tribal elites succeeded in sharpening the Hutu/Tutsi division.

However, writers stressing the ancient roots of nations are correct, too, because national myths (myths they are) almost always draw together some bits and pieces of common history or culture. It is a very selective process and hard to predict which bits and pieces will prevail. Why do these myths take the form they do? Why does political socialization work sometimes, or for a time, and not other times? We're back to fundamental questions: What identities are important for what purposes? Why are persons loyal? Why do old political affiliations wane and die, and new ones emerge?

Part of the reason that states persist, of course, is that their governments all exercise some coercion along with attempts to socialize and persuade. Some governments exercise a lot of coercion, which calls to mind General Pinochet, Haitian leaders or the KGB. An identity can to some extent be imposed, although most are not. For example, you might have been told a few years ago that, like it or not and whatever your other identities (e.g. Armenian Catholic), you were a citizen of the Soviet Union. But Mansbach and I argue, loyalties are largely an exchange phenomenon. Persons are loyal only when they are getting benefits in exchange, including the not to be underestimated psychological satisfaction that may come from being associated with a group and its ideology. Conversely, loyalty tends to diminish when the costs of association persistently seem to exceed benefits.

De-anthropomorphizing the state has an additional analytical virtue, forcing us to ask again: who or what is the state, and whose interests does it really serve? Despite statist propaganda, government elites are rarely representative of the entire populace. Under-representation of particular ethnic or other groups in the institutions of government does make it difficult for the state even to pose as a 'higher' and 'neutral' servant of the public interest. The general citizenry does not benefit equally, and many are benefiting hardly at all, from either the direct largesse or trickle-down from state programmes. Nevertheless, no government will survive long if it is not benefiting someone, at a minimum a corrupt elite stratum (e.g. an old-style Latin American dictatorship) and sometimes a great many persons indeed.

We should not leap to accept the old dubious argument that poverty and oppression are the major causes of violence. Throughout history, most of the violence has been perpetrated by elites who are doing quite well, thank you, via the states and empires that they dominate – motivated by greed rather than need. The scholarly literature on the subject tells us that those who have most to gain from violence are normally the slowest to resort to it, except when conditions suddenly go from bad to intolerable. Much more volatile are middle-class setbacks after a period of rapid progress. Ironically, then, the more economic and social progress we make, the greater risk of explosive downturns. We should also keep in mind that elites exist at all levels of society, not just in an upper stratum. Once a pattern of violence sets in, it is often difficult to stop, not only because violence can evolve into a 'culture' or way of life (death) but also because elites among the group(s) involved tend to develop significant status, psychological and sometimes material stakes in the continuation of violence. Just as governments of states may serve narrow interests, the same can be true of anti-government leadership. Were *any* peace to be firmly secured in the Arab–Israeli zone of conflict or Northern Ireland, Hamas and IRA/Protestant extremists would weep bitter tears.

LOOKING AHEAD

The Westphalian state has had a pretty good run as a model for a few hundred years and it may be that the world is moving on – perhaps even hurtling on. The challenges do appear to be intensifying in the present era. In fact, the Westphalian state model has been realized to a large extent only in Europe and not everywhere, satisfactorily, there. It is instructive to think of Italy, caught in the identity crossfire among cities, regions and the Mafia. In much of what used to be called the Third World (another transient identity), we observe only an alien European form plastered over age-old tribal reality.

Where do we go from here, both within and beyond existing states? As I have noted, although rearranging boundaries forcibly from the outside is still likely to meet widespread resistance, boundaries are being rearranged in a number of places from the inside and, in any event, are constantly being transcended by ever-greater transnationalism. Some state-centric theorists insist that nothing has really changed because mini-nationalisms all want their own state. That is a silly argument, not least because it is absolutely certain that few of them will ever have anything of the sort.

The entire world is groping for new political arrangements for which we simply do not always have the appropriate ideas, forms or words to describe. There are hundreds of international functional regimes, including many that never make the headlines, that are exercising significant amounts of control over particular issues like fishing, telecommunications and river pollution. In the very birthplace of the Westphalian state, the Europeans are forging a European Union, but its precise nature is still evolving. Will it ultimately reflect federal principles; confederal, subsidiarity, consociationalism – or what? The experiment is in some respects (not all, for there have been many political unions) unprecedented. When the smoke clears on the battlefields of some of the former Soviet republics, Yugoslavia and elsewhere, there will have to be formulae invented to knit smaller units together in selective ways to form larger. One can foresee autonomy arrangements for certain minorities and economic (re)integration for limited sectors of the economy.

In sum, fission and fusion will occur in the future as it has in the past, although with innovative forms and increasingly complicated interrelationships that are appropriate for our highly interdependent world on the eve of a new millennium. New identities and loyalties will form, and older ones will be resurrected or adapted to suit changed circumstances. Multiculturalism as a vague idea may have some pragmatic utility insofar as it encourages at least toleration and maybe even appreciation of 'other' persons, beliefs, and lifestyles. Nevertheless, it is essential for us to recognize that the sheer range of potential identities and loyalties in a global culture experiencing 'fragmegration' goes far beyond anything advocates of multiculturalism have traditionally addressed. Demands for minority rights (when everyone is a minority in some important context), ethnic autonomy and/or national self-determination – although not for basic *human* rights – will likely do much more harm than good. They are hopelessly dated and inadequate 'solutions' to the crises of institutions and identity that lie ahead for us all.

NOTES

1. This essay is a revised version of a paper originally presented at the Second Pan-European Conference in International Relations, Paris, France, 13–16 September 1995.
2. T.H. White, *The Once and Future King* (New York: Ace, 1987), 638–9.

3. Ibid.
4. See especially Yale H. Ferguson and Richard W. Mansbach, *Polities: Authority, Identities, and Change* (Columbus: University of South Carolina Press, 1996); 'The Past as Prelude to the Future: Changing Loyalties in Global Politics', in Yosef Lapid and Friedrich Kratochwil (eds), *The Return of Culture and Identity in IR Theory* (Boulder: Lynne Rienner, 1995); 'Between Celebration and Despair: Constructive Suggestions for Future International Theory', *International Studies Quarterly*, Vol. 35, No. 4 (December 1991), 363–86. Some of the ideas in this essay are expressed in the foregoing works and also in Yale H. Ferguson, 'Ethnicity, Nationalism, and Polities Great and Small', *Mershon International Studies Review*, Vol. 38, Supplement 2 (October 1994), 241–6; and 'Ethnicity, Nationalism, and Global Politics: Continuity and Change', paper for Commission of History of International Relations session on Multiculturalism, 18th International Congress of Historical Sciences, Montréal, Canada, 27 August–3 September 1995.
5. John J. Mearsheimer started the exchange with his 'The False Promise of International Institutions', *International Security*, Vol. 19, No. 3 (Winter 1994/5), 5–49. It continued in *International Security*, Vol. 20, No. 4 (Summer 1995). See Robert O. Keohane and Lisa L. Martin, 'The Promise of Institutionalist Theory', 39–51; Charles A. Kupchan and Clifford A. Kupchan, 'The Promise of Collective Security', 52–61; John Gerard Ruggie, 'The False Premise of Realism', 62–70; Alexander Wendt, 'Constructing International Politics', 71–81; and John J. Mearsheimer, 'A Realist Reply', 82–93.
6. Keohane and Martin, 'The Promise of Institutionalist Theory', 38, 46–7.
7. Wendt regards 'critical IR theory' (correctly in my view) not as a single theory, rather a 'family of theories that includes postmodernists (Ashley, Walker), constructivists (Adler, Kratochwil, Ruggie, and now Katzenstein), neo-Marxists (Cox, Gill), feminists (Peterson, Sylvester), and others.' Having the two claims 'in common no more makes critical theory a single theory than does the fact that neorealism and neoliberalism both use game theory... Some critical theorists are statists and some are not; some believe in science and some do not; some are optimists and some are pessimists; some stress process and some structure.' Wendt, 'Constructing International Politics', 72.
8. How 'shared knowledge' can exist anywhere but 'in actors' heads', to this reader, is far from obvious. Perhaps they are keeping it in their notebooks or libraries?
9. Wendt, 'Constructing International Politics', 71–2.
10. Keohane and Martin, 'The Promise of Institutionalist Theory', 46.
11. Wendt, 'Constructing International Politics', 75.
12. Keohane and Martin, 'The Promise of Institutionalist Theory', 47.
13. Wendt, 'Constructing International Politics', 75.
14. Mearsheimer, 'A Realist Reply', 93.
15. Alexander Wendt, 'The Agent–Structure Problem in International Relations Theory', *International Organization*, Vol. 41, No. 3 (Summer 1987), 335–70.

16. Alexander Wendt, 'Anarchy is What States Make of it: The Social Construction of Power Politics', *International Organization*, Vol. 46, No. 2 (Spring 1992), 391–425.
17. Peter Sahlins, *Boundaries: The Making of France and Spain in the Pyrenees* (Berkeley: University of California Press, 1989), 5–9.
18. James N. Rosenau, *Turbulence in World Politics* (Princeton, NJ: Princeton University Press, 1990).
19. Francis Fukuyama, *The End of History and the Last Man* (New York: Free Press, 1992).
20. Samuel P. Huntington, 'The Clash of Civilizations?', *Foreign Affairs*, Vol. 73, No. 3 (Summer 1993), 22–49.
21. See 'On The Clash of Civilizations', *Foreign Affairs*, Vol. 72, No. 4 (September/October 1993), 2–26.
22. *Foreign Affairs*, Vol. 72, No. 5 (November/December 1993).
23. *The New York Times*, 29 May 1995, 9.
24. Ibid.
25. *The New York Times*, 24 May 1995, A19.
26. Books in English include: Benedict Anderson, *Imagined Communities: Reflections on the Origin and Spread of Nationalism* (London: Verso Editions and New Left Books, 1983); John A. Armstrong, *Nations Before Nationalism* (Chapel Hill: University of North Carolina Press, 1982); Karl Wolfgang Deutsch, *Nationalism and Social Communication: An Inquiry into the Foundations of Nationality* (Cambridge: MIT Press, 1953); Ernest Gellner, *Nations and Nationalism* (Ithaca: Cornell University Press, 1983); Eric J. Hobsbawm, *Nations and Nationalism since 1780* (Cambridge: Cambridge University Press, 1990); Hans Kohn, *The Idea of Nationalism*, 2nd edn (New York: Macmillan, 1967); William H. McNeill, *Polyethnicity and National Unity in World History* (Toronto: University of Toronto Press, 1986); Daniel Patrick Moynihan, *Pandaemonium: Ethnicity in International Politics* (Oxford: Oxford University Press, 1993); William Pfaff, *The Wrath of Nations: Civilization and the Furies of Nationalism* (New York: Simon and Schuster, 1993); and two books by Anthony D. Smith: *The Ethnic Origins of Nations* (Oxford: Oxford University Press, 1986) and *National Identity* (London: Penguin, 1991).

3 Culture, Power and International Negotiations: Understanding Palau–US Status Negotiations
Peter Black and Kevin Avruch

INTRODUCTION

Not even one-tenth of the way into his magisterial, and never self-wounding, recounting of his years as Richard Nixon's national security advisor, Henry Kissinger recalls his first visit (in that capacity) to Italy: 'I have always loved the stark beauty of the country and extraordinary humanity of its people.' He goes on:

> But every visit confirmed that Italy followed different political laws and had a different concept of the role of the state from that of the rest of Western Europe. Perhaps Italians were too civilized, too imbued with the worth of the individual to make the total commitment to political goals that for over a century and a half had driven the rivalries and ambitions of the other countries of Europe.

Dr Kissinger proceeds, then, to speculate on why this is so, reflecting mainly on Italy's rich, troubled history, its ambivalent relationship to the papacy, and so on. In the next paragraph, however, the scholarly professor reminds us that, by 1969, he is no longer leading a contemplative life by the Charles River, but a rather more muscular one by the Potomac. 'Whatever the reason' for Italy's apparent uniqueness, Kissinger continues,

> each visit left me with the feeling that its primary purpose was fulfilled by our arrival at the airport. This symbolized that the United States took Italy seriously; it produced photographic evidence that

Italian leaders were being consulted. This achieved, Italian ministers acted as if they were too worldly-wise to pretend that their views on international affairs could decisively affect events.[1]

As is so often the case with contemplation of international relations in the latter half of the twentieth century, Henry Kissinger provides a scenario of paradigmatic clarity; certainly he illuminates the trinity of our title. In those passages he begins as the worldly Harvard scholar affectionately ruminating on cultural difference and ends as the Assistant to the President for National Security Affairs offering one of his not-so-subtle instructions in the culture of power: instructions, that is, as to where in the great scheme of world power *circa* 1969 Italy stood. Given his biography, this is not a surprising switch. He is, after all, European-born, and thus heir to that long German fascination with Italy and Italian culture. Yet he also was the employee of a President whose views on the significance of Italy, or at least the Italian lira, were captured for all time on the Watergate tapes.

Kissinger's remarks exemplify the thesis of this chapter. The seasoned practitioner (the 'player') in international relations may be intuitively, and even self-consciously, attuned to matters of culture; but too easily the player allows 'power' to overmaster this intuition. Meanwhile, the scholar of international relations starts and ends with *power*; all too often there seems not even a Kissingerian intuition of culture.

ON THE ABSENCE OF CULTURE IN INTERNATIONAL RELATIONS

Among other things, culture focuses our attention on differences – among states or, more precisely, among societies as they are reduced to the shorthand of states. Therefore, one does not have to look far for the reasons for culture's absence in mainstream conceptualizations of international relations. The well-known dominance of the field since the 1950s by the so-called realist paradigm rendered culture not merely epiphenomenal, but invisible and mute. The realist paradigm saw the international system in terms of states, conceived as undifferentiated, monolithic actors, acting with a rational calculus to maximize security (among other utilities) by marshalling and projecting power to coerce adversaries and co-opt allies. The state system was a balance of power system, set in a larger (and implicitly presumed) context of global disorder and ever-impending chaos.[2]

Any one of the major assumptions of realist thinking has the effect of rendering culture invisible, for each entails uniformitarianism. First, the assumption of undifferentiated states suppresses any possible differences among them, or at least renders differences among states essentially mono-dimensional: states only need be distinguished from one another by their relative (i.e. susceptible to an ordinal ranking) possession of power. Second, the assumption of rationality in the behaviour of states suppresses any considerations of other modes of reasoning and/or decision-making imperatives. Third, the assumption (linked inextricably to rationality) of utilities-maximizing (e.g. 'security') imposes, *a priori*, a single, universalizing metric.[3] Finally, all this suppression of *difference* in favour of *sameness* is possible because the strong force holding the entropic system of states together is power. Power is the ultimate utility and the fundamental resource; it is *the* reality that drives 'realism'. The state system is conceived to conform to the laws of this reality. It thus resembles nothing so much as that old Rutherford–Bohr model of the atom; a miniature solar system of hard, solid-bodied entities, drawn to and repelled from one another and revolving around denser nuclei.[4]

Perhaps much of the above should be placed now in the past tense, since realism and balance-of-power thinking is no longer regnant as it once was. Realism always had its philosophical counterpart in international relations: a position faintly praised (and so damned) as 'idealism'. This view stressed beliefs, values, ideologies and ideas as motors of international affairs. At first glance idealism is more sympathetic and amenable than realism to a cultural perspective. After all, a concern with culture is itself historically linked to idealist and 'mentalist' – *subjectivist* – concerns. There is a crucial difference, however. Much of the idealist perspective reduces to a mentalism that is itself universalized, based on, say, presumptions about natural law and human nature. In its liberal, utopian guise, idealism replaces the will to dominate of the realists with the will to cooperate.[5] Again the effect is to eradicate difference in favour of sameness, and culture is about difference.

The other late challenger to the hegemony of realism can be understood in terms of our analogy of the realist's state system to the Rutherford–Bohr atom. Physicists no longer conceive of the orbital subatomic particles as solid and irreducible particles; instead these particles are seen as swirling constellations of massed charges and potentialities – miniature stochastic subsystems of considerable activity. What now counts is that which *constitutes* the apparent particles. Here is an analogy for the state system: rather than conceive of states as monadic and monovocalic, speaking authoritatively with one (governmental) voice in the name of their citizens, states are now seen as (sometimes unstable) tropes, metonyms for competing congeries of internal ethnic, regional, racial or class interests. Domestic politics affect international politics (nowadays a truism) and, more profoundly, more often than not they thoroughly undermine pretensions of state-level rationality or maximizing behaviours. This ('quantum mechanical') view of the international system brings us closer to considering cultural differences, in fact, than the idealist view does. Here we deal, for example, with matters of ethnic identities and nationalist discourses, with suicidal irredentisms and genocidal ethnic cleansings, with operationalized primordialisms of one sort or another that have little to do with rational decision-making or problem-solving. Here we find ourselves, as often as not, in the realms of passion and ontology, of situated differences among states and (now) their peoples.[6]

CULTURE AND INTERNATIONAL NEGOTIATIONS

One area of international relations thinking that has appeared relatively more open to the admission of cultural perspectives has been that concerned with international negotiations. We suspect this is so because it is an area that allows active practitioners to contribute to the debates. It is also an area in which analytical attention can be focused on problems of interstate communication, not just authoritative, self-evidently maximizing 'decision-making'. Communication implies the existence of interlocutors, while decision-making may be (wrongly) reduced to an autistic, hermetically sealed blackbox process. The existence of interlocutors means that it is harder to lose sight of the fact that negotiations proceed through the interactions of individuals who are always situated actors (if not always as floridly individualistic as Henry Kissinger). There is a small, but growing, literature on culture and negotiations by 'insiders': professionals and practitioners.[7] Some specialists in international relations, not themselves practitioners or professional diplomats, have also recently taken up this area.[8]

Nevertheless, even in the area of negotiation, there is a lingering resistance among most practitioners and theorists to treat culture as a 'variable' capable of affecting ultimate outcomes. As Zartman and Berman indicate, this resistance stems from two separate arguments.

The first holds that negotiation is, at some deep structural level, a 'universal process, utilizing a finite number of behavioral patterns, and that cultural differences are simply differences in style and language ... variations, albeit important, on a basic theme'.[9] The second argument is that there exists by now an international diplomatic culture, to which new diplomats – even those from Third World or 'non-Western' cultures – are soon enough socialized. We might add a third argument, a precipitate of political realism, that holds that whatever the status of culture – deep or surface structural, universalized (uniform) or particularistic – it is inevitably trumped by power.

Each argument invites a different sort of counter-argument. The idea that a deep, pan-human process is involved in all negotiations takes us into the deepest waters philosophically; it has to do with old questions about 'how natives think' (ourselves included, of course). But practically speaking – in terms of pursuing international or intercultural negotiations successfully – the deepest questions are beside the point.[10] Even if the universalistic position is granted, one must still face the more germane, if humbler, issue of how much 'interference' or inefficiency is introduced to negotiations by inadequate attention paid to cultural, even stylistic, differences. How soon before differences in degree become differences of kind? To appeal to the analogy of language (as Zartman and Berman do), it is one thing to argue that English and Arabic, say, are at the deepest structural levels of neurological functioning, the 'same' (linguistic or cognitive) entity. It is another to underestimate their impressive differences, or to expect that translations can be done by *anyone*, or that once done by a bilingual speaker, they are unproblematically transparent. Put bluntly, knowing that all human languages are the same at some level is small comfort if you are suffering sudden chest pains at a small hospital in Palau, there are no English speakers around and you are unable to speak any Palauan.

The second argument – there is a universal culture of diplomacy – holds in effect that (at least in the diplomatic world), we all now speak the same language anyway. One response (among several) to this argument is that even assuming one's 'native culture' can be leached out in diplomatic training – a large assumption – the argument still goes wrong by, in effect, over-privileging diplomats. How often do diplomats, with whatever cosmopolitan sensibilities, shape the foreign policies of their states? The settlements they reach through negotiations ultimately must be acceptable to political (civilian or military) leadership. Diplomats are responsible to political figures and their political constituencies, to the prejudices of the masses and to mass public opinion. And, by the nature of things, political leadership is often more embedded in, and reflective of, indigenous culture(s) than is the diplomatic corps. This is true, we maintain, for Europe and North America. It is more true in the so-called Third World, where Oxbridge or Sorbonne-educated diplomats often must answer to their leader in the person of, say, Idi Amin Dada. Alternatively, some Idi Amin tires of his Stanford-educated foreign minister and appoints his village-educated kinsman to the post. Moreover, as Raymond Cohen has pointed out, whereas in negotiations around narrow, technical issues diplomats are more likely to predominate over politicians and the effects of cross-cultural differences may be relatively muted, 'the more emotive, "political", and public the issue, the more likely are cross-cultural effects to be felt.'[11]

In other words, it is precisely in times of international crisis when the political stakes are highest (a time of 'international chest pains' as it were), that culture matters most. Culture mattered, for example, when a policewoman was shot in London and the Foreign Office found itself negotiating with Libyan representatives in 'Peoples' Bureaus' rather than embassies; it mattered when the United States found its embassy and diplomats held hostage by Iranian 'students'; and, we suspect, it mattered when Tariq Aziz returned from a crisis meeting with James Baker, to brief Saddam Hussein on some of the finer points of international law.

Perhaps the last example cited, from one of the many preludes to the Gulf War, is a good introduction to the third argument marshalled against culture: that, in the end, power trumps everything else. To update the Napoleonic quip, God is on the side of the aircraft carriers, the stealth bombers and the Tomahawk missiles. Even Cohen, who has written persuasively of interstate cultural misunderstandings as creating costly 'dialogues of the deaf', agrees that the effects of culture are limited in any situation in which *force majeure* can be invoked, where, that is, the 'power discrepancy between two states is so great that the weaker has no choice but to comply with the will of the stronger'.[12]

This statement is a specimen of what might be called 'the native's point of view' among scholars and especially practitioners of international negotiations. It is a kind of local common sense, seldom contested and rarely held up to critical scrutiny. It has the tautological quality of much common sense, though, and is, after all, a cultural expression. The culture which generates such a discourse is, like any culture, a social production, which in turn is used in the interpretation of social action – negotiations, here. And like a tribal culture on any remote and isolated atoll, it remains blind to itself. We are speaking here about the culture of power.

We have already indicated some of the flaws in that culture (of power) as a mode of operating in the international arena by noting the critiques of power politics and the realist paradigm raised by many scholars within international relations. The use of power may indeed be one 'solution' to any problem in international relations,[13] but at what costs (even to the stronger state), over what period of time (*force majeure* is usually efficient in the shorter, rather than the longer term) and, most importantly, in lieu of what other sorts of solutions, solutions that are in the long run less costly and more likely to avoid future confrontations?[14] Power is not a simple 'primitive' in the international (or any other) system. The decision to project power is itself a culturally constituted act, as are the forms of and rationale for its projection. And power projected *cross-culturally* is doubly constituted – once in its projection, and again in its reception. Between the projection and reception, cultural differences muddy the waters. The 'clear' and 'unambiguous' meanings of a projection of power often seem much less clear some months or years afterward. Need we mention the messy and inconclusive results of the Gulf War?

Perhaps the Gulf War is not an entirely appropriate example of power asymmetry. After all, the American-led coalition forces stopped short of marching on Baghdad and removing Saddam at least in part to avoid unacceptable casualties from remaining Iraqi forces; Iraqi power in the conventional sense of military force apparently was still a factor to be reckoned with. The imbalance of power, even after Iraq's military rout in Kuwait, turned out to be not as absolute as many had calculated. Thus for the remainder of this chapter we turn to an extended case study of a set of negotiations in which all – and we mean all – power, as defined conventionally, was held by one of the parties. The case under study involves ongoing negotiations on the status of Palau, part of the former US Trust Territory of the Pacific. We chose it because it shows how culture and power are intertwined and intermixed, and how blindness to cultural differences, a blindness on the part of both parties, can cause problems of communication to appear truly intractable.

The point we wish to demonstrate is that many of the serious difficulties that bedevil negotiations can be traced to what we call 'cultural blindness', the failure of the parties to perceive the profound differences in meaning that each ascribes to important features of the negotiations. This blindness ultimately arises from deep, if largely unconscious, ethnocentrism, especially, in this case, the ethnocentrism of those with the power.

More generally, while it would be wrong to claim that solid, long-lasting, mutually desired and self-enforcing outcomes are unreachable in the face of cultural blindness, we do assert that an awareness of cultural difference will increase the probability that such outcomes can be achieved. And as we show, without such awareness the negotiation process is almost guaranteed to be that infamous 'dialogue of the deaf'.

UNDERSTANDING PALAU–US STATUS NEGOTIATIONS

Negotiations Terminable and Interminable

1994 saw the culmination of close to 20 years of negotiations between the governments of the United States and Palau (a Pacific archipelago) aimed at the transformation of their relationship from one in which the US administered the islands under a United Nations mandate to one in which Palau is 'freely associated' with the US as a sovereign nation.[15] Thus the speech given to the United Nations Trusteeship Council by Palau's representative in that year truly earned the name given by that Palauan wit who had called it 'Palau's *Final*, Annual Farewell Address to the Trusteeship Council'. The joke? Palauan representatives (and often the same person) had been bidding good-bye to the Trusteeship Council on the occasion of the imminent termination of Palau's trusteeship status with monotonous regularity for more than a decade. It should be no surprise then that the Palau–US status negotiations became notorious for their tortuous history, a history which led to one anti-climatic false conclusion after another.

The power differential between the two negotiating partners is one reason why the history of the discussions between the last UN trust territory and the last superpower has been so remarkable. Palau is a society of approximately 15,000 people and at the time the talks commenced was an American dependency. By any measurement known to *realpolitik* Palau was a society with zero power. The US, on the other hand, was... The United States of America, the Most Powerful Nation the World Has Ever Seen. This is the calculus which no doubt lay behind a very revealing indiscretion attributed to then National Security Advisor Kissinger at the start of the 1969 negotiations which preceded the direct Palau–US talks. 'There are only 90,000 people out there', he said, referring to the Trust Territory before it fractured into its constituent parts, 'who gives a damn?'[16]

Why these negotiations should have dragged on so long and produced so many surprising twists and turns makes an interesting question. Here, this question provides us with a useful case study, one which dramatically illustrates the way the culture of power can be disconcerted (and not so temporarily) by the power of culture.

Two Stories

For some it has proved tempting to view the length and difficulty of the negotiations as a morality play – and there is a small but growing literature which takes this stance. One version has it as a David and Goliath tale in which the wily and righteous resistance of a tiny but environmentally sensitive, and thus anti-nuclear, indigenous population is deployed against the hegemonic colossus of the modern world – nuclear-armed, deep-pocketed and without principles. The violence and disorganization in Palau directly or indirectly related to these negotiations are, in this Manichean view, the results of machinations set in play by the CIA, the Pentagon or simply the military-industrial complex. And this is not a view to be casually dismissed given the existence of an official 1963 study which laid out in detail the steps the American government should take to manoeuvre Palau and the other Micronesian societies out from under the United Nations' roof and into permanent association with the United States, a transformation necessary (so the report claimed) for America's national security.[17]

Another, much more cheerful version of the tale is occasionally heard. It is found mostly in the documents submitted by the State Department to the United Nations and in Congressional testimony. It is the story of how a patient (if at times bumbling and inattentive) protector shepherded its weak and small dependant onto the world stage, fending off challenges mounted by foreign, radical, uninformed and Machiavellian elements whose real agendas had nothing to do with the well-being of the Palauan people. This version cannot be rejected out of hand either given, for example, the unlikely assortment of 'allies' with whom various parties on the Palauan side were associated at various times.[18] Yet, whatever the merits of these two competing (and curiously complementary) versions of the history of the status negotiations, no one (at least no one of whom we are aware) has claimed that the negotiation process itself was anything but confused, troubled and extraordinarily drawn out. And, regardless of who was wearing the white hat and who the black, that feature of this history calls out for analysis. Before beginning, however, it is necessary to sketch in the political background.

Deconstructing a Trust Territory

The United States captured Palau in 1944 together with the other areas of Micronesia which had been administered by the Japanese under a mandate from the League of Nations. Palau and these other administrative districts was the United States Trust Territory of the Pacific Islands. The USTTPI became the only one of the United Nations' trusteeships to be designated a 'strategic trust', which meant that while routine supervision of the US mandate was delegated to the Trusteeship Council, an organ of the General Assembly, any final decision on matters relating to its status was relegated to the Security Council.

In 1975, it became apparent to the Palauans that Palau was not destined to play a leading role in any new political entity emerging out of the Trust Territory. Two of the original districts had already struck out on their own: the Northern Mariana Islands to become a US commonwealth and the Marshall Islands to become an 'independent' republic, freely associated with the US. Significant segments of the Palauan elite decided that Palau too should seek a separate future and in 1975 Palau's legislature established a Political Status Commission to investigate alternative futures.

The splintering of the Trust Territory was a consequence of a decision made earlier by the American government to seek termination of the UN mandate. The motivations for that decision appear clear enough: the terms of the mandate obliged the US to provide for the social, economic and political advancement of the Micronesian inhabitants of the Territory so that they could exercise their inherent right of self-determination. Under these terms of reference, the colonial character of the American regime in Micronesia could become only an increasingly embarrassing impediment to US purposes both in Micronesia and in the UN.

Termination thus represented for the US a kind of tidying up from the aftermath of the Second World War which would allow the prosecution of the Cold War to proceed according to its own logic and without the distraction of what was increasingly seen as an archaic and less and less defensible arrangement. For the Micronesians, it represented something quite different, or rather *somethings* quite different because the Micronesian peoples, especially their political elites, saw a variety of possible opportunities and threats opening up before them as the reality of the American demand for a new status was borne in upon them. That demand shattered the fragile unity of Micronesia, as first one district then another sought to create a separate future, especially *vis-à-vis* the Americans. In doing so they came up against what many in the US government saw as fundamental US stakes.

National Interests

America's initial postwar security concerns in Micronesia were almost entirely negative, arising as they did from the bloody struggle to sweep from the islands the heavily fortified Japanese. Japanese forces had emerged out of Micronesia to strike at Allied positions in 1941–2, and it was back through Micronesia that Americans had fought on their way towards the Japanese home islands. Never again, the thinking went, would the US allow a foreign power to interpose itself between North America and Asia. This doctrine went by the name of 'strategic denial'. It had as its corollary the rather interesting provision that there was nothing of any importance to the US in Micronesia itself.

By the mid-1960s (the time of the decision to seek termination of the Trusteeship) that 'dog in the manger' corollary was beginning to evaporate, especially with respect to Palau. Pentagon planners were attracted to the possibilities of its first-class harbour, large (by Micronesian standards) land area and short distance from the Philippines (about 500 miles). These strategic possibilities and interests put severe constraints on the kinds of political relationships the US was willing to work out with Micronesia. Referring to Micronesia in 1973 the US Secretary of Defense, James Schlesinger, said:

> The region not only surrounds the access routes to Guam, but also those to the Near East, and our sources of raw materials can be controlled from Micronesia. Moreover a North–South line of communication, of greater and greater importance, passes through the region, linking our Northern allies, Japan and Korea, to our allies and friends in the South, Australia and New Zealand, The Philippines and Indonesia. In the strong sense of the term, the US must remain a Pacific power.[19]

Like that notorious 1969 statement by Henry Kissinger referred to earlier, this is a specimen of the discourse of the culture of power which in its seeming clarity renders inaudible other ways of talking about the same geopolitical space and shrinks the room for manoeuvre of the parties on both sides to almost nothing. Once the issue was framed in these terms, genuine independence for Micronesian societies became a very dubious proposition for American policymakers.

Making things even more complicated for the American side, termination would require a plebiscite in Micronesia acceptable to the Security Council, a body where the Soviet Union, Cold War enemy and anti-imperial spokesman, held a veto. Such a plebiscite would stand constitutionally in Micronesia and legally in international law as a Wilsonian act of self-determination. Thus, the balloting questions themselves and the validity of the voting process *vis-à-vis* the criteria for free and fair elections have loomed large in these discussions. Somehow the Soviets would have to give their imprimatur to a process leading to an outcome in which fundamental American security interests were served. And the other people involved, that is the inhabitants of the Trust Territory, would also have to go along. Nowhere has achieving this latter requirement been more difficult for the US than in Palau.

From Dependant to Partner

The Palau that made the decision in 1975 to seek its own future was a society in ferment, a complex and deeply divided place with an intense political life. A large number of American Peace Corps volunteers were living and working in Palau, frequently on intimate terms with their hosts. More and more Palauans were entering the administration at a higher and higher level and the American-derived representative bodies and offices were attracting more and more social attention. The first wave of young people was returning from American colleges, universities and law schools. All these phenomena had the unintended consequence of demystifying the US presence for both Palauans and Americans.

The intense contradictions between American ideals and the colonial reality had always made the Trust Territory something of an anomaly, but with the steady 'Americanization' of Palau fewer and fewer people on either side of the administrative apparatus could sustain belief in the premises, conscious and unconscious, which underlay the Trusteeship. Succeeding those premises (of protection, dependency, inequality, progress and betterment) came another set, equally fictitious, but easier to sustain. These premises held that Palau and the US were somehow equivalent entities, able to negotiate as equal partners. Both societies, it was held, would be represented in those talks by negotiators who had the power to bind their respective peoples to agreements, negotiators whose legitimacy was thought to rest ultimately on the will of these peoples, expressed through majority rule voting. This perception was fundamental to the negotiating premises upon which bargaining about the future was based. In other words when the US looked at Palau in the 1970s, it no longer saw a traditional society ruled by custom and chiefs; instead it saw (or pretended to see) a version of itself.

This is not the place to detail the history of the Palau status negotiations. Such an account, even in outline, would require more space than we have available.[20] It is sufficient to note that in 1982, after a number of false starts, negotiators from the two sides agreed upon a revised draft of a Compact of Free Association to govern the future Palau–US relationship. The Compact has been more or less accepted by the American government but it has yet to be ratified by Palau, leading to many attempts to renegotiate its terms. The difficulty in Palau has resided in contradictions between certain clauses in the Compact and certain articles in Palau's Constitution.

Impasse

Free association proclaims itself as a contractual arrangement between sovereign and independent states, freely entered into, in which various rights and duties are transferred from one to another on a *quid pro quo* basis for a specified period of time. In the Palau case, the specified rights and duties mostly had to do with the security interests of the US, that is, base rights in the islands. The *quid pro quo* mostly was money – large amounts of money. During the years of negotiations leading up to the initialling of the draft Compact, political institution building in Palau continued apace. In 1980, a constitution drafted by a Constitutional Convention was adopted which ushered in a period of almost complete local self-government. A largely ceremonial House of Chiefs added a bit of local flavour, but in most respects the Constitution of Palau created the institutions and offices of something like a miniature United States. Sixteen states, derived from the old District of Palau Municipalities, which were mostly the old indigenous villages of traditional Palau, were created.These states were federated under a national government with a bicameral legislature, an independent judiciary and an executive branch led by a president and vice-president. All this for a society of fewer than 16,000 people.

One clause of the new constitution almost immediately became the source of great tension and discord, both within Palau and between it and the Americans. That clause imposed a ban on the introduction of hazardous materials, including nuclear material, into the territory of the new Republic, a ban that could only be overturned with the agreement of 75 per cent of the voters. It did not take long to see that this clause directly conflicted with those sections of the Compact which gave the US military rights in Palau. The US armed forces, after all, are nuclear-armed and large numbers of its most important naval vessels are nuclear propelled.

By the early 1980s the shape of the impasse was clear: Palauan society was attempting to constitute itself and its future relationship with its colonial ruler on the basis of two organic documents which directly contradicted each other. Neither could be changed without great difficulty. To change the salient clauses of the constitution required the consent of 75 per cent of eligible voters; to change the Compact required the US government to abandon what it viewed as its national security interests. The next dozen years were taken up with attempts to square this circle.

In 1994 success was finally achieved, but it is small exaggeration to say that it came about through a constitutional manoeuvre only marginally different from one which had failed previously and which perhaps was made possible simply because none of the players had the strength left to object. Success has come, only after eight plebiscites, three national elections, the assassination of the first Palauan president, the suicide of the second, political violence including murder, firebombings and intimidation, strikes, layoffs and furloughs, law suits almost beyond number, a multi-million dollar default by the Republic, a failed constitutional amendment, numerous congressional hearings, scathing reports written by the US General Accounting Office, Amnesty International, the United Nations, journalists and special pleaders of various persuasions, attempt after attempt by the Palauan side to reopen negotiations on the Compact and, probably most crucial of all, the disintegration of the Soviet Union.[21]

It is this last point that catches our attention. What, we ask, could have been going on that was so difficult to resolve that it required a superpower collapse before closure could be reached? Others may argue about the precise values to assign to the various factors (learning, exhaustion, etc.) that have led to the final conclusion of the termination process. All will agree on the importance of the transformation of the context in which the process was unfolding.

Context Transformation

Consider for a moment the widely believed rumour that the Americans discreetly footed the bill for the final Soviet inspection of the Trust Territory. This inspection was a necessary fig leaf before the USSR could vote to accept the termination of the Trust relationship in those parts of Micronesia which had already made their new constitutional arrangements. It was carried out shortly before the Soviet Union came to its own impecunious termination. The fact alone that this rumour exists and circulates is impressive. It is difficult to imagine stronger evidence of the transformation of the international context in which the termination process was unfolding.

The US embarked on the process of termination at least in part to eliminate the possibility that the USSR could interfere in what was regarded as an area vital to US national interests; the logic of strategic denial seemed to require this. Paradoxically, the USSR's disintegration removed not just the incentive to termination but also one of the major impediments to its successful conclusion, since the possibility of a Soviet veto had been one of the strongest cards in the hands of the Compact's opponents. Moreover, the winding down of the Cold War eliminated much of the energy behind the US desire for bases.

Timing, they say, is everything. When that much speculated upon day finally dawned and the US withdrew from its Philippine bases, those Palauans who had counted on such an eventuality to increase the value of the potential bases in their islands and thus the leverage they could bring to bear in the negotiations, found themselves in an unexpected situation. Instead of being in a position of strength, with a suddenly enhanced ability to extract concessions, including vastly increased transfer payments from the US Treasury, they found one of their prize assets losing its value. Post-Cold War shrinkage of the Pentagon budget meant that the combined actions of mother nature and the Philippine Senate did not drive the Americans back to bargaining anew with Palau as had been widely predicted. And it is hard to imagine the US Congress, with no clear strategic threat involved and with bases being closed in many home districts, appropriating money to compensate Palau so that the US could spend yet more money to build replacements for the bases at Clark Field and Subic Bay.[22]

Finally, the acquisition of external allies by the anti-Compact forces in Palau was made much more difficult by the end of the Cold War. Palau, which for a brief period in the 1980s had occupied a position on the agendas of activists in a number of countries, has moved back even further into the shadows.

Non-Cultural Obstacles

There are important reasons for the delay that cannot be assigned to the realm of culture, first among which are those associated with the effects of social scale. Palau must be one of the smallest societies ever to seek nation-state status; indeed accepted notions of nationhood are challenged by the possibility of an independent, sovereign Palau. Palau is so small and so economically dependent on the United States that the problematic act of imagination necessary for its creation as a nation is not 'imagining community' but imagining *sovereignty*.

Palau's small size meant that very small numbers of people could exert enormous influence on the outcome of events; for example, a swing of less than 200 voters in one key ballot would have concluded the process years earlier.[23] Furthermore, Palau's small scale meant that leaders were socially linked to a very high percentage of the total population by ties of kinship, business, church membership and education. Looked at from the other direction, very few people in Palau were more than one or two network links away from a leader. Hence the idea of isolating policy-makers and negotiators from the issues and passions of the moment so that long-term interests could be formulated and sought makes little sense.

On the US side also, scale played a role. Palau was never a major American preoccupation and in the massive, complex and shifting web of bureaucracies which formulated and implemented the connection between the superpower and the rest of the planet, a continuous process of education and re-education was necessary as agendas and personnel shifted and agencies gained and lost power. Few of the many opportunities for miscues, missteps and mistakes which this process presented were missed.

Both sides were badly and continuously divided internally. These internal divisions were constantly shifting, but at any one time important American and Palauan factions could be found which opposed some feature of any proposed resolution of the impasse. This situation was most acute in Palau, where a tiny, already splintered society had adopted a government structure with built-in separation of powers and a plethora of new offices which, given the demographics of leadership in such a micro- (proto-) state, almost guaranteed the emergence of very severe conflicts of interest.

Divide and rule, either intentionally or unintentionally, is a well-known colonial strategy, but here it proved counter-productive. Divisions within Palauan society made reaching agreement with the US position very difficult. Palauans were not mere passive objects, however. Their intimate knowledge of how the US government worked proved very useful to them at different times. Playing one agency, faction or even branch of the American government off against another, they too practised a kind of divide and rule, if from the bottom up.

These and other features of the social organization of the two sides and the strategies they adopted bear some of the weight for the long delay in reaching closure, but not all of it. Further, their consequences would have been dealt with much more productively had it not been for that pervasive indifference to cultural difference characteristic of the American side.

Differences in Power, Differences in Culture

With the exception of a tiny group, whose remote home islands were included within the boundaries of first the District and now the Republic, the indigenous inhabitants of Palau are linguistically and ethnically a single people. As a society, then, Palau was culturally quite homogeneous and its culture has been classified by ethnologists as Micronesian. Americo-Micronesian might better describe the current neo-colonial Palauan socio-cultural world, however. This is especially evident in the political and legal spheres.

Palau's traditional political life was composed of a constantly shifting pair of alliances, each internally organized by rank, which linked together all the villages and thus all the people of Palau and which incessantly struggled with each other for dominance. A network of ranked and competitive lineages and clans, made up of people matrilineally related and led by elders and chiefs, provided a kinship base for social organization which meshed with the village-based residential system. Traces of these indigenous structures are still actively important. To these local forms of social organization have been added a whole panoply of American-inspired political institutions based on principles of universal suffrage and residence-based representative democracy. Permeating the whole of Palauan politics, both 'traditional' and 'modern', is the deep (local) wisdom that life is to be lived competitively and statuses organized by rank.

Palauan society has been long characterized by tendencies towards ranked hierarchy and bilateral competition. These two interrelated and fundamental cultural themes have persisted under the long sequence of colonial regimes which have administered the islands – Spanish, German, Japanese, American – and they have structured Palauan life at all levels.[24] Their dynamic interplay produces a political life characterized by an unstable hierarchy of opposed pairs of social units, with those at each level incorporating those below and subsumed by that above. Each named social group, whether residential or kin-based, competes with its paired opponent at its own level while at the same time being part of a nested hierarchy. The entire social order is bifurcated into *bital*, opposing yet complementary 'sides' or 'legs' or 'halves' at each level of inclusiveness. *Bital ma bital* characterizes both opposition of units at one level and their coordination at another level when they become part of a larger *bital* facing its own opponent. *Bital ma bital* thus translates as 'half and half', or 'half versus half' depending on the context. Of course actual social life is much more complex than this simplified model indicates, but *bital ma bital* informs Palauan thinking about social life from genealogy to cosmology. It remains the key to understanding Palauan political process.

And what of American culture? Notoriously hegemonic, it may be categorized under a variety of well-freighted rubrics: individualistic, modern, postmodern, Western, global, democratic and/or imperial. The US and Palau emerge from quite separate historical trajectories and thus, regardless of the degree of 'Americanization' in Palau, culturally the two societies remain strikingly different.

The cultural differences which were salient in the history of the negotiations are many and include the differing meanings of such fundamentals as *land*, *money*, *constitution*, *law* and *voting*, as well as such 'customary matters' as the proper role of chiefs and women in political life and even the morality (or lack of it) of the Second World War. We shall focus here on one particular realm having to do with the cultural meanings given to the social organization and performance of negotiating units. For efficiency's sake, we largely restrict ourselves to American (mis)understandings of the Palauan side.

We certainly do not wish to imply that Palau has avoided badly misreading American culture but it is the case that the preponderance of ignorance, as well as the preponderance of power and wealth (an unsurprising correlation in colonial history), lay with the Americans.

Therefore in what follows we will primarily attend to the ways that an unreflective, uncritical reliance on American cultural models by the US side led to failures of understanding.

Teams and Sides

Americans and Palauans both frequently drew on a 'team' metaphor in talking about the negotiations, but instead of a US-style cooperative group subsuming individual goals in the pursuit of a collective good, the Palauans seem to have meant something else. A glance at the way baseball is played in Palau begins to illustrate this meaning.

The Palauans learned baseball from the Japanese and it has become a favourite sport. Groups of friends, villages and hamlets all form the basis for teams which compete. Naturally enough, the level of play varies: sometimes it reaches awe-inspiring heights of brilliance and at others equally awe-inspiring depths of incompetence. Often such heights and depths are achieved by the same team during the same game, sometimes even in the same inning. The key factor seems to be the quality of the first move. If the first player makes a good play – say spearing the ball with a diving catch and winging it towards a baseman to start a double play – his whole side (and even at times the entire field) is likely to respond with brilliant moves of their own, as each person seems to draw energy and inspiration from the possibilities of perfection aroused by that first performance. But if he bobbles the ball, then a cascading series of errors is likely to result, as each player in turn withdraws his attention and even at times his physical engagement from the game. By the time that sequence of (attempted) plays finishes, most people on the field will be busily demonstrating their lack of connection with what was going on by gazing off into the distance, talking to someone in the crowd, or even wandering off in search of a snack. Whether the sequence is one of error or brilliance, though, the game will proceed to the next episode, and both possibilities will again await realization.

To the great consternation of the Americans, moments in the negotiating process demonstrated each of these Palauan configurations. Thus, just when the conclusion was reached that the Palau side was uncommonly canny, deploying a well-coordinated tactical game plan in which everyone was skilfully playing their roles in the unfolding of some master strategy, something would happen and the Palau side suddenly would no longer be much of a team (in the American sense of course). Instead of 'hanging in there', as American common sense dictates one should when faced with an obstacle, the Palauan negotiating team either literally or figuratively disassembled itself in ways very similar to a baseball team that made a bad play. Even if people from the American side had been familiar with the Palauan style of baseball, it is unlikely they would have drawn this correlation or learned from it. Baseball, after all, is America's favourite pastime, and if those Micronesians were playing it differently, then they were just playing it wrong.

As problematic as the 'play' of the Palau 'team', from the American point of view, was its size. The 'oversized' delegations which Palau sent to the talks in such places as Guam, Hawaii, New York and Washington generated much cynical American talk about *per diem* expenses and vacation trips. Why else would so many people show up for the talks? In the US context, where institutionalized nervousness about 'junkets' is endemic, such a question makes good local sense. Behind this cynicism might well have been irritation that the size of Palau's delegation made it difficult if not impossible for the US to discover or constitute locally powerful leaders ('chiefs') with whom and through whom control could be maintained – a common colonial aim. Palau subverted this goal by presenting the Americans with a moving cloud of constantly shifting 'leaders'.[25]

To account for the size of the delegations it is not necessary to paint anyone as either pettily venal or heroically anti-colonial, nor is it necessary to classify the Palauans as bad team players for repeatedly 'dropping the ball'. In fact such labelling probably was part of the reason things did not proceed more smoothly; it was simply the application of self-confirming American cultural knowledge. The cultural knowledge which Palauans use in their production and interpretation of social action, including negotiating future political status, is quite different from that used by Americans. There is little if any evidence that the US government ever noticed this.

Leadership in Palau

In a world of hierarchy and bilateral competition, the task of leadership is different from that in a world of bureaucratic representation. Leadership in Palau requires keeping the subunits that compose one's side satisfied that their ends are being served so that the 'balanced opposition' between them which has produced a side to lead does not evaporate. Should that happen – and it does – the leader becomes an ex-leader.

The leader's achievement of personal ends in such a situation requires another kind of balance, one in which those personal ends and the communal ends of the *bital* and its subunits are not seen to be in competition. This explains why one of the elaborate Palauan metaphors describing different paths to power talks in terms of a lizard. The cold-blooded reptilian nature of the creature is not salient. Rather, the metaphor points at the way this species of lizard, by continuously manoeuvring to stay out of sight, always reaches the top of the tree unnoticed by any observer.[26]

The groups Palau sent to negotiate with the US were always groups of leaders and that accounts for their size. To embody all the forces and factions of Palauan social life salient to the creation of Palau's future and sustain them in balance while the negotiations dragged on required the presence of all those persons who constituted, and whose statuses as leaders were constituted by, those very forces and factions. Because all those persons were also ambitious politicians in their own right, in their competition with one another they shifted sides with bewildering (to the Americans' eyes) facility. And when things went wrong, as they did on several occasions, the group stopped being a unified '*bital*' of any sort and fragmented into its several elements. This happened most dramatically after the two presidential deaths, when there seems to have been a very marked falling back to lower levels of balanced opposition before a new inclusive configuration was recreated. Whatever the circumstances and motivations behind those two national tragedies – and the political struggles surrounding the Compact and the constitution are surely implicated – among their consequences was a marked dissolution and later reconstitution of the Palauan side of the negotiations.

Thus, the composition and performance of the groups which Palau sent to negotiate on its behalf were no exception to the *bital ma bital* pattern characteristic of Palauan social life in general. It is impressive to note that we have found nothing to indicate that the US was even aware of this pattern, let alone of its possible role in how the negotiations played out. And that ignorance had consequences, not least the painful and destructive prolongation of the talks. The tantalizing possibility exists that, unnoticed by its ruler/negotiating partner, the Palauan side was attempting to enter into a relation of balanced opposition with it, *bital ma bital*.

American negotiators also brought their own metaphors with them, of course. They just did not notice that they were metaphors. For example, they talked of 'the table', of getting to it, of putting all their cards on it, of dealing with people on this side and on that side of it. Those same people who unreflectively talked about tables (with all their implications of direct, face-to-face, seated, calm discussions) occasionally noted the name of the legislative body which Palauans had created in their new constitution. If they had ever reflected on that name – *Olbiil Era Kalulau*, or House of Whispers – they might have seen how another society was imagining political life and then might have noticed their own imaginings.

CONCLUSIONS

The departure point of our case study was the failure of a set of bilateral negotiations to reach early and easy closure, a particularly instructive failure given the astronomical difference in power between the two sides. What is revealed here is not just the inability of power easily to override culture, but something more subtle – the way the culture of power is oblivious to itself.

While acutely conscious of the discrepancies in the power of the two societies, policy-makers and negotiators on the American side at least seem to have remained resolutely blind to the differences in culture. This blindness, in turn, we argue, arose from the failure of the US side to recognize the deeply American assumptions with which its negotiators and policy-makers were operating.

Even on those rare occasions when the American side took note of Palauan culture, as they were forced to when Palauans talked of such 'traditional' matters as chiefs and the role of a clan's women in controlling the allocation of titles and land, they seemed oblivious to the peculiarly American meanings in which they themselves were trafficking. It is almost as if they were saying to the Palauans, 'You have culture (i.e. customs) but no power; we have power (i.e. money and weapons) but no culture.' Such a stance grows out of a profound lack of cultural awareness.

By cultural awareness in this context we refer to an awareness that a difference may exist in the way the social world is understood and that this difference may play a role in the course of negotiations. Furthermore, such an awareness rests on the willingness to make explicit the cultural assumptions which all parties carry – the self as well as the other. Because American ideas about both the issues and the processes involved remained largely unexamined, Palauan understanding of these matters remained invisible to the Americans. And because those understandings stayed invisible, the talks were protracted and difficult and Palauan society was subjected to a decade of destructive stress and pressure, the consequences of which are still untold.

The US, in its desire for finality, in its insistence on the power of votes and signatures to bind whole societies forever, and in its presentation of the talks as though between equals sitting across a table, was operating on many of the premises and assumptions which have traditionally operated in the international arena. The Palauans, with a tradition of keeping settlements provisional, with a strong desire to give hereditary leadership an active role in any decision with society-wide implications, and with their peculiar genius for organizing virtually every interaction (including elections, negotiations and signing ceremonies) into a display of hierarchical competition, were not operating on those same assumptions and premises.

Taking a longer view, it might well be that in the emerging world culture a single set of premises and assumptions will continue to govern international negotiations. It is a pretty resilient culture model after all. But the breakdown of the old international regime and the creation of a new one is going to involve many more of the kinds of encounters that we have analysed here.

As increasing numbers of previously unrepresented peoples enter the world arena, international negotiations will increasingly involve attempts to reach accords across deep cultural divides. An attention to culture in such circumstances may be difficult, but it is important. Its difficulty lies in the blindness of power to anything but itself; its importance lies in the trauma that such blindness can inflict on those caught up in its path.

ACKNOWLEDGEMENT

The authors wish to thank B.W. Black for her unflagging assistance.

NOTES

1. H. Kissinger, *White House Years* (Boston, MA: Little, Brown and Company, 1979), pp. 100–1.
2. The *locus classicus* of this view, for the twentieth century at least, is to be found in Hans Morgenthau's *Politics among Nations: the Struggle for Power and Peace* (New York, NY: Alfred A. Knopf, 1956).

3. See K. Avruch and P.W. Black, 'Ideas of Human Nature in Contemporary Conflict Resolution Theory', *Negotiation Journal* (Vol. 6, No. 3, 1990), pp. 226–7.
4. There is one significant difference from the miniature solar system. There were in effect two suns. In the heyday of realism in international relations, the Cold War, the 'nucleus' was considered a dual, bipolar entity: the West and the East, with weaker states revolving around the strong centres of the US and the USSR.
5. M. Banks, 'The International Relations Discipline: Asset or Liability for Conflict Resolution?', in E. Azar and J. Burton (eds), *International Conflict Resolution: Theory and Practice* (Brighton: Wheatsheaf Books, 1986), p. 10.
6. See, among many others, J.W. Burton, *Global Conflict: The Domestic Sources of International Crisis* (Brighton: Wheatsheaf Books, 1984); D.L. Horowitz, *Ethnic Groups in Conflict* (Berkeley, CA: University of California Press, 1985); and J.V. Montville (ed.), *Conflict and Peacemaking in Multiethnic Societies* (Lexington, MA: Lexington Books, 1991). Preceding these voices was that of Clifford Geertz, who argued that the postcolonial struggles of 'new' states were inseparable from internal cultural dynamics: see *Old Societies and New States* (Glencoe, NY: The Free Press, 1963).
7. We mean works that are analytical of culture and negotiation, not merely memoiristic, and we limit ourselves here to Americans. First, we note the importance of Edward T. Hall, who was on the staff of the US State Department's Foreign Service Institute (FSI) in the 1950s, and introduced many of the ideas on intercultural communication to young and future diplomats. Consider also Edmund Glenn, who was chief of the State Department's translation services for many years, *Man and Mankind: Conflict and Communication between Cultures* (Norwood, NJ: Ablex, 1981), and works by Glen Fisher, a diplomat and former dean at the FSI, *International Negotiation: A Cross-Cultural Perspective* (Yarmouth, ME: Intercultural Press, 1980) and *Mindsets: The Role of Culture and Perception in International Relations* (Yarmouth, ME: Intercultural Press, 1988). See also H. Binnendijk (ed.), *National Negotiating Styles* (Washington, DC: Foreign Service Institute, US Department of State, 1987).
8. See particularly R. Cohen, *Culture and Conflict in Egyptian-Israeli Relations: a Dialogue of the Deaf* (Bloomington, IN: Indiana University Press, 1990); and *Negotiating across Cultures: Communication Obstacles in International Diplomacy* (Washington, DC: United States Institute of Peace Press, 1991). See also I.W. Zartman and M.R. Berman, *The Practical Negotiator* (New Haven, CT: Yale University Press, 1982), pp. 224–9. A cross-cultural approach to conflict and conflict resolution at levels below the state can be found in K. Avruch, P.W. Black and J.A. Scimecca (eds), *Conflict Resolution: Cross-Cultural Perspectives* (New York, NY: Greenwood Press, 1991).
9. Zartman and Berman, *op. cit.*, in note 8, p. 226.
10. For a precise definition of 'intercultural' conflict, see K. Avruch and P.W. Black, 'The Culture Question and Conflict Resolution', *Peace & Change* (Vol. 16, No. 1, 1991), pp. 37–8.

11. R. Cohen, *Culture and Conflict, op. cit.*, in note 8, pp. 14–15.
12. Ibid., p. 15.
13. A 'solution', perhaps, in the draconian sense that genocide is indeed one 'solution' to interethnic problems.
14. These are just the sort of questions John W. Burton has asked for many years in his conflict-resolution based critique of power politics and realism; see, for example J.W. Burton, *Conflict: Resolution and Prevention* (New York: St. Martin's Press, 1990). On the other hand, Burton has a constricted sense of culture. See, K. Avruch and P. Black, 'A Generic Theory of Conflict Resolution: a Critique', *Negotiation Journal* (Vol. 3, No. 1, 1987), pp. 87–96, 99–100; and J.W. Burton and D. Sandole, 'Expanding the Debate on Generic Theory of Conflict Resolution: A Response to a Critique', *Negotiation Journal* (Vol. 3, No. 1, 1987), pp. 97–9.
15. A few words about two key terms are necessary. Palau is also Belau. We follow the convention used in the islands. Palau is the preferred term when English is used and Belau when Belauan is used. Second, we include within the term 'negotiations' all communications of whatever nature between the two sides concerning the issue of Palau's future relationship to the United States.
16. Cited in W.J. Hickel, *Who Owns America?* (Englewood Cliffs, NJ: Prentice Hall, 1971), p. 208.
17. *Report of the US Survey Mission to the Trust Territory of the Pacific Islands* (Washington, DC: The White House, 1963). The anti-compact perspective informs, *inter alia*, R. Aldridge and C. Meyers, *Resisting the Serpent: Palau's Struggle for Self Determination* (Baltimore, MD: Fortkamp Publishing Company, 1990); C. Lutz (ed.), *Micronesia as a Strategic Colony: The Impact of U.S. Policy on Micronesian Health and Culture* (Cambridge, MA: Cultural Survival, 1984); S.Roff, *Overreaching in Paradise: United States Policy in Palau Since 1945* (Juneau, AL: Denali Press, 1991); J. Anglim, 'Palau: Constitution for Sale', *Bulletin of Concerned Asian Scholars* (Vol. 22, No. 1, 1990), pp. 5–20; and L. Wilson, 'Women of Belau: Confronting US Military Policy in the Pacific', *Radcliffe Quarterly* (June 1993), pp. 14–16.
18. Pro-compact narrative may be found in official reports, e.g. US Department of State, *Trust Territory of the Pacific Islands: 37th Annual Report to the United Nations* (Washington, DC: US Government Printing Office, 1984) and administration testimony in, e.g., US Senate, *To Approve the Compact of Free Association*, Hearings Before the Committee on Energy and Natural Resources, 98th Congress, 2d Session, No. 98–1067, 24 May 1984; and to some extent in, *inter alia*, A. Leibowitz, *The Last Trusteeship: The Struggle over Palau* (manuscript); and A. Ranney and H. Penniman, *Democracy in the Islands: The Micronesian Plebiscites of 1983* (Washington, DC: American Enterprise Institute for Public Policy Research, 1985).
19. J. Winkler, *Losing Control: Towards an Understanding of Transnational Corporations in the Pacific Islands Context* (Suva, Fiji: Pacific Conference of Churches, 1982), pp. 23–4.

20. For the history of the negotiations, see K. Nakamura, 'Letter to Leadership of Fourth Olbiil Era Kelulau from the President of Palau Regarding Implementation of the Proposed Company of Free Association Between the Republic of Palau and the United States of America', Serial 0318-93 (Koror, Palau: Office of the President, 12 May 1993); G. Smith, *Micronesia: Decolonisation and U.S. Military Interests in the Trust Territory of the Pacific Islands* (Canberra: Australian National University Press, 1991); E. Wood, 'Prelude to an Anti-War Constitution', *Journal of Pacific History* (Vol. 28, No. 1, 1993), p. 67; J. Dorrance, *Micronesian Crosscurrents and the US Role in the Western Pacific: A Case Study of US Interests, Objectives and Policy Implementation with Recommendations for Change* (Washington, DC: National War College, 1975); D. Shuster, 'Elections, Compact and Assassination in the Republic of Palau', *Pacific Studies* (Vol. 12, No. 1, 1988), pp. 23–48; and V. Uherbelau, 'Closing Statement: 60th United Nations Trusteeship Council', New York, NY, 17 May 1993.

21. Among the most important of these reports are A. Boss *et al.*, *Report of the International Observer Mission, Palau Referendum, December 1986* (New York: International League for Human Rights, Minority Rights Group, 1987); L. Christopher, *Palau's Evolving Relationship to the United States*, Report No. 88-442F (Washington, DC: Congressional Research Service, 1988); S. Solarz *et al.*, 'Problems in Paradise: US Interests in the South Pacific', Report of a Congressional Delegation to the South Pacific, 5-16 August, 1989, 101st Congress, 2d Session (Washington, DC: US Government Printing Office). US General Accounting Office, *US Trust Territory: Issues Associated with Palau's Transition to Self-Government*, Publication 89-182 (Washington, DC: US Government Printing Office, 1989). See also R. Parmentier, 'The Rhetoric of Free Association and Palau's Political Struggle', *The Contemporary Pacific* (Vol. 3, No. 1, 1991), pp. 146–58.

22. Nevertheless, an unnamed source travelling with Secretary of State Christopher stated that the US intended to remain a military power in Asia: 'Investment in the next several years will be in the direction of much greater mobility so that in the event of disobliging circumstances we could cross the Pacific very quickly.' See D. Zabarenko, 'US to Beef up Military in Asia', *Honolulu Star-Bulletin*, 26 July 1993, p. A-1.

23. D. Shuster, 'Politics, Ethnicity and Violence in Palau: The Furlough Period' (Laie, HI: Brigham Young University, Institute for Polynesian Studies, 1990, ms).

24. For the history of Palau, see, among others, K. Nero, *Cherechar a Lokelii: Beads of History of Koror, Palau 1780–1983*, PhD dissertation, University of California, 1987. For recent ethnographic analyses, see C. Ferreira, *Palauan Cosmology: Dominance in a Traditional Micronesia Society* (Gothenburg: Acta Universitatus Gothoburgensis, 1987); R. Parmentier, *The Sacred Remains: Myth, History and Polity in Belau* (Chicago, IL: University of Chicago Press, 1987); and D. Smith, *Palauan Social Structure* (New Brunswick, NJ: Rutgers University Press, 1983). For *bital ma bital* as metaphor, see R. and M. Force,

'Keys to Cultural Understanding', *Science* (Vol. 133, No. 3460, 1961), pp. 1202–6.
25. D. Rubinstein, personal communication, 1993.
26. R. McKnight, *Competition in Palau*. PhD dissertation, Ohio State University, 1960.

4 International Political Economy as a Culture of Competition[1]
David Blaney and Naeem Inayatullah

INTRODUCTION

That the international political economy is competitive is not controversial. Competition usually is seen as endemic to the anarchic structure of international life. As members of an international society, states are constituted as independent actors who must rely primarily on their own resources and efforts to achieve their goals and purposes. This requirement of 'self-help' becomes 'competitive self-help' where the goals and purposes of states are incompatible. If, as we are often told, states are compelled to define important goals in terms of relative gains, then competition assumes a prominent and defining role in international life.

Such a characterization is only bolstered when we consider that states are embedded within a capitalist global division of labour. Although the expansive and integrative logic of capitalism has incorporated the globe into a single economic space, a genuinely world economy, political boundaries continue to demarcate this singular space into national units because, in part, these boundaries operate as distributive devices. Thus, states compete both for market shares for their firms and regions in the world market and to promote and attract the development of technologically advanced and high-profit firms and industries within their boundaries. Whether we see the state as guarantor of the economic welfare and security of its citizenry or as concerned primarily with its own capacities, competition retains its force as a prominent feature of international society.

We do not mean to claim by this that competition exhausts the character of international social life. Certainly, alternative practices are widespread, although these tend to be established in relation or opposition to competition.[2] Thus, few would question that competition remains a core concept of social theory. However, competition is rarely, if ever, given a self-consciously theoretical treatment. This neglect is itself suggestive of the hold that a culture of competition has on our imagination – that we can legitimately treat competition as given. Our aim is, then, to redress this absence of theory. We suggest that competition is a meaningful scheme, a social practice involving the juxtaposition of certain values and principles which constitute the self and construct its relation with others. More specifically, our argument is that international political economy is a particular culture, constituted importantly by the continuing attempt to mediate the opposition between the principles of equality and hierarchy through the staging of competitions. On the one hand, the modern practice of competition constructs actors as formally equal and independent competitors in contradistinction to a fixed hierarchy of status. On the other hand, competitive practices continue to join this formal status of equality to a hierarchy revealed within a social process of staging competitions. Thus, the hierarchies revealed in modern competitive practices stand simultaneously as an expression of the equality of actors and as a vitiation of that equality.

The notion that the structures and processes of international political economy are 'cultural' remains controversial, despite the increasing concern with cultural questions or issues within international relations. Perhaps best known, although somewhat hysterical in tone, is Samuel Huntington's declaration that in the wake of the Cold War international conflict will be 'cultural', that battles will be fought between the primordially distinct 'civilizations' of the West and its competitors, Confucian East Asia and Islam.[3] Others read the assertions of cultural pluralism versus a Western society of states against a longer historical context and within a deeper theoretical vision.[4] The issue has been defined in large part by the project of Hedley Bull and Adam Watson to trace the evolution and expansion of an originally European society of states across the globe. This expansion of the European state system by force and example created a single (albeit multicultural) society of states, thereby inspiring various forms of resistance and revolt which threaten the background of common norms, values and purposes that order international society.[5] Still others raise cultural questions against the backdrop of the globalization of production and consumption facilitated by the emergence of a world economy. The process of globalization may be seen (and perhaps celebrated) as a harbinger of the emergence of a global culture/civil society and the attendant political possibilities of global management, if not deliberation,[6] or castigated as the destruction of diversity or the dissolution of culture itself.[7] Perhaps both accounts are overdrawn as we encounter processes of cultural diversification and localization alongside, even as responses to, these globalizing processes.[8] Although culture has arrived as a topic of conversation, its status as a category within IR/IPE theory remains unclear. Establishing culture as a category of IR/IPE is a task beyond the ambitions of this chapter.[9] We do hope, however, to suggest the overall plausibility of our account of the logic of international political economy as a culture of competition and a competition and hierarchy of cultures. We organize our discussion into four sections. The first section maps the set of oppositions or tensions evoked by the use of 'culture' and discusses the implications of a social constructivist approach. The second section sketches out the structure of meanings and purposes defining the 'cultural' logic of competition. Here, we emphasize the way a peculiar juxtaposition of the principles of formal equality and competitively revealed hierarchy is central to the social practice and purposes of competition. We draw on numerous theorists and analysts, especially the work of Friedrich Hayek, in developing our account of this cultural logic. Although our ultimate purpose is to dispute Hayek's political conclusions (as we do more clearly in the conclusion), we find Hayek invaluable as an 'informant' on the meaningful structure of a culture of competition. In the third section, we demonstrate that the interweaving of the logics of sovereignty and the capitalist global division of labour similarly counterposes principles of formal equality and revealed hierarchy. International social life is thereby constituted both as a culture of competition and as a competition and hierarchy of cultures. Fourth, and by way of conclusion, we argue that the sense of 'innate' inferiority and 'natural' superiority attached to formally equal individuals within a culture of competition is the central social contradiction of that structure of meaning and purpose. Highlighting this contradiction focuses our attention on the failure of modern society to come fully to grips with the meaning of the transition from traditional hierarchy to modern equality – a confusion that drives the modern social actor to construct the other as ripe for subordination and exploitation. We close by hinting at a reinterpretation of competition as a spur to the pursuit of excellence within the self through contact with others.

CULTURE AND SOCIAL CONSTRUCTION

In what sense can we think of international political economy as culture? Answering this question requires that we tread on the dangerous conceptual terrain of definitions of culture.[10] Without attempting an exhaustive review or some synthesis, we suggest that the use of 'culture' evokes two related tensions or oppositions.[11] First, the use of the term points to a distinction between culture and nature, and the cultural and the natural. 'Culture' suggests human activity and creative capacities; the human capacity to construct, live and aesthetically express a form of life; human action to embrace and practise as well as to critique and reform the 'values and visions' of an inherited form of life.[12] To use a different language, human beings live in the world according to a certain 'vision' or 'cultural representation'. This 'vision' sustains cultural life, constituting a way of life's specific identity in relation to the larger cosmos – its particular conception of what it means to be a human community in the world.[13] Thus, human artifice is contrasted with the fixities and givens of nature, and the human being is freed and determined as a cultural being. This is not to free the species from material existence, but to suggest that humans 'live in the material world ... according to a meaningful scheme of [their] own devising.'[14]

Second, the use of 'culture' at once points to universality and commonality *and* to partiality and diversity. 'Culture' refers us to the universal in human experience – the meaningful and constructed quality of human existence – and to the particular commonalties constructed as the basis of distinctiveness in relation to others. We should note that increasingly the universality evoked by 'culture' as central to human existence and the commonalties forming a distinct community are joined in claims about the arrival of a global culture.[15] However, the term 'culture' still strongly signals that human artifice is multiple: 'culture' continues to appear as 'cultures' and seems to stand in tension with the joining of concepts implied by the idea of a global culture. It remains important, then, that a way of life is not only an ongoing process of self-definition, but that each way of life defines itself as a distinct identity in relation to others.[16] Thus, the language of 'culture' draws our attention to the construction and maintenance of a meaningful and purposeful scheme of existence as a common, yet still multiple, human project.

With this 'sense' of culture in mind, we can begin to think about what it would mean to construct international political economy as a culture of competition. Central to our claim is the idea that competition is not a 'fact' of nature.[17] Rather, competition is a social construction, a particular structuring of meaning and purpose which informs competitive social practices and gives competition its central role within the cultural logic of modern society. We emphasize the socially constructed quality of social life because the metaphor of 'construction' allows us to de-reify competition as a social practice that has been naturalized or taken for granted, potentially identify an agency responsible for motivating, activating or operating competitive social practices, investigate the structure of meaning – the goals, purposes and values – that actors as competitive agents hold and upon which they act, and highlight possibilities for a transformation or reinterpretation of the structure of meaning informing and enabling competition. Despite these potential gains, we believe that the addition of the language of 'structure' serves as a necessary counterweight to a pure or naive constructivism. The idea that the social world is a world of meaning and purpose does not entail that agents acting on the basis of a particular set of meanings and purposes will necessarily achieve the intended results. Therefore, we do not focus on possible agentic source(s) of competition – states, multinational corporations, producers of knowledge, etc. – in our constructivist account of competition. If we point to a source, shaping and perpetuating our current practice of competition, it is the deep confusion about the meanings and purposes that lies at the heart of a modern culture of competition and our (read: human beings, with varying degrees of reflexivity and resistance) willingness and/or compulsion to live according to this confusion. The organization and confusion of meaning and purpose structuring the practice of competition appears in our work, then, as analogous to a structural constraint. It must be stressed, though, that we conceive such a structure as simultaneously internal to the individual actors and as constitutive – as both constraining and enabling of the individual actor as a certain kind of agent. We accept this residue of structural analysis as the necessary overlap of structural and constructivist practice.[18]

THE MEANINGFUL STRUCTURE OF COMPETITION

Our point of departure, then, is that competition is not a fact of nature, but a social practice. In this section, we will sketch out the meaningful and purposeful structure of competition in modern social life. Although our eventual purpose – to expose the antinomies of this cultural logic – is quite foreign to Friedrich Hayek, his voice looms large in our account here because his work stands as a powerful exploration (and defence) of the meaning and purpose of competition. Indeed, his account of the cultural logic of competition is mostly supported by others who have been compelled to lay out that logic as a prelude to an apology or critique.

Competition, in our age at least, presumes and expresses the formal equality of the individuals or selves brought into competition. At the same time, competitive situations assume and establish a ranking (or hierarchy) of achievement or value – winners and losers, gold, silver, and bronze, top ten lists, etc. How can these principles be reconciled? Within the cultural logic of competition, hierarchy is not necessarily seen to violate the formal equality of individuals because competitions in principle are not to be decided by prior difference in social status. Rather, hierarchies are to be based on individual differences, which are made manifest in the competition itself.[19] The way a culture of competition joins formal equality and revealed hierarchy requires more careful examination.

Friedrich Hayek helps us understand this logic where he describes competition as a kind of experiment, as a 'discovery procedure'.[20] The staging of competitions both assumes and is a means to the discovery of these individual differences; that is, competitions require that individuals adopt competitive strategies to mobilize and display their particular quality and quantity of ability, skill, or effort. Where a ranking is established in relation to individual efforts and achievements, the individual's position in the hierarchy is taken, perhaps inevitably, as a sign of the self's merit or value relative to others,[21] although we cannot assure a perfect correspondence between merit and rewards due to the contingencies of human interaction – the role of luck /chance in competitive activities or games.[22] In other words, the individual establishes his or her value in a modern society in good part through a process of comparison with others made possible by the staging competitions. The hierarchy of value established through competition and the formal equality of individuals seem to coexist only uneasily. However, within this cultural logic, competition is not normally seen as the source of hierarchy. Rather, as Hayek explains, the rankings produced by competition merely reflect 'one of the most distinctive facts about the human species' – 'the boundless variety of human nature' and 'the wide range of differences in individual capacities and potentialities'. These differences are taken to exist logically prior to, or to be given outside of, the competition itself. This is not inconsistent with the fact that being immersed in competitive practices may spur individuals to prepare themselves or enhance their combination of skills and effort, perhaps adopting the methods of successful competitors as models, because these individual differences, whether innate or cultivated, are seen as belonging purely to the individual, apart from or outside of the social practice of competition. This introduces the possibility of social mobility across successive competitions because competitions act to uncover a hierarchy latently present in the individual and independent traits of the competitors at a certain point in time, not some fixed distribution of skills or achievements. Thus, a culture of competition treats hierarchy as an underlying set of individual differences merely expressed in the competitive interactions of formally free and equal individuals.[23]

Though these competitive interactions are central to a certain kind of social order,[24] Hayek's language is consistent with the way a culture of competition establishes and defines the fact of hierarchy as 'natural': hierarchies are seen to be intrinsic to human populations as a set of traits potentially revealed and ranked in competitions. Competition appears, then, as no more than a set of rules designed to reveal what is already latently present in nature. In this ethical context, we cannot challenge the justice of hierarchy itself or hierarchies revealed by adequately designed rules for competition. At most, we can question specific rankings based on either the inadequacy of particular sets of rules to perform the task of ranking or on violations of adequate rules because they fail to recognize the formal equality of the competitors.[25]

In a culture of competition, we might be led to consider hierarchy and hierarchies as beyond ethical concern since they are treated as given and thereby unamenable to human design. But for Hayek, competition expresses central social values, and the revelation of hierarchies serves important social purposes. We can be most specific about these values and purposes by focusing on the market as the central site within a culture of competition where competitions are staged and a hierarchy of skills and effort revealed and (however imperfectly) rewarded.[26]

Most importantly perhaps, the market, as a discovery procedure, embodies and expresses the status of competitors as equally individual and independent (albeit needy)[27] selves. Competitors come to the market with a right to property, as property owners and 'freely contracting individuals'.[28] The discovery procedure employed by the market is also valued in a culture of competition because it is linked to the achievement of certain social goods. The system of rewards organized by the market not only unleashes human productive efforts, it directs those efforts to producing the things needed by others, crucial because the market fosters a situation of economic interdependence. The market also exposes less productive efforts and validates more productive ones, thereby providing models of effective competitive strategies and generating greater wealth at the cost of fewer resources and efforts. Thus, as Hayek explains, the competitions staged in the market are valuable because they generate wealth and improve the chances that each individual will have his or her 'separate and incommensurable ends' met.[29]

To summarize, the market actualizes a certain set of 'values and visions': the good life possible in a culture of competition is realized where wealth is generated via competitive mechanisms that embody the status of selves as individual, independent and formally equal actors.

INTERNATIONAL POLITICAL ECONOMY AS A CULTURE OF COMPETITION

The cultural logic of competition is also a constitutive feature of international social life. International political economy comprises an interweaving of the logics of sovereignty (the realization of the equality and independence of political communities in a society of states) and global capitalism (a hierarchical ordering revealed in the competitions staged in a world market). Together these interwoven practices form the 'constitutive horizon'[30] of international social life as a culture of competition.

Sovereignty, the independence of states and the absence of a supreme political authority,[31] conjures up for most international relations theorists the image of a war-filled 'state of nature', billiard ball states and the anarchy problematic.[32] However, this 'state of nature' was 'founded'. As Cornelia Navari argues:

> is not there something odd about the 'state of nature' which constitutes international relations – namely, the fact that it did not always exist? The fact that it was an *established* state of nature which emerged out of something that went before . . . [?]

And indeed the state of nature did have to be founded. It was scarcely natural to the men of the time that social organization be cut off from external authority, formed into billiard balls and the space between emptied. The notion of the state as a billiard ball is a convention; it was instituted. That condition of affairs is maintained by other conventions, such as non-intervention and recognition, which were also instituted. To say simply that the space between is 'empty' is not true. It is 'empty' in the sense that for certain purposes the state is a billiard ball.

But the space is full of conventions which maintain that image. It is also full of the convention that societies must become states for certain purposes.[33]

As this makes clear and as is crucial to Hedley Bull's distinction between system and society, a society of states is more than merely a pattern of interaction among otherwise isolated political communities. Rather, a society of states is a set of historically constructed social practices stabilized by and made meaningful in terms of a more or less common form of (international) social life. In terms closer to Bull's, a society of states requires that there be a set of recognized norms and principles, of common values and purposes, which give shape and meaning to the interactions among states and give the society its value and meaning to the participants.[34] Thus, a society of states is (a) culture in that it stands as a specific way of assigning meaning and value, a specific way of organizing international social life such that states are constituted and valued as billiard balls.[35]

To be more precise, the principle of sovereignty was elaborated as a response to the hierarchical social order of Christendom, the idea that outside forces (God, pope, emperor) determine the life of each 'community', weaving them into a single 'Christian Commonwealth'.[36] The establishment of a society of sovereign states gives force to the idea that final authority should rest within each independent community, that each community is, in this sense, self-determining. The idea is that each political community should be governed by rules, norms, goals and purposes which belong to it in some strong sense, which express the 'values and visions' implicit in the community's conception of the good life.[37] Ideas of national, popular or territorial self-determination are all versions of this idea implicit in sovereignty.[38]

The principles of the equality of states and the obligation of tolerance appear as corollaries of sovereignty and community self-determination. Leo Gross explains that the principles of equality and the coexistence of separate political communities were made central to the society of states at its inception:

> In the political field, [the Peace of Westphalia] marked man's abandonment of the idea of a hierarchical structure of society and his option for a new system characterized by the coexistence of a multiplicity of states, each sovereign within its territory, equal to one another and free from any external earthly authority.[39]

It is this conception of an international society embracing, on a footing of equality, the entire human race irrespective of religion and form of government which is usually said to have triumphed in the seventeenth century over the medieval conception of a more restricted Christian society organized hierarchically, that is, on the basis of inequality.[40]

In principle, each political community is recognized as a sovereign equal, possessing the same rights and duties. This equality of status implies a duty or an obligation by each political community to respect the sovereignty of others,[41] to allow different versions of the good life to be played out – free from unwanted interference – behind the protection of sovereign boundaries. Of course, various forms and degrees of unwanted intrusions continue to occur, but the principle of sovereignty allows us to identify these as 'interventions'[42] and, to the extent that sovereignty directs state action, the principle allows a relatively safe place in which a community's vision can be implemented. It is in this sense that the principles of equality and tolerance of individual difference are constitutive of and made manifest in a society of states.

We must stress again that states are treated as formally equal and independent sovereigns because of their presumed value as sites or receptacles for the realization of the 'values and visions' of peoples or cultures. That cultures neatly map onto states or that states can adequately represent or contain cultures remain problematic ideas and are sources of some dissatisfaction with sovereignty,[43] yet 'nation-ness' remains 'the most universally legitimate value' of our time. In fact, the force of the logic of sovereignty compels that cultures or forms of life be 'imagined' primarily as political communities (bounded in relation to others and equally sovereign as states), as nascent states, or as relatively autonomous actors within multi-nation states.[44] Thus, whatever the limits of the state as a container of the 'values and visions' of a political community, it is principally as or inside a state (acting within a society of states) that a form of life must seek to realize the 'values and visions' which express and by which it constructs its identity.

We can say, then, that in international social life each state or political community is thought of as an independent and equal self, with a sense of itself and a series of projects or goals and values associated with expressing that identity. Any such identity has implications for economic 'policy'. The identity of a political community might incorporate or exclude capital accumulation and economic growth for its own sake, represented, for example, by developmentalists and ecological movements respectively. Nevertheless, it is important to recognize that even simple reproduction, or zero growth, requires the creation of wealth; that is, realizing the projects, the values and visions, of any political community depends on some degree of wealthiness, compelling wealth creation as a necessary element of social life. The idea of sovereignty accounts for this compulsion by reserving and protecting the state's rights to its own resources and efforts as means to realizing its purposes. Charles Tilly notes that this idea is central to the principle of self-determination:

> If . . . a people controls a state of its own, it has the collective right to exclude or subordinate members of other populations with respect to the territory and benefits under control of that state.[45]

It is not unfair, then, to see sovereignty as the attribution of a 'collective property right' within contemporary international political economy. Charles Beitz writes:

> The requirement of respect for a state's domestic jurisdiction functions as a kind of collective property right for the citizens of that state – it entitles the state to exclude foreigners from the use or benefit of its wealth and resources except on terms that it voluntarily accepts.[46]

Sovereign boundaries thereby demarcate a space for the pursuit of a community's 'values and visions' as well as bounding and protecting the resources and efforts to be drawn upon as means to realizing that form of life. In addition, the claim of this right by a state establishes by implication an equal right of other communities to reserve their resources and wealth for their own purposes. In this way, sovereignty constitutes and demarcates forms of life as discrete political *and* economic units.[47]

The rule that each state must rely on its own resources and efforts is often labelled as the requirement of 'self-help'. This requirement, although sometimes a hardship, is also defended as a virtue practised by the truly independent and as supportive of the self-realization of the community. In other words, the independence of political communities is thought to be more secure and more fully realized where the community is self-supporting. However, the requirement of self-help also places political communities into competition. Competitions among states in the international political economy are often thought of as being staged in two separate spheres – the world economy and the strategic sphere of military competition. We need to examine in some detail the structuring of meaning and purpose which links and differentiates these two spheres of competition and the place competition occupies in defining the nature of political communities and the relations between them in contemporary international social life.

Economic competition takes place within the world market, a system of mutual dependence in which each political community must produce for the needs of others in order to secure its own livelihood. Thus, each political community is established as both producer and consumer, as both needy and provider of the needs of others, within a global division of labour.[48] It might be thought that the world economy is more appropriately seen as an economic interaction of individuals and firms. While this characterization is accurate at one level, we ought not to forget that the practice of sovereignty authorizes states as collective economic actors. The consequences of such an authorization are outlined and bemoaned by Hayek:

> It is neither necessary nor desirable that national boundaries should mark sharp differences in standards of living, that membership of a national group should entitle us to a share in a cake altogether different from that in which members of other groups share. If the resources of different nations are treated as exclusive properties of these nations as wholes, if international economic relations, instead of relations between individuals, become increasingly relations between whole nations organized as trading bodies, they inevitably become the source of friction and envy.[49]

Indeed, the idea of the 'trading state' is seen as a crucial concept in understanding the history, particularly the contemporary history, of international political economy.[50]

States, as sovereigns and thereby as 'trading bodies' within a competitive world market, are assigned a complicated role in both maintaining/policing the competitions staged by the world market and in participating as producers and consumers in those competitions. As the guardians of a competitive international economic order, states must establish the enabling conditions, the 'social structure of accumulation', which set the rules of the competitions and give the world market its purpose as a generator of wealth on a global scale. This includes a role as guarantor of the property rights of individuals and firms, including the establishment and maintenance of a set of international economic institutions which ensure the stability and enforce the rules of a competitive world economy.[51]

Once secured by the actions of independent states, the market is thought to operate as a 'discovery procedure' on a global scale, rewarding the uses of resources and efforts which best serve the needs of others. As an independent producer, each political community acquires its share of global wealth according to the market value of its contribution (that is, the contribution of its individuals, firms and regions) to global production in the meeting of needs within the world economy. As an independent consumer, each state is able to draw on global wealth to support its cultural self-expression only to the point allowed by that market valuation of its contribution. Because each state must provide and develop its own capacity to realize its purposes, state is pitted against state in an effort to acquire shares in global production. It is not surprising, then, that states engage in an intense global competition to create conditions within their boundaries and for their firms globally to secure world market shares and promote the development of technologically advanced and high-profit production capacities by their firms and within their boundaries.[52] Although not properly described as a zero-sum game, these processes of 'competitive self-improvement'[53] secure gains for some states at the expense of others, relatively and absolutely in varying combinations. In this way, the competitions staged within the world economy appear to uncover not only a hierarchy of individuals and firms, but also a hierarchy of political communities.

Just as in a single society, competition is applied in a world market in order to realize important purposes and express basic values. First, staging economic interactions as competitions is seen to spur global production and enhance the possibility of meeting the needs of political communities and their members. The reasoning is that because the market reveals and rewards (even if imperfectly) a hierarchy of resources and efforts devoted to meeting needs, each state (the individuals, firms and regions within it) will direct their resources and efforts to producing those things to which both the rewards are greatest and their given capabilities are best suited. And, as Adam Smith teaches, because wealth is limited by the extent of the market, securing the operation of a world market promotes the expansion of wealth and increased chances of meeting needs on a global scale. In this context, the ongoing economic competitions staged within the world market are valued because they are seen to increase global wealth and the chances for each political community to acquire the wealth it requires to express and realize its form of life.[54]

Second, a competitively revealed hierarchy of states is valued because it is seen as providing models for the proper and successful organization of political communities as economic actors. Where the success of cultural self-expression depends on 'competitive self-improvement', the resultant hierarchy of state capacities appears also as a valuation of cultures.[55] This feature of international political economy is captured in a vocabulary of gradations of economic success and potential. Advanced economies are contrasted with backward economies. Modern societies are contrasted with the traditional, where modernization represents a strategy for future economic success. Likewise, countries are developed and less developed, or somewhat optimistically characterized as developing. On one side, this conceptual vocabulary suggests that the hierarchy revealed by competition is a hierarchy of cultural forms, abilities and efforts. On the other side, this hierarchy suggests a model (or some set of models) for organizing cultural forms as relatively successful economic competitors. A political community's chances of realizing its form of life within the world economy comes to depend on adapting its 'values and visions' to accommodate competitive development strategies or industrial policies. The revealed hierarchy of cultural forms provides information to political communities about what works and what doesn't in a culture of competition, thereby contributing to the process of wealth generation around the globe.

Third, this hierarchy of political communities is also validated because it expresses and is a realization of the sovereignty of political communities. The independence and formal equality of communities is expressed in their status as economic units, possessing a sovereign property right. The sovereign property right recognizes and constructs the individuality of political communities, demarcating the space within which the distinctive traits of each separate community are contained or realized. Relevant individual differences in productive resources, capacities, and efforts are treated thereby as logically prior to or separate from the global competition itself (perhaps even as facts of nature).[56] Thus, the competitions staged by the world market retain their legitimacy because competition can be seen as uncovering the hierarchy latent in the individual differences of multiple forms of life. We can say, then, that economic competition in the international political economy also reflects a peculiar juxtaposition of the principles of equality and hierarchy: competitions staged by the world market among formally equal bearers of property rights produce a ranking of forms of life as the revelation of a hierarchy latent in the individual differences of independent communities.

Competition in the military sphere is entangled with economic competition in international social life, but also stands as an analytically separable expression of the cultural logic of competition. In the contemporary society of states, each state must be concerned to protect the identity of its political members, to secure through self-help the well-being and safety of its community. Interactions between communities may be experienced as threatening to the identity of each because the other community represents an alternative set of 'values and visions' which may spill over boundaries. A culturally defensive attitude is sharpened where some communities attempt to impose their way of life on others. Such impositions may be motivated and legitimated by the claim of a hierarchy of forms of life presumably uncovered by the successful conquest itself or as revealed in some other sphere thought of as competitively discovering a latent superiority and inferiority. Such threats and violations are made increasingly severe because the principle of self-help, while limiting the state's ability to realize and defend the identity of the political community to its own resources and efforts, provides the means by which some states may effectively lay claim to the resources and efforts of others. More specifically, inequalities in wealth-acquiring capacities between communities may generate conflict 'when the boundaries between the communities limit ... access to wealth.'[57] Those with less access to wealth given current boundaries might channel their resources so that they could attempt forcibly to alter their borders and their access to wealth. Those with greater capacities might use their advantage in resources and wealth as a tool for pillaging those less favoured and less capable of resisting such intrusions. In Hayek's terms, this demarcation of states as political *and* economic units creates a 'contest of force', 'clashes of power'.[58] Such a context of threats and resort to force prompts states to organize themselves in part as 'units of protection', erecting 'fortifications and fortresses' in order to deflect these threats.[59] Some have referred to this mutual vulnerability as a 'security dilemma'.[60] In a security dilemma, each state's effort to defend the integrity of its political community appears as a potential threat to other states' efforts to do the same, prompting augmentation of each state's fortress and a greater threat to all others. In such a situation, though the security of the political community is a crucial aim of each state, it is fully achieved by none.

Strategic competition is destructive, then, not only physically, but also of important social purposes of international political economy. At the same time, for apologists of a culture of competition such an assessment stands as only a partial analysis of a society of states. Though potentially destructive and creative of varying degrees of mutual insecurity, strategic competition is seen to give order to the system and thereby to promote (perhaps paradoxically) the survival or security of its individual units. We need to examine these two sides of the social practice of strategic competition more closely, because this purported purpose of competition in IPE has no direct parallel in a market society where government is taken for granted.

On the one side, strategic competitions establish a hierarchy of states, a ranking of 'powers'. Inequalities among powers become a *de facto* basis for the exercise of threats or the deployment of force by the stronger in order to coerce the weaker. Where such coercion operates, the stronger are able to dictate to the weaker, including dictating in part the rules and principles ordering international relations. States appear as divided between those that can dictate the laws and those that must obey them, violating the idea of states as sovereign equals and leaving the relatively weak subject to the threats of the stronger. In this sense, processes of strategic competition do less to realize and express the values of sovereignty (independence, equality and tolerance) and more to transgress them.[61]

On the other side, the hierarchy uncovered by strategic competition is understood to fulfil an important social purpose: it is said to support order and the norms and principles of a society of states by identifying those states capable of playing a key role in maintaining that order. The staging of strategic competitions allows distinctions to be drawn between Great, Middle and Small Powers.[62] The necessity of strategic competition is claimed because, where such distinctions are blurred, strategic competitions are required to clarify the relative position of states.[63] Such clarification is crucial because in a global culture of competition powerful states are recognized as having a special responsibility to bear in maintaining international order. Hedley Bull writes:

> great powers are recognized by others to have, and conceived by their own leaders and peoples to have, certain special rights and duties. Great powers, for example, assert the right, and are accorded the right to play a part in determining issues that affect the peace and security of the international system as a whole. They accept the duty, and are thought by others to have the duty, of modifying their policies in the lights of the managerial responsibilities they bear.[64]

The role of the Great Powers, then, is 'to contribute to international order ... by managing their relations with one another ... and by exploiting their preponderance in such a way as to impart a degree of general direction to the affairs of international society as a whole.'[65] This special managerial role is only possible where states are joined in a society of common norms, values and goals so that the special contribution of these powers in maintaining that society is recognized and accepted by at least most states, although force also plays some (and not unimportant) role in maintaining this situation.[66] That there is widespread acceptance of this role, at least by those states giving direction to international order but also by many which value that order, is suggested by the continuing incorporation of this 'diplomatic norm' into the organizational structures of international society – the Concert of Europe, the League of Nations, the United Nations[67] – and continuing calls for today's Great Powers to assume their role as guarantors of international peace and security, even perhaps at the cost of (re-)colonization.[68]

This analysis exposes the central role of force in strategic competitions and simultaneously in maintaining (for the most part) the independence (if not the equality) of states. We should not conclude, then, that force is unbridled in this situation. Rather, force is at once recognized and utilized as well as constrained.[69] The legitimacy of the special role of the Great Powers depends on their ability to constrain themselves and moderate the destructive consequences of strategic competition across the globe.[70] That competition is indeed moderated is suggested in that the collapse of the 'fortress' in the event of attack does not 'ordinarily presage the destruction of the state as such or of the "way of life" of its inhabitants'. Rather, the preservation of political communities has been given increasing weight, not only as norm, but in the practice of states, including that of the Great Powers.[71] What is normally at stake in strategic competitions is the status of states as powers and the role each state will play – marginal or substantial – in the management of the affairs of international society or some regional system.

Thus far, we have treated strategic competition as if it were primarily a matter of military strength. However, we know that in international political economy, economic capacities are crucial to long-term strategic competitiveness.[72] It is also the case that economic competitiveness alone as well as the need to secure the conditions for the world market have received increasing weight in the postwar era as a component of the state's responsibility to protect the 'values and visions' of its political community. Because economic competitiveness is also treated as a strategic concern, the logic of Great Powership is applied in the economic sphere as well. The Great Powers (including economic powers without substantial military clout) have come to act as guardians of the rules governing the world market. The predominant role that the advanced industrial societies play formally in the management of the international financial and trading institutions and informally via the Group of 7 and other fora for consultation on economic policy is an illustration of the implementation of this principle.[73] The debate about the status of Japan and Germany as Great Powers, including their possible status as Permanent Members of the Security Council stands as another, although unresolved, attempt to apply this thinking in international social life.

In sum, competition and the competitive processes we take either as given in themselves or as the causal effect of the given structure of anarchy reveal themselves as a certain structuring of meaning and purpose. International political economy stands, then, as a peculiar intertwining of the principles of equality and hierarchy mediated by the staging of competitions. The modern practice of competition joins the formal equality and independence of actors (in their role as sovereign competitors) with the hierarchy revealed by the competitions staged in the world market. This hierarchy stands as an expression of the status of actors as formally equal and independent because its represents, not some fixed hierarchy of social status, but a hierarchy revealed in a process of competition which presumes and manifests this initial status of equality.

BY WAY OF CONCLUSION: THE ANTINOMIES OF A CULTURE OF COMPETITION

What, then, is the significance of seeing competition as cultural and IPE as a culture of competition? Our analysis reveals that the cultural logic of competition involves a very precarious balancing. First, a culture of competition is formed by holding together an understanding of important purposes and values as *social* and a treatment of individuals as ontologically primitive, as in some sense *natural*. On the one hand, competition expresses and realizes the equality and independence of individual actors as competitors at the same time that they uncover rankings of achievement and effort. This discovery function of competitions is harnessed by society to serve important purposes, as in the creation of wealth by the competitions staged by the market. Thus, whatever its origins or its status in relation to some idea of human nature, competition is given a social construction – is seen to embody social meanings and is harnessed to serve important social values.

On the other hand, the individual actor, though socially recognized (constituted?) as equal and independent, is treated as given primordially; that is, given prior or external to the social construction of a culture of competition. In competitions, individual characteristics are given as natural, not socially constructed. Indeed, the power and value of competition is that it reveals these natural differences. Because the process of competition is not seen to create the character or traits of individual actors, the ontologically primitive individual is protected or severed from the social process. To put it in other terms, the self is formed prior to the social.

Thus, a culture of competition utilizes competing methodologies for self-understanding and competing systems of reference in order to make sense of the world. An idea of a socially constructed world is set in tension with a pre-social individual. International political economy expresses this tension in the opposition between the construction of the social meaning and purpose of the outcomes, structures, institutions, regimes, etc., produced by the interactions of individual actors and the pre-social quality of these actors and their motivations and needs.[74] Thus, a culture of competition is understood (paradoxically and problematically) as requiring the construction of the social world by pre-social individuals.

Second, a culture of competition rests on an uneasy juxtaposition of the principles of equality and hierarchy. Individual actors are socially constructed as equals in form; each is formally equal as a competitive property owner within the market or as a sovereign political community within a (competitive) society of states. The hierarchies constructed within a culture of competition are not thought to violate this initial social condition because they are treated as natural, and, thereby, as prior or external to the social condition of equality. Thus, hierarchy is not fully accepted as a *social* condition. Rather, hierarchies of wealth and power are constructed as *natural*, and treated as givens of international political economy.[75]

However, this solution to the 'problem' of inequality in a culture of competition succeeds only to the extent that we allow the problematic idea of the construction of social life by pre-social individuals. As we have seen, the idea that hierarchy is socially constructed is disallowed by treating the needs, motivations, capabilities, etc. of individual actors as pre-social. If we come to see both the self (the individual, the sovereign political community) and the hierarchy of selves (whether domestic or global) as constructed within social life,[76] the project defined by a culture of competition begins to totter if not collapse. The sense of 'innate' inferiority and 'natural' superiority attaching itself to (socially) equal individuals or political communities is revealed as the central social contradiction of a culture of competition.

If this account of the structuring of meaning and purpose in competition and competitive self-other relations is correct, then it appears that we have yet to come fully to grips with the meaning of the transition from traditional hierarchy to modern equality that simultaneously constituted the individual as self and the political community as sovereign. It is this continuing inability to make sense within our modern idea of equality that enables and compels the modern social actor to construct itself as a competitor in relation to others and to construct others simultaneously as dangerous and threatening and as ripe for subordination and exploitation. Perhaps only when difference is not translated into rank, as 'inferiority' or 'superiority' in relation to an other, we might redeploy competition as a search for excellence within which the rich difference of the other becomes a catalyst for an appreciation of the potential richness of the other within the self.[77]

NOTES

1. An earlier version of this paper was presented at the International Studies Association, Washington, D.C., 28 March–1 April 1994. We would like to thank John Agnew, Craig Murphy, David Levine, Nick Onuf, Matt Davies and the editors of this volume for their helpful suggestions.
2. See, for example, James N. Rosenau, *Turbulence in World Politics: A Theory of Change and Continuity* (Princeton: Princeton University, 1990); Ernst B. Haas, *When Knowledge is Power: Three Models of Change in International Organizations* (Berkeley: University of California, 1990); and R.B.J. Walker, *One World, Many Worlds: Struggles for a Just World Peace* (Boulder: Lynne Rienner, 1988).
3. Huntington's article, 'The Clash of Civilizations?', *Foreign Affairs* 72:3 (Summer 1993), pp. 22–49, engendered a strong response in the pages of *Foreign Affairs*. See especially the response by Fouad Ajami, 'The Summoning', *Foreign Affairs* 72:4 (September/October 1993), pp. 2–9. Huntington tends to treat the terms 'civilization' and 'culture' as synonymous (see p. 22). This practice is not uncommon. For a brief history of the relation between these two terms, see A.L. Kroeber and Clyde Kluckhohn, *Culture: a Critical Review of Concepts and Definitions* (New York: Vintage, 1963), pp. 15–25.
4. See, for example, Ali A. Mazrui, *Cultural Forces in World Politics* (London, Nairobi, and Portsmouth: James Currey and Heinemann, 1990); R.B.J. Walker, 'The Concept of Culture in the Theory of International Relations', and Richard A. Falk, 'Culture, Modernism, and Postmodernism: A Challenge to International Relations', both in Jongsuk Chay (ed.), *Culture and International Relations* (New York: Praeger,

1990), pp. 3–17 and 267–79 respectively; Nicholas J. Rengger, 'Culture, Society, and Order in World Politics', in John Bayliss and N.J. Rengger, (eds), *Dilemmas of World Politics: International Issues in a Changing World* (Oxford: Clarendon Press, 1992), pp. 85–103; Adda B. Bozeman, *The Future of Law in a Multicultural World* (Princeton: Princeton University Press, 1971); Alan Pleydell, 'Language, Culture and the Concept of International Political Community', in James Mayall (ed.), *The Community of States: A Study in International Political Theory* (London: Allen and Unwin, 1982), pp. 167–81.

5. See, especially, Hedley Bull and Adam Watson (eds), *The Expansion of International Society* (Oxford: Clarendon Press, 1984), Adam Watson, *The Evolution of International Society: A Comparative Historical Analysis* (London and New York: Routledge, 1992), and Adam Watson, 'Systems of States', *Review of International Studies* 16:6 (1990), pp. 99–109. The unease of a multicultural international society is examined particularly well by Bull and Watson in the 'Conclusion' and Bull in 'The Revolt against the West', both in *The Expansion of International Society*, pp. 425–35 and 217–28 respectively. The centrality of the Bull / Watson project to current debates is suggested by Barry Buzan, 'From International System to International Society: Structural Realism and Regime Theory Meet the English School', *International Organization* 47:3 (1993), pp. 327–52 and Ole Waever, 'International Society – Theoretical Promises Unfulfilled', *Cooperation and Conflict* 27:1 (1992), pp. 97–128.

6. See, for example, Ronnie D. Lipschtz, 'Reconstructing World Politics: The Emergence of Global Civil Society', *Millennium* 21:3 (1992), pp. 389–420; Paul Ghils, 'International Civil Society: International Nogovernmental Organizations in the International System', *International Social Science Journal* 133 (August 1992), pp. 417–29; and, in a more critical spirit, Craig N. Murphy and Enrico Augelli, 'International Institutions, Decolonization, and Development', *International Political Science Review* 14:1 (1993), pp. 71–85.

7. See, for example, P. Iyer, *Video Night in Kathmandu* (New York: Knopf, 1988); A Mattelart, *Transnationals and Third World: The Struggle for Culture* (South Hadley: Bergin and Garvey, 1983); E. Gans, *The End of Culture: Toward a Generative Anthropology* (Berkeley: University of California, 1985); and Wolfgang Sachs, 'One World', in W. Sachs (ed.), *The Development Dictionary* (London: Zed Books, 1992).

8. See Jonathan Friedman, 'Culture, Identity and World Process', in Daniel Miller *et al.* (eds), *Domination and Resistance* (London: Unwin and Hyman, 1989), pp. 246–60 and 'Being in the World: Globalization and Localization', *Theory, Culture and Society* 7:2–3 (1990), pp. 311–28; Arjun Appadurai, 'Disjuncture and Difference in the Global Cultural Economy', *Public Culture* 2:2 (Spring 1990), pp. 1–24; Ulf Hannerz, 'Notes on the Global Ecumene', *Public Culture* 1:2 (Spring 1989), pp. 66–75; and Anthony D. Smith, 'Towards a Global Culture?', *Theory, Culture and Society* 7:2–3 (1990), pp. 171–91.

9. Several recent articles attempt this more ambitious task. See Thomas H. Eriksen and Iver B. Neumann, 'International Relations as a Cultural System: an Agenda for Research', *Cooperation and Conflict* 28:3 (1993),

pp. 233–64, and Marco Verweij, 'Cultural Theory and the Study of International Relations', *Millennium* 24:1 (1995), pp. 87–111. See also Naeem Inayatullah and David L. Blaney, 'Knowing Encounters: Beyond Partiality and Parochialism', in Y. Lapid and F. Kratochwil (eds), *The Return of Culture and Identity in IR Theory* (Boulder: Lynne Rienner, 1995).

10. We do not attempt to enumerate the contents of cultural life if such an enumeration is possible. Others have attempted such a list. See the various enumerations in Kroeber and Kluckhohn, *Culture*, especially pp. 182–90. In the international relations literature, Ali Mazrui has ventured such a list of seven functions of culture as a basis for definition. Culture provides: (1) 'lenses of perception and cognition'; (2) 'motives for human behavior'; (3) 'criteria of evaluation'; (4) 'a basis for identity'; (5) 'a mode of communication'; (6) 'a basis of stratification'; and (7) 'a system of production and consumption'. See Mazrui, *Cultural Forces*, pp. 7–8 (stress removed).

11. In this section we rely heavily on Walker, 'The Concept of Culture', and Kroeber and Kluckhohn's *Culture*.

12. The phrase in quotation marks is Walker's from 'The Concept of Culture', p. 3.

13. Here we draw on the language of Ashis Nandy, *Traditions, Tyranny and Utopias: Essays in the Politics of Awareness* (Delhi: Oxford University, 1987), and Tzvetan Todorov, 'A Dialogic Criticism?', in Todozov, *Literature and its Theorists: A Personal View of Twentieth Century Literature* (Ithaca: Cornell University, 1987), p. 160.

14. Marshall Sahlins, *Culture and Practical Reason* (Chicago: University of Chicago, 1976, p. viii. Sahlins elaborates this point later (at p. 209) in the text:

> ... nature is to culture as the constituted is to the constituting. Culture is not merely nature expressed in another form. Rather the reverse: the action of nature unfolds in the terms of culture; that is, in a form no longer its own but embodied as meaning. Nor is this a mere translation. The natural fact assumes a new mode of existence as a symbolized fact, its cultural deployment and consequences now governed by the relation between its meaningful dimension and other such meanings, rather than the relation between its natural dimension and other such facts. All of this of course within material limits.

Perhaps similarly, Kroeber and Kluckhohn (*Culture*, pp. 12 and 368) place culture as 'superorganic', as an 'intervening variable' between human beings as organisms and the human environment.

15. See, for instance, the claims of Francis Fukuyama, 'The End of History', *The National Interest* 16 (1989), pp. 3–18; V.S. Naipaul, 'Our Universal Civilization', *New York Times* (5 November 1990); and Lucian W. Pye, 'Political Science and the Crisis of Authoritarianism', *American Political Science Review* 84 (1990), pp. 3–19. See also the citations in note 6.

16. We draw on Thomas Eriksen's formulation that cultural identity is 'relational and processual'. Thus, it is possible to emphasize the process of maintaining a sense of cultural identity – integrity and bound-

edness – in relation to the wider world, rather than the preservation of some 'fixed, monolithic entity,' or immutable cultural essence. Thomas H. Eriksen, 'The Cultural Context of Ethnic Differences', *Man* 26:1 (1991), pp. 127–44.

17. This is an issue not so easily decided by evidence, as Alfie Kohn suggests, though he weighs in against the claim that competition is natural. See Alfie Kohn, *No Contest: The Case against Competition* (Boston: Houghton Mifflin, 1986), chapter 2. Our argument might be stated in this way: though the physiological qualities of the species make it amenable to competition (as well as cooperation we might add) the specific character of competition – its meaningful and purposeful character in the modern era – cannot be read off from the 'facts' of nature. In the international relations literature it is Kenneth Waltz who makes (perhaps) the strongest case against reading competition as a natural fact in his rejection of 'first image' thinking in *Man, the State, and War* (New York: Columbia University, 1959), chapters II and III. Of course, our account of competition as a structure of meaning and purpose deviates from Waltz's view of competition as a causal effect of anarchy.

18. George Marcus and Michael Fischer, *Anthropology as Cultural Critique: An Experimental Moment in the Social Sciences* (Chicago: University of Chicago Press, 1992), p. 78, approvingly cite Raymond Williams to the effect that explanations necessarily 'merge ... the understanding of their subject's point of view in circumscribed social settings with the difficulties of also representing accurately the penetration of larger forces'. Following Marcus and Fischer, we aim, then, to present the 'outside forces' of political economy as 'an integral part of the construction and constitution of the "inside" ' (p. 77).

19. See Isaac Kraminick, 'Equal Opportunity and the Race of Life', *Dissent* 28:2 (1981), pp. 178–87.

20. Friedrich A. Hayek, *Law, Legislation and Liberty. Vol. 3: The Political Order of a Free People* (Chicago: The University of Chicago Press, 1979), pp. 67–8.

21. Hayek hopes to dispute the idea of 'rewards to merit' as the legitimating value of a modern competitive society, directing our attention to other purposes, that we highlight below, although he acknowledges the general appeal of and to that notion. See Friedrich Hayek, *Law, Legislation and Liberty. Vol. 2: The Mirage of Social Justice* (Chicago: University of Chicago Press, 1976), chapter 8.

22. Hayek, *Law, Legislation and Liberty. Vol. 2*, pp. 72–8, 115, and Frank H. Knight, *The Ethics of Competition and Other Essays* (London: Allen and Unwin, 1936), p. 56.

23. See Friedrich Hayek, *The Constitution of Liberty* (Chicago: University of Chicago, 1960), chapter 6. The quoted phrases are from p. 86.

24. See Friedrich A. Hayek, *Law, Legislation and Liberty. Vol. 1: Rules and Order* (Chicago: University of Chicago Press, 1993) and Thomas E. Flanagan, 'Hayek's Concept of Constructivism', in J. M. Porter (ed.), *Sophia and Praxis: The Boundaries of Politics* (Chatham, NJ: Chatham House, 1984) on the need for rules and order (albeit without an orderer) in Hayek's system.

25. See Hayek, *Law, Legislation and Liberty. Vol. 2*, pp. 71, 123–4. This is consistent also with Robert Nozick's argument in *Anarchy, State, and Utopia* (New York: Basic Books, 1975), pp. 150–82.
26. It should be clear by now that we do not use the terms 'competitive' or 'competition' to refer to the internal structure of markets. Competition is not a static state, as in the parameters and equilibrium solution of a model of perfect competition. Rather, competition is a process, a series of competitive struggles and strategies. See Joseph A. Schumpeter, *Capitalism, Socialism and Democracy* (New York: Harper Colophon, 1976), chapter VII, and Paul J. McNulty, 'Economic Theory and the Meaning of Competition', *Quarterly Journal of Economics* 82 (1968), pp. 639–56.
27. Needs, like the skills and efforts of individuals, are treated as given prior to or outside of the market and the competitions it stages.
28. Knight, p. 49. For Hayek, the market is both an expression of and the unintended outcome of the particular and independent actions of individuals. See, for example, Hayek's *Law, Legislation and Liberty. Vol. 2*, p. 107. Marx is also eloquent on the status of the individual in the market in *Capital*. Vol. I (New York: Vintage, 1977), chapter 1 and in his discussion of Aristotle's limited capacity to conceive the economy (pp. 151–2). See also Karl Marx, *Grundrisse* (New York: Vintage, 1973), pp. 243–5; G.W.F. Hegel, *Elements of the Philosophy of Right*, ed. Allen W. Wood (Cambridge: Cambridge University Press, 1991), Part 1, Sections 1 and 2 (on 'Property' and 'Contract') and Part 3, Section 2 (on 'Civil Society'); and David P. Levine, *Economic Theory. Vol. I: The Elementary Relations of Economic Life* (London, Henley, and Boston: Routledge and Kegan Paul, 1978), chapter 1.
29. We express this argument mostly in language drawn from Hayek, *Law, Legislation and Liberty. Vol. II*, chapter 10 (the quoted phrase is from p. 107) and *The Constitution of Liberty*, chapter 5. See also the discussion of the valuation of individuals and the social good of wealth production within a society centering on competition in Knight, pp. 47–53, and Justin Rosenberg, *The Empire of Civil Society* (New York: Verso, 1994), chapter 5. These themes of the mutual dependence of economic actors and the spur to human production are central to Adam Smith, *The Wealth of Nations* (New York: The Modern Library, 1937), Book I, Chapter 1, and Karl Marx, *Capital. Vol. III* (New York: International Publishers, 1967), p. 250 and *Grundrisse*, pp. 325 and 541. James A. Caporaso and David P. Levine, *Theories of Political Economy* (Cambridge: Cambridge University, 1992), chapter 2, provide a nice summary discussion of the treatment of these themes in the classical political economy tradition.
30. The phrase in quotation marks is drawn from R.B.J. Walker, *Inside/Outside: International Relations as Political Theory* (Cambridge: Cambridge University Press, 1993), p. 9.
31. Hinsley is quite succinct. Sovereignty is the 'idea that there is a final and absolute political authority in the political community ... and no final and absolute authority exists elsewhere'. F.H. Hinsley, *Sovereignty*, 2nd edn (Cambridge: Cambridge University Press, 1986), p. 26.

32. Richard K. Ashley, 'Untying the Sovereign State: A Double Reading of the Anarchy Problematique', *Millennium* 17:2 (1988), pp. 227–62.
33. Cornelia Navari, 'Knowledge, the State and the State of Nature', in Michael Donelan (ed.), *The Reason of States: A Study in International Political Theory* (London: Allen and Unwin, 1978), p. 119.
34. Hedley Bull, *The Anarchical Society: A Study of Order in World Politics* (New York: Columbia University Press, 1977), chapter 1, and Adam Watson, 'Systems of States'.
35. Likewise, Eriksen and Neumann, 'International Relations as a Cultural System', p. 239, cite Bull's notion of 'international society' as an important starting point for a cultural analysis of international relations.
36. Leo Gross, 'The Peace of Westphalia – 1648–1948', in Richard Falk and Wolfram Hanrieden (eds), *International Law and Organization* (New York: J.B. Lippincott, 1968), p. 54.
37. See Michael Walzer, 'The Moral Standing of States: a Response to Four Critics', *Philosophy and Public Affairs* 9:3 (1980), pp. 209–29, and Robert H. Jackson, 'Martin Wight, International Theory and the Good Life', *Millennium* 19:2 (1990), pp. 261–72.
38. On the connection of state sovereignty and the principle of self-determination, see Yael Tamir, 'The Right to National Self-Determination', *Social Research* 58 (1991), pp. 565–90, and Allen Buchanan, 'Self-Determination and the Right to Secede', *Journal of International Affairs* 45 (1992), pp. 348–65. Of course the right to secession/self-determination may conflict with the current drawing of sovereignties. For a detailed discussion of the tensions involved, see Hurst Hannum, *Autonomy, Sovereignty, and Self-Determination: The Accommodating of Conflicting Rights* (Philadelphia: University of Pennsylvania Press, 1990).
39. Gross, 'The Peace of Westphalia', p. 54.
40. Ibid., pp. 59–60.
41. Hinsley, *Sovereignty*, p. 158, and Martin Wight, 'The Origins of the States-System: Chronological Limits', in Hedley Bull (ed.), *Systems of States* (Leicester: Leicester University Press, 1977), p. 135.
42. See Cynthia Weber, 'Reconstructing Statehood: Examining the Sovereignty/Intervention Boundary', *Review of International Studies* 18 (1992), pp. 199–216, and Hedley Bull, 'Introduction', in H. Bull, (ed.), *Intervention in World Politics* (Oxford: Clarendon Press, 1984), pp. 1–6.
43. See Walker, 'The Concept of Culture', Rengger, 'Culture, Society, and Order', and Richard A. Falk, 'Culture, Modernism, Postmodernism'.
44. The quotation is from Benedict Anderson's important account of this 'imagining' process in *Imagined Communities: Reflections on the Origin and Spread of Nationalism* (London: Verso, 1983). For a similar set of claims about the salience of nationalism and international statehood, see Anthony D. Smith, *Nationalism in the Twentieth Century* (New York: New York University Press, 1979), 'Introduction: The Formation of Nationalist Movements', in Anthony D. Smith (ed.), *Nationalist Movements* (New York: St. Martin's, 1976), and 'Towards a Global Culture?'.
45. Charles Tilly, 'National Self-Determination as a Problem for All of Us', *Daedalus* 122:3 (1993), p. 29.

46. Charles R. Beitz, 'Sovereignty and Morality in International Affairs', in David Held (ed.), *Political Theory Today* (Stanford: Stanford University Press, 1991), p. 243.
47. Justin Rosenberg provides a compelling account of the demarcation of the economy as a distinct sphere in relation to the political life necessary to a capitalist society. See Rosenberg, *The Empire of Civil Society*, especially chapter 5.
48. See Naeem Inayatullah and David L. Blaney, 'Realizing Sovereignty', *Review of International Studies* 21:1 (1995), pp. 3–20; Raymond Vernon and Ethan B. Kapstein, 'National Needs, Global Resources', *Daedalus* 120:4 (1991); Robert B. Reich, 'What is a Nation?' *Political Science Quarterly* 106:2 (1991), pp. 193–209; and Sally Falk Moore, 'The Production of Cultural Pluralism as a Process', *Public Culture* 1:2 (Spring 1989): 26–48.
49. Friedrich A. Hayek, *The Road to Serfdom* (Chicago: University of Chicago Press, 1944), p. 220.
50. See Richard Rosecrance, *The Rise of the Trading State: Commerce and Conquest in the Modern World* (New York: Basic Books, 1986).
51. See, for example, Janice E. Thomson and Stephen D. Krasner, 'Global Transactions and the Consolidation of Sovereignty', in Ernst-Otto Czempiel and James N. Rosenau (eds), *Global Changes and Theoretical Challenges: Approaches to World Politics* (Lexington: Lexington Books, 1989), pp. 196–8, 214–16; James Mayall, 'The Liberal Economy', in James Mayall (ed.), *The Community of States*, pp. 96–111; David K. Tarullo, 'Logic, Myth, and the International Economic Order', *Harvard International Law Journal* 26:2 (1985), pp. 533–52; and Stephen Gill and David Law, 'Global Hegemony and the Structural Power of Capital', in S. Gill (ed.), *Gramsci, Historical Materialism and International Relations* (Cambridge: Cambridge University Press, 1993), pp. 93–124. The term 'social structure of accumulation' is from Gill and Law, p. 95.
52. This description is drawn from Susan Strange, 'States, Firms and Diplomacy', *International Affairs* 68:1 (January 1992), pp. 1–15; Reich, 'What is a Nation?', pp. 201–2; and Clyde V. Prestowitz, Jr, 'The Fight over Competitiveness: A Zero-Sum Debate?', *Foreign Affairs* (July/August 1994), pp. 186–9.
53. Charles Bright and Michael Geyer, 'For a Unified History of the World in the Twentieth Century', *Radical History Review* 39 (1987): 69–91.
54. Smith, Book IV, chapter 1. Also, see Craig Murphy's detailed discussion of this logic in *International Organization and Industrial Change* (New York: Oxford University Press, 1994).
55. See the related claims of Gustavo Esteva ('Development') and C. Douglas Lummis ('Equality'), in Wolfgang Sachs (ed.), *The Development Dictionary* (London: Zed Books, 1992).
56. The construction of productive capacities as facts of nature is clear in Ricardo. In contemporary theories, factor endowments, whether conceived as natural or constructed endowments, are treated as given outside of the process by which returns from trade are determined. See Robert Gilpin, *The Political Economy of International Relations* (Princeton, NJ: Princeton University Press, 1987), chapter 5.

57. David P. Levine, *The Fortress and the Market* (manuscript, 1991), p. 39.
58. Hayek, *Serfdom*, pp. 220–1.
59. John H. Herz, *International Politics in the Atomic Age* (New York: Columbia University Press, 1959), pp. 14 and 40.
60. See Ashley, 'Untying the Sovereign State'; Robert Jervis, 'Cooperation Under the Security Dilemma', *World Politics* 30 (1978), pp. 167–214; and John H. Herz, 'Idealist Internationalism and the Security Dilemma', *World Politics* 2 (1950), pp. 157–80.
61. See Ian Clark, *The Hierarchy of States: Reform and Resistance in the International Order* (Cambridge: Cambridge University Press, 1989), pp. 218–19, and Bull, *Anarchical Society*, p. 205.
62. Bull employs all of these gradations, plus the idea of 'quasi-states', in *Anarchical Society*, chapter 9. All of these terms are common usages, except for the idea of 'quasi-states' which has recently become popular in academic circles only due to the efforts of Robert H. Jackson, *Quasi-States: Sovereignty, International Relations, and the Third World* (Cambridge: Cambridge University Press, 1990).
63. We adapt the analysis of Geoffrey Blainey, *The Causes of War* (New York: The Free Press, 1988), chapter 8.
64. Bull, *Anarchical Society*, p. 202.
65. Ibid., p. 207.
66. In Bull's terms, the Great Powers maintain a 'hegemony', based on some combination of force and legitimacy. See *Anarchical Society*, pp. 215–18. This usage appears somewhere between a Gramscian and a realist notion of hegemony as Stephen Gill and David Law draw the distinction in *The Global Political Economy* (Baltimore: Johns Hopkins University Press, 1988), pp. 76–80.
67. Ibid., p. 202, and Clark, *Hierarchy of States*, p. 113 and chapters 6, 8, and 9.
68. See Paul Johnson, 'Colonialism Back – and not a Moment too Soon', *New York Times* 18 March 1993, and Robert Jackson, *Quasi-States*.
69. Clark, p. 21.
70. The general failure of the superpowers to refrain from acting as major sources of conflict contributed to the low level of legitimacy accorded superpower conflict. See Clark, chapter 9 and Bull, chapter 9.
71. Herz, *International Politics in the Atomic Age*, pp. 61, 71–5.
72. The interrelation of military and economic power is well captured in Paul Kennedy's *The Rise and Fall of the Great Powers* (New York: Random House, 1987). While there is no simple correlation between military strength and a country's wealth at any one point in time, Kennedy makes clear that economic success is necessary to sustain military strength for any length of time. Certainly, Kennedy also suggests the role that military power may play in economic success although this relationship may be weakening in the present.
73. See Clark, pp. 175–8, Watson, *Evolution of International Society*, chapter 25; and Mayall, p. 103.
74. This case is not hard to make in relation to neorealist and neoliberal international political economy. The case is more difficult to make in relation to Marxian IPE because this tradition holds to the intrinsic sociality of actors. However, Marxist method itself tends to explain the

specificities of social forms of life as particular expressions of an external and prior nature of human beings as social producers. See David L. Blaney, 'Individual, Class, and Communism: The Self and Marx's Social and Political Theory', Ph.D. dissertation, University of Denver, 1990, chapter 1.

75. Again, this conclusion is difficult to dispute for the neorealist and neoliberal frameworks. This is not to say that individual scholars may not be concerned about the question of international inequality, but that their intellectual system of reference gives them little scope for questioning hierarchy. Here the Marxian tradition is at its best, although we would argue that the most fruitful construction of the Marxian critique of inequality depends on the social construction of individuality in modern social relations. See Inayatullah and Blaney, 'Realizing Sovereignty', for a social constructivist reading of Marx.

76. See Peter L. Berger and Thomas Luckmann, *The Social Construction of Reality* (Garden City, NY: Anchor, 1966); Lev S. Vygotsky, *Thought and Language* (Cambridge, MA: MIT Press, 1962); Heinz Kohut, *The Restoration of the Self* (New York: International Universities Press, 1977); Inayatullah and Blaney, 'Realizing Sovereignty'; Rob Walker, *Inside/Outside*; and Alexander Wendt, 'Anarchy is What States Make of it: The Social Construction of Power Politics', *International Organization* 46:2 (Spring 1992), pp. 391–425.

77. See David L. Blaney and Naeem Inayatullah, 'Prelude to a Conversation of Cultures in International Society? Todorov and Nandy on the Possibility of Dialogue', *Alternatives* 19:1 (1994), pp. 23–51.

5 Neorealist Claims in Light of Ancient Chinese Philosophy: the Cultural Dimension of International Theory[1]
Roland Bleiker

> There is that mountain! There is that cloud! What is 'real' about them? Remove the phantasm and the whole human *element* therefrom, you sober ones! Yes, if you could do *that!* If you could forget your origin, your past, your preparatory schooling – your whole history as man and beast! There is no 'reality' for us – nor for you either, you sober ones ... [2]

INTRODUCTION

The key concepts of the neorealist approach to international theory were developed by Western scholars, largely based on analyses of interactions among Western states.[3] Yet one of the paradigm's main purposes is to transcend time and space in order to recognize patterns in the recurrence of international conflict. Can any such intellectual endeavour be free of prejudices and cultural biases?

I argue that neorealist thought – and indeed any form of intellectual endeavour – is strongly influenced by time-and place-specific values. This is not to say that the neorealist conceptual framework is void of explanatory power. But even if it can account for the existence of a majority of conflicts in the present world system, neorealism is based on subjective assumptions and therefore limited to a specific historical and cultural realm. A greater awareness of these ethnocentric biases could contribute to a substantial refinement and improvement of neorealist explanations. Tolerance of alternative discourses could aid academics and policy-makers alike in the avoidance of armed conflicts and, eventually, lead to the construction of a global order that is more just and less prone to violence than the present anarchical self-help system.

The issue of reification in the explanation of interstate conflict is, of course, not a new one. Critical theorist approaches to international theory have also drawn attention to systems of exclusion and the problems involved in theorizing independently from time-and place-specific contexts. Thus, rather than adding to the already existing extensive theoretical inventory on the subject,[4] this chapter attempts to approach the issue from a new angle. The objective is to probe neorealist claims for ethnocentric biases by examining them in light of a tradition of thought that is concerned with the same issues – war and peace – yet has emerged in an entirely different historical and cultural setting: ancient Chinese philosophy. Hence, this paper focuses on ideas about, rather than actual practices of, warfare. The rationale behind this approach is the belief that ideas, if they become hegemonic not only on a societal, but also on an inter-societal level, are instrumental in shaping 'reality' and thus practices of war and peace.

The first two sections outline some of the factors that give rise to suspicion about ethnocentrism in neorealism and present the potentials and problems of a comparison with Chinese philosophy. The subsequent substantive sections deal with three sets of issues on which the two strains of thought diverge. First, I compare the ontologies of the relevant approaches. The focus rests on the use of levels of analysis, the academic and institutional organization of the search for knowledge, and the key questions posed in the approach towards war and peace. Second, I examine the two intellectual traditions' attitudes towards reason and the search for solutions to the problem of war. Third, I concentrate on variations in the perceptions of the international system and the actors that comprise it.

THE 'WHETHERS' AND 'WHITHERS' OF ETHNOCENTRISM

In his *tour d'horizon* of international theory, K.J. Holsti suggests that theories belong to one paradigm, the classical (realist) one, if they rely on the following three assumptions: (1) that the proper focus of study is the causes of war and the conditions of peace/security/order; (2) that the main units of analysis are the diplomatic-military behaviours of the only essential actors, nation-states; and (3) that states operate in a system characterized by anarchy (the lack of central authority).[5]

Most of these key assumptions are embedded in a deep-rooted intellectual tradition. Elements of neorealist thought can be recognized, or so at least it is claimed, in Thucydides' analysis of the Peloponnesian war, in the philosophical treatises of Niccolò Machiavelli, Thomas Hobbes and Jean-Jacques Rousseau, as well as in the (pre-structuralist) realism of E.H. Carr and Hans Morgenthau. These thinkers derived their hypotheses largely from the study of conflict within a particular, relatively homogeneous cultural environment – the European state system. Serious and culturally sensitive anthropological studies about warfare in other cultural spheres were not available until, at the beginning of the twentieth century, the (structural) functionalism of Malinowski and Radcliff-Brown introduced more systematic and culturally sensitive forms of ethnographies.

Even today, cultural homogeneity characterizes theories of international relations. Europeans and North Americans develop the major insights and paradigms. An empirical study suggests that in the 1980s scholars of anglophone countries, particularly the United States and Great Britain, dominated the field of international theory.[6] As did their intellectual ancestors, these authors derive their theories by and large from analyses of Western historical cases, particularly from the post-Westphalian European state system and its later global expansion. Only rarely do they consider patterns of warfare in premodern and non-Western contexts.

One way of recognizing the implications of this cultural domination in neorealist thought is to take a step back, leave the field of international theory for a moment and glance at the self-critical debate within contemporary continental philosophy. At least since Nietzsche, Western philosophy has been preoccupied with questions about the meaning of its own existence. Should philosophy come to an end because all claims of truth have a spatial and temporal dimension? Should we focus solely on hermeneutics, genealogy or deconstruction because objective knowledge has remained an unattainable dream?[7]

While fragmented into many schools and dispersed at many fronts, contemporary philosophy agrees on at least one thing: a return to a Platonic search for an independent and ahistoric truth is not just anachronistic, but simply impossible. The French philosophical tradition represents the extreme form of distrust towards so-called metanarratives,[8] but even the relatively normative German critical theorists assume that reality is socially constructed and knowledge is intrinsically linked to the expression of basic human interest.[9]

Language is one of the reasons for this consensus within contemporary continental philosophy. All forms of intellectual expression depend on language. Languages are never neutral. They reflect particular values and ideas. Each language is the embodiment of a specific image of reality and, therefore, creates a cultural consensus that conditions each author's perceptions and thoughts. Each individual is, from the first day of his/her life onward, submitted to distinct cultural and linguistic influences and experiences that reflect a certain *Weltanschauung*. One's subsequent actions and thoughts cannot be completely neutral and objective because they are shaped by the reflection of specific cultural values.[10] Thus, ethnocentrism is not an evil academic trap to be avoided or eradicated at all cost. Rather, ethnocentrism is a subtle and unavoidable natural constraint that requires careful awareness, cultural sensitivity and tolerance in the formulation of theoretical propositions.

What, then, is the relevance of these findings for neorealism? In light of the linguistic conditioning of all intellectual endeavors and the anglophone domination of realist thought, our focus should shift from the 'whether' to the 'whither' of ethnocentrism. The task becomes one of trying to identify the elements of realist thought that are most likely shaped by specific spatio-temporal values and to recognize the subjectivity involved in the interpretation of the causes of conflict and the conditions for the establishment of peace.

This chapter attempts to approach this objective by examining neorealist claims in light of ancient Chinese philosophy, a system of thought that is also concerned with warfare, yet emerged uninfluenced by Western international theory. In order to compare realism with an entirely non-Indo-European stream of thought, I solely focus on Chinese philosophy during the Spring and Autumn (711–481 BC) and the Warring States (480–221 BC) period, which roughly corresponds to what Karl Jaspers called the Axial period. Focusing primarily on specific thoughts within the two most influential schools, Confucianism and Taoism, the article refrains from examining competing contemporary thoughts and later influences on Chinese philosophy, such as neo-Confucian addenda to *the Analects*, the spread of Buddhism or the more recent contact with Western ideas and ideologies.

There is no neutral stance from which an objective comparison between neorealism and Chinese philosophy can be conducted. No matter how seriously and well researched one approaches the issue, the structure of the English language forces the examiner to impose alien concepts on Chinese ideas because they can only be expressed through references to values, experiences, terminologies and structures that possess meaning and identity within the Western cultural tradition. Thus, the present study does not pretend to be an objective cross-cultural comparison. It certainly does not suggest that Chinese philosophy projects a better world or provides more insight into war and peace than neorealism does. Rather, it is my intention to follow Nietzsche's advice that in order to investigate our (European) morality from a certain distance, one should proceed like a wanderer who desires to know how tall the towers of a city are: he/she must leave the city.[11] I am thus employing Chinese philosophical ideas, heterogeneous as they are, as a means through which to leave the cultural hegemony of the realist city in order the examine the subjective and reified foundations over which its towers of reality are built.

DISCOURSE, PRACTICES AND THE SOCIAL CONSTRUCTION OF 'REALITY'

> This world of nations has certainly been made by men, and its guise must therefore be found within the modifications of our own human mind.[12]

Historians tend to agree that what could be called realist power politics characterized the political situation at the time when the classical Chinese texts were written. During the preceding period, the early Chou dynasty, there was no conflict among competing political entities because the patronage of a single emperor guaranteed unity. From about 770 BC on, the order of this so-called Golden Age started to crumble, the empire disintegrated and several independent states emerged. Louis Walker describes this epoch, the Spring and Autumn period, as one of disorder, central importance of state power and uncontrolled struggle for superiority.[13]

Rather than concluding, as structural realists would, that this system of competitive sovereign states inevitably breeds conflict, Chinese philosophers chose to envisage a world in which cultures interact without being dominated by the structural features of anarchy. I will discuss these alternative worldviews and their implications in more detail later. At this point may it suffice to observe that not one of the major Chinese philosophers of the time accepted the practices of warfare and the political structures of the time as naturally given. This tendency has been explained in various ways. The Confucian vision of orderly and hierarchical relations between individuals and aggregates of individuals is usually presented as an attempt to find the lost 'Tao', to re-establish the order and the harmony that existed during the preceding Chou, Shang and Hsia dynasties.[14] However, a full appreciation of the Chinese refusal to accept existing practices and structures as the sole reality can only be reached by touching upon the issue of dualism.

The way we perceive the interaction between dualistic entities has a crucial bearing on whether 'reality' is accepted as given or, rather, as subject to human will. International theory and Western conceptualizing in general have traditionally been based on the juxtaposition of antagonistic bipolar opposites, such as rational/non-rational, good/evil, just/unjust, war/peace or chaos/order. One side of the pairing is considered to be analytically and conceptually separate from the other. The relationship between the bipolar opposites generally expresses the superiority, dominance or normative desirability of one entity (such as peace) over the other (such as war). David Hall and Roger Ames argue that such dualist conceptualizing leads to *ex nihilo* or 'transcendent philosophies'.[15] According to these doctrines, unconditioned elements determine the fundamental meaning and order of the world, such as, in neorealist thought, the structure of the international system defines the behaviour of the nation-states.

Drawing upon the Taoist and Yin–Yang school, the dominant approaches in Chinese philosophy explicitly try to avoid dualistic conceptualizing. Instead of thinking in the form of dichotomies, opposites are considered complementary because neither side can exist by itself. Since peace (or any other concept) can only prevail by virtue of its opposite, war, both form an inseparable and interdependent unit (yin and yang) in which one element is absolutely necessary for the articulation and existence of the other. Hall and Ames claim that operating along these forms of conceptual polarity leads to 'immanental philosophies'.[16] This is to say that events and actors are always interdependent, that there is no transcendent source which determines actions. Structures mediate thoughts and behaviour of agents, but the will of agents also influences structures. From this view, structures are not accepted as given and unchangeable, particularly the ones that may be responsible for a great deal of conflict.

Thus, rather than accepting the implications of the existing order, Chinese philosophers focused on human abilities to overcome the negative consequences of the existing 'realities'. The effects of this approach were not uniform. On a truly international level, the Chinese vision of world order had little or no impact because Confucian ideas never came even close to being hegemonic on a global scale. Yet, on the societal and to some extent also on the regional, inter-societal level, interactions among individuals and aggregates thereof were highly influenced by Confucian *leitmotifs*. A.C. Graham even argues that should ideas indeed have an impact on social forces, the Axial period in China was an example of tremendous success.[17]

The issue of ideas and their shaping of structures is central to the arguments presented by the critics of neorealism. Expanding what had already been a key concern of Nietzsche's writings, critical theorist approaches to international theory assert that the fundamental principles of international politics are subject to continuous change and that the direction of this change is at least partly a function of how we perceive and approach 'reality'. Not only is there no objective 'reality', but realities are always constructed. In short, discourse shapes practices. Hence, Robert Cox argues that there is no theory outside a specific spatio-temporal context, that 'theory is always for someone and for some purpose'.[18] There are, in Cox's view, two types of theory: problem-solving theories and critical theories. Problem-solving theories, of which neorealism is an example, consider the prevailing structures of the world as the given framework for action. They study the workings and impacts of the international system or address the problems that it creates. Such theories not only accept the existing order as given but also, intentionally or unintentionally, sustain it.[19] Critical theories, by contrast, attempt to transcend the existing world order with the objective of comprehending how it was created and how it could give way to less violent alternative orders.

Markus Fischer recently articulated the structuralist counter-argument to the critical theorist position.[20] Based on his studies of discourses and warfare practices in medieval Europe, he claimed that the lack of a central protection and regulatory institution forced states to engage in realist power politics despite contrary communal discourses, a hypothesis that would undermine the critical theorists' claim that discourses shape practices.

Both viewpoints, the structural-realist and the critical theorist, seem unconvincing in an extreme articulation. A radical existentialist view that credits agents and ideas with unlimited ability to shape the course of history is certainly difficult to accept. Anarchy is the condition under which interaction among states takes place today and its powerful structural impact cannot be neglected or avoided. Yet, this does not mean that structure exists and exerts influence independently of human agency. Ideas have a bearing on the formulation of policies. For example, a Clausewitzian and a Confucian perspective are likely to lead towards entirely different state behaviour, even if the system in which they operate is anarchic. Carl von Clausewitz considered war not as an aberration or a substitute for negotiations, but rather as a logical pursuit of diplomacy through other means.[21] Such a viewpoint influences decision-making because it not only delivers the explicit rationale for initiating and conducting interstate war, but also imbues the action with philosophical and moral legitimacy. By contrast, a Confucian-oriented foreign policy is less likely to resort to violent means because it foresees the dissemination of influence not through wars, but via non-violent and persuasive methods such as education and indoctrination.

Several studies have suggested that the implicit and explicit theoretical concepts of policy-makers have a crucial impact on the occurrence of wars. For example, K.J. Holsti, basing himself on an extensive survey of the issues over which armed conflicts were conducted between 1648 and 1989, argues that politicians' understanding of wars have influenced both the result of peace settlements as well as the emergence of subsequent conflicts.[22] Alexander Wendt goes a step further. He claims that anarchy does not necessarily have to create a security dilemma. The only 'logic' of anarchy is the one that is created by practices. As he puts it, 'self-help and power politics are institutions, not essential features of anarchy. Anarchy is what states make of it.'[23]

Thus, even if the structure of the international system cannot be changed immediately, discourses on war and peace can have a bearing on policy formulation and, consequently, on the occurrence and avoidance of conflict. With this aspect in mind I now explore some of the differences between neorealism and ancient Chinese philosophy.

ONTOLOGICAL DIFFERENCES IN THE STUDY OF WAR AND PEACE

> The origin becomes of less significance in proportion as we acquire insight into it.[24]

In his influential analysis of international politics, *Man, the State and War*, Kenneth Waltz differentiates between three approaches to the study of interstate conflict. Depending on whether the causes of war are seen in 'man' (i.e. individuals), the attributes of specific states or the nature of the state system, he labels them first, second or third image analyses.[25] Most of the early and several contemporary theories, such as those of Kant, Grotius, Hobbes and Morgenthau, belong to the first and second categories. While appreciating the general concept of power employed by these authors, neorealism has shifted the focus of inquiry to a structural level. It is not human nature or the attributes of states, but the systemic forces of the anarchical international system that are responsible for the recurrence of interstate conflict. In the absence of a global regulatory institution, the units of the system, sovereign states, must seek security through maximizing their own defence capacities. This gives rise to a security dilemma, a vicious circle of continuous competition and conflict, according to which the very exercise of one state's security is a threat to the neighbouring states.

Such a structural explanation of conflict is alien to Chinese philosophy. The main subjects of study are individual ethics and societal order, i.e. first and second image analyses. It is generally assumed that if harmony is reached at this level, global peace will follow automatically. Even Chinese philosophers who indirectly elaborate theories of international relations, such as Confucius or Han Fei Tzu would, in Waltz's definition, be 'reductionist' because they only study the behaviour of units, not the impact of the system.[26] The very idea of separating among several levels of analyses is absent in Chinese philosophy. These differences in ontology are partly a reflection of how the search for knowledge is pursued.

The West has witnessed a long tradition of splitting up the organization of intellectual endeavour. Assuming that the world cannot be explained by one single theory, that there is a need for demarcation, academia was separated into several fields. The social sciences alone are divided into various subfields. International theory is only one of the subfields of political science, coexisting with others that range from political philosophy to comparative politics. Neorealist international theory in turn is concerned with only one particular type of armed conflict: interstate war. Even within this already narrowly defined area of investigation, there has been a tendency towards increased specialization on particular aspects or issues, such as regimes, alliances or integration. The reifying tendencies involved in this approach are obvious if we accept Michel Foucault's thesis that subdivisions of social knowledge do not represent an objectively existing 'reality' but, rather, constitute time and place specific rules and methods that control the production of discourses, systems of exclusion designed to define what is right and wrong, true and untrue, moral and immoral.[27]

Chinese philosophers do not share the belief that focusing on one precisely demarcated field of study will produce Pareto-optimal conditions for academic research. The rejection of dualist conceptualizing is at the origin of this holistic approach. Since elements of bipolar opposition cannot exist by themselves and are defined always in relation to one another, events are seen as interdependent occurrences. Thus, Waltz's search for monocausality and his contention that one realm has to be separated from all the others in order to deal with it intellectually[28] is contrasted by the less parsimonious but equally convincing argument that the whole is greater than its parts, that the search for knowledge cannot, even for analytical reasons, be fragmented into different subfields. Consequently, Chinese philosophers reject intellectual endeavours that separate inquiries about conflict from philosophy, economics, religion and other fields of study.

This is not to judge the adequacy or intellectual usefulness of holism in comparison to academic specialization. I am only suggesting that the two approaches tend to produce different outcomes. As a result of a holistic view, as prevalent in Chinese philosophy, the concern about war is only one theme among many. Armed conflict is inevitably linked not only to politics, but also to issues such as religion, economics, even ethics and individual self-fulfilment. This direct link of conflict with human nature, history and culture implies that a (Chinese) theory about war and peace cannot exist outside of a time-and place-specific context. Quite to the contrary, the separation of international theory from other academic fields may create a vacuum that can lead to a search for atemporal structures that permanently mediate change. This view suggests that war is caused, and peace can be found independently of particular historical and cultural circumstances.

Another ontological consequence of these varying approaches to knowledge can be seen in perceptions of history. Operating along linear understandings of time, international theory is mainly concerned with locating the causes of war. Among the crucial questions to be asked, Waltz points out, are 'why does this occur?', and 'what causes what?'[29] It is only after finding out the answers to these questions he claims that the conditions for peace can be sought. Aetiological (cause–effect) analysis plays a much smaller role among Chinese philosophers. In spirit with rejecting dualist thinking, they do not perceive history as a continuum of past, present and future but, rather, fuse these perceptions of time into a state of immediate awareness which takes the form of immanent or cyclical perceptions of history.[30] From this nonlinear perspective of time, the search for a solution takes place independently from cause–effect analyses. Most experts agree that the main focus of Chinese philosophy is not searching for the truth, but locating the 'Way' (the *Tao*), not understanding the world, but making 'man' great; not determining the causes of war, but establishing the conditions for peace.[31]

This difference in ontological approaches between East and West is not only manifest in conflict studies. Michel Foucault's analysis suggests that similar patterns of difference and exclusion are also reflected in the practice of medicine.[32] Confirming this hypothesis, Ted Kaptchuk points out that Western medicine is primarily concerned with either isolating disease categories or defining agents of disease. Its objective is to detect a precise cause for a well-defined and self-contained illness. Chinese medicine, being embedded in a holistic cultural *Weltanschauung*, does not focus on specific disease entities. It does not trace symptoms back to causes. Instead, it concentrates on understanding the relationship of one organ to the whole, on patterns rather than causes of disharmony. Hence, restoring an overall balance between the body's yin and yang forces takes precedence over questions of cause and effect.[33]

The field of medicine also reflects the difference between transcendental Western and immanental Eastern philosophies. Kaptchuk notes that Western medicine, in trying to discover pathological mechanisms behind apparent symptoms, attempts to discover the underlying causes of an illness independently from a specific patient or spatio-temporal circumstances. Chinese medicine, by contrast, only rarely relies on a transcendent body of theory. It considers the patterns of a patient's signs and symptoms as unique and therefore does not try to find solutions outside the idiosyncratic sphere of a particular patient.[34]

REASON, CONFLICT AND THE SEARCH FOR PEACE

> Once I, Chuang Chou, dreamed that I was a butterfly and was happy as a butterfly. I was conscious that I was quite pleased with myself, but I did not know that I was Chou. Suddenly I awoke, and there I was, visibly Chou. I do not know whether it was Chou dreaming that he was a butterfly or the butterfly dreaming that it was Chou.[35]

Drawing on the Greek tradition, the belief in reason, logic and science guides Western thought. International theory does not diverge from this pattern; reason and logic prevail in analyses and solutions of most theoreticians. It has been common in the West to argue, as Max Weber did, that the power of *logos*, of defining and of reasoning was unknown to Chinese philosophers, that they were preoccupied with narratives while being ignorant of the 'empirical-aetiological', rational-formalist' and 'speculative-systematic' approaches that were essential to Hellenic, Occidental, Middle Eastern and Indian philosophies.[36] More recently researchers have claimed, however, that rational discourses were much more prevalent in ancient China than previously assumed.[37] Sophists like Hui Shih and Kung-sun Lung as well as the later Mohists, in an almost mirror-like image of the early Wittgenstein, rely heavily on reason and logical puzzles in their analyses. Hence, Graham concludes that Chinese philosophy was not unaware of the power of reason and *logos*, but that its most influential schools knowingly opposed or at least rejected an unlimited faith in it.[38] This scepticism towards reason is most pronounced in Confucianism, the Yin–Yang school and Taoism. It finds its most explicit representation in Chuang Tzu's anti- rationalism, contained in his second of seven 'Inner Chapters', called 'The Sorting Which Evens Things Out'.[39]

Variations in the attitude towards reason influence the study of conflict in several ways. Drawing on Aristotle's concept of teleological action, the realist tradition generally assumes that under normal circumstances individuals and states act rationally, which is to say that policies result from a thought process that attempts to maximize utility through cost-benefit analyses. This assumption is the fundamental base, or even the *raison d'être*, of several approaches to the study of conflict, such as balance of power and game theories, or Robert Gilpin's application of economic (rational choice) theory to international politics.[40] Following from this assumed rational behaviour of states, the realist tradition concludes that the actions of states can also be understood in rational terms.[41]

Confucians and particularly Taoists point out that the process of choosing between goals or options is often a spontaneous and intuitional, rather than a rational process. They assume that before making an apparently conscious decision, subconscious and instinctive factors decide the outcome of the decision-making process. Hence, Chinese philosophers tend to reject a rational and logical analysis as appropriate for examining the dynamics of human thought and interaction. Rather, an assessment of particular phenomena should be based on such factors as detached awareness, instinct, wisdom and spontaneity.

Confucians and Taoists thus favour a discursive, correlative or narrative approach, which takes the form of poems, stories or aphorisms.

This contrasts with Hans Morgenthau's contention that 'a theory of politics must be subjected to the dual test of reason and experience'.[42] Chuang Tzu not only repudiates the utility of reason to a philosophical endeavour, he also questions the relevance of experiences for illuminating the issue of war and peace. Experiences, he would undoubtedly argue, cannot test (realist) theories because experiences are always judgements which are already mediated by a moral prejudice about what is right and wrong. Chuang Tzu's famous butterfly story, quoted at the beginning of this section, exemplifies this scepticism about the existence of single reality. In its typical non-dualistic form, it rejects the distinction between reality and unreality, object and subject, right and wrong. The only way to liberate oneself entirely from these misleading structures is to undo and overcome the dualistic pairings, to break free from the prejudices and delusions built up by intellectually acquired and semantically conditioned thought patterns. Thus, aesthetics and the search for emptiness through meditation become essential in the establishment of truth or, as Lao Tzu expressed it, 'one who knows does not speak, one who speaks does not know.'[43]

In contrast to this mystical approach, the dualistic concepts which gave rise to the Taoist rejection of a single and objective reality are essential to many approaches within Western social science. In the tradition of the Enlightenment, realists generally assume the existence of a concrete and objective world, a reality that exists independently of human perceptions, a reality that can be understood as well as assessed as long as our theoretical and analytical approaches are rational and systematic enough. Theories are only convincing if empirical examinations can validate them or, at the very least, if they successfully pass the scrutiny of Popperian falsification tests.

Despite the prevalence of these positivistic ideas within the realist tradition, Waltz himself is sceptical of purely empirical and heuristic methodologies. In the opening chapter of his *Theory of International Politics* he criticizes the induction of causes from observing and adding up facts and data. Instead, he presents a creative method of theory-building that focuses on isolation, abstraction, aggregation and idealization. Waltz argues in an almost Taoist way that explanatory power is gained not by staying close to reality, but by moving away from it.[44] Yet, as soon as we closely examine the product of Waltz's theory-building, similarities with Chuang Tzu or Lao Tzu vanish. The above mentioned differences relating to aetiology and levels of analysis set the two views of war and peace as far apart as they could possibly be. Even Waltz's contention that theories are speculative processes without any claim to truth finds little or no reflection in his actual explanation of interstate conflict. Neither does the structural theory presented in his latter chapters deal with the ramifications of his astonishing earlier presentation of 'reality' as a continuously changing human artifact. The role that (realist) theorizing plays in the creation of (realist), realities' is even more ignored by the numerous researchers who subsequently tested and refined Waltz's premises in order to present a systematic, rational and quasi-scientific interpretation of modern warfare.

The differences between realist and Chinese perceptions of reason also left their mark on the respective searches for peace. The only way out of the security dilemma is a situation in which the individual acts rationally and is able to assume that everyone else does so too, as in Waltz's interpretation of Rousseau's stag hunt parable.[45] Most non-realist Western schools equally rely on reason. Martin Wight points out that theories which assert conceptions of global justice are based on the supposition that 'man' is a rational and social animal. As a result, 'his' rational nature leads 'him' to conform to a global order based on morality.[46] Immanuel Kant links reason to a didactical process. Human beings are, in his view, egoistic as well as rational. Paradoxically, it is the egoistic nature of individuals and the resulting occurrence of increasingly destructive wars which inevitably drives human beings toward greater respect for justice based on rationality.[47] Reason is also crucial to the solution advocated by the utilitarian tradition, which, according to Bentham, holds that besides public opinion, a rational body of international law is essential for the avoidance of war.[48] Even the critical theorist approach, at least in its Habermasian or Apelian form, attempts to promote social justice primarily with a communicative and intersubjective theory of rationality.

These rational approaches to conflict resolution are much less prevalent in Chinese philosophy. Chuang Tzu would refute such solutions as misleading and, in a Western sense, as 'unreasonable'. An assessment of a particular problem and the solution to it does not, as already mentioned, require reason, but should be based on such factors as detached awareness, instinct and wisdom. Confucius equally rejects the establishment of peace through rational institutions such as laws, preferring instead an aesthetic approach that sustains a harmonious order through such elements as rituals and music.[49] Relying again on Chuang Tzu's ability to capture the essence of the matter in a few words, solutions cannot be based on reason because:

there is nothing that is not the 'that' and there is nothing that is not the 'this'. Things do not know that they are the 'that' of other things; they only know what they themselves know.... Because of the right, there is the wrong, and because of the wrong, there is the right. Therefore the sage does not proceed along these lines (of right and wrong, and so forth) but illuminates the matter with Nature. This is reason.[50]

The differences between the logical realist approach and the embodiment of this anti-rational, Tao-oriented approach to 'reason' find their clearest and perhaps most consequential manifestation in the perceptions the two streams of thought have of the nature of the international system.

PERCEPTIONS OF THE INTERNATIONAL SYSTEM AND ITS ACTORS

Speculations about the state of nature play an important role in Western philosophies and indirectly in international theory. This importance is partly derived from the belief that by knowing how individuals behaved in the state of nature, one could conclude which human characteristics are natural and which are artificially acquired by the influence of civil society. Descriptions of the state of nature vary from author to author, ranging from a peaceful, independent and egalitarian Rousseauesque version to the Hobbesian state of war. Despite these differences, Western philosophers usually assume that anarchy (the absence of a central regulatory authority) was the most important feature of the state of nature.

Chinese philosophers are less explicit in their speculations about this subject. Among the few who explicitly elaborated on the state of nature was Mo Tzu, whose speculation bears many similarities with the anarchical, disharmonious and conflict-prone description provided by Thomas Hobbes and John Locke.[51] Taoist and even Confucian texts could also be interpreted as projecting a state of anarchy, or at least some form of initial equality among human beings. In a surprisingly Rousseauesque way, the *Analects* (the most reliable source of Confucian doctrines) state that 'by nature men are alike. Through practice they have become far apart.'[52] However, this analysis of social dynamics differs from Confucius' normative viewpoint.

The important elements of the Confucian doctrine assume the existence of a preordained natural order. Central to Confucianism are the five cardinal relationships which characterize all human interactions in a very ordered and hierarchical way. They are sovereign–subject, father–son, old–young, husband–wife and friend–friend. It is likely that Rousseau would have criticized Confucius for not having reached the state of nature in his analysis, for speaking about civil 'man' and not savage 'man'. However, Rousseau himself argues that inquiries into this question cannot be based on scientific measurements and historic facts, for they are hypothetical and conditional reasoning.[53] Hence, the Confucian perception of a naturally hierarchical order cannot be regarded as right or wrong, it can only be acknowledged to exist.

This issue is of direct relevance to the pursuit of study of International Relations because international theory has traditionally equated the interaction of individuals in the state of nature with the relationship among sovereign states in the international system. Among the authors who elaborate on this link, which Hedley Bull called the 'domestic analogy', are Spinoza, Hobbes, Locke, Rousseau, Kant, as well as the more recent realist theorists.[54] Thus, the state of nature and therefore the international system are characterized as decentralized and anarchic, which provides the *raison d'être* for most neorealist claims.

Chinese philosophy, in accordance with the emphasis on the *Tao*, is more critical in applying the 'domestic analogy'. The link between the state of nature and the international system is drawn only when this is compatible with the advocated conditions for peace. The idea of an anarchical international system is virtually absent from the Chinese philosophical tradition. Benjamin Schwartz even goes so far as to argue that the entire Chinese world of thought shares one cultural assumption, which is:

> the idea of a universal, all-embracing sociopolitical order centering on the concept of a cosmically based universal kingship; the more general idea of the primacy of order in both the cosmic and human spheres; and the dominant tendency toward a holistic 'immanentist' view of order.[55]

The philosophy which provides the rationale for this vision is Confucianism. The five cardinal relationships, the norms of behaviour within the family and the idea that all power should reside in one single ruler, are applied to civil society and to the international system. Each 'unit' in this sino-centric system has, according to its ability and function, a precisely defined place within a pyramidal international structure that ties the common citizen with the Chinese emperor and ultimately with Heaven itself. The system is perceived to be a universal one, characterized by a set of tightly arranged hierarchical relationships.

Not only Confucianism, but also most other Chinese philosophies, assume the existence of order in the international system.[56] Taoists, despite their commitment to *laissez-faire* principles and (anarchic) individual freedom, point out that the cultivation of inner virtues automatically leads to harmony among individuals and states. Mo Tzu, although supposing conflict in the state of nature, advocates a cosmic order which is 'produced and maintained by the purposeful cooperation of Heaven, spirits, and men of good'.[57] This theory assumes that if the wisest man is chosen as the universal king of all civilizations, peace and global indivisible love will automatically follow.[58] Even the Chinese legalist school, which can in many ways be compared to the realist tradition in international theory, projects a certain image of universal order. In principle, legalists admit that the nature of the international system is conflictual because every state's objective is to maximize power. However, legalists stress that since every ruler is trying to become a hegemon by making his state paramount over all others, the end-product is the establishment of a global order.[59]

It is not my intention to equate the Chinese vision of global order through hierarchy with a state of harmony or justice. Patriarchal and hierarchical Confucian principles have led to a great deal of oppression and discrimination. I only intend to use the Confucian vision of a global order to compare and contrast it to the neorealist concept of an anarchical international system that forces states to live in permanent competition with each other. Most realist hypotheses, such as the security dilemma or balance of power theories, depend on this assumed anarchy and would lose all meaning in the context of an orderly and hierarchical perception of the international system, no matter how oppressive and unjust its structure is. The only forms of hierarchy that penetrate realist thought are the ones that result from variations in prestige, the distribution of power or unequal divisions of labour. In Raymond Aron's words, the oligopolistic character of the international system allows the main actors to influence the system more than the system can influence them.[60] However, realist perceptions of power hierarchies that operate within an anarchical system are different from the Confucian vision, because they do not rest on the assumption that the hegemon is legally established and formally recognized by the subordinate powers.

Confucianism also repudiates another essential assumption of neorealism, the contention that sovereign nation-states are the only consequential actors in the international system. From a Chinese viewpoint, interactions take place among cultures, not states. The very expression of 'Middle Kingdom' embodies the idea of cultural superiority, i.e. China being the moral leader and the centre of humanity. As a result, it was perceived to be China's primary responsibility, as Adda Bozeman points out, 'to introduce civilization into less privileged adjoining areas and thus prepare the barbarians for their ultimate inclusion in the world state'.[61] As opposed to armed conflicts being considered inevitable within a (realist) anarchical system, analysts tend to agree that given Confucius' rejection of power politics as an agent of diplomacy, the extension of the Chinese cultural realm to 'barbarian' areas is supposed to take place in a nonviolent way, through education, virtuous example, persuasion, indoctrination, immigration and social intercourse.[62]

CONCLUSION

This study suggested that neorealism and ancient Chinese philosophy diverge in at least three main subject areas: their ontologies, their treatment of reason and their perceptions of the international system. The ontologies of the two intellectual traditions further differ in three ways:

(1) Neorealism separates among several levels of analysis and limits its approach to one principal level, the systemic one. The impact of the structure of the international system on the formulation of state policies explains the reoccurrence of interstate conflict. This monocausal and parsimonious approach stands in contrast to the Chinese tradition, which focuses on the behaviour of individuals, and aggregates thereof, without limiting itself to precisely defined levels of analysis.

(2) In order to maximize the search for knowledge, the West has divided academia into various fields and subfields. The relative separation of the studies on international relations from other disciplines may be one of the factors that led to the neorealist search for a structural and ahistoric analysis. The rejection of dualism and the resulting holistic framework of Chinese philosophy links the study of war with, among others, philosophy, religion,

and culture. It does not attempt to understand the ramifications of conflict outside specific spatiotemporal circumstances.
(3) Dualistic conceptualizing and linear perceptions of history partly explain the prevalence of cause-effect analysis in the neorealist approach to conflict. The key issue to be addressed is 'why do states go to war?' This question is only of minor relevance to Chinese philosophers. Cyclical and immanental perceptions of time as well as the belief in the social construction of reality led them to reject aetiology in favour of searching the conditions for peace independently from the causes of war.

The role of reason occupies a pivotal position in neorealist studies of conflict, but only a minor one in the Chinese approach to the problematique. This difference manifests itself in at least three ways:

(1) In the realm of epistemology, neorealists generally assume that under normal conditions individuals and states act rationally. Chinese philosophers point out that the process through which actors choose among several options is dominated by intuition and spontaneity.
(2) Following from this first point, neorealists conclude that the behaviour and actions of states can be understood through rational means. They apply a rational and logical analysis to the study of war and assume, albeit not in general agreement, that scientific-empirical research methods can test or at least falsify the established theories. Chinese philosophers, rejecting the prevalence of reason in epistemology, tend to approach the issue of conflict through narrative or correlative means that are based on detached awareness and wisdom. Scepticism about the existence of a single truth and reality makes testing of theories irrelevant to them.
(3) The realist search for peace, to the extent that this is of concern to an aetiological approach, is based on reason. An escape from, or containment of, the security dilemma can only be hoped for if a state acts rationally and can assume that others do so too. Chinese philosophers tend to reject this solution as misleading and, instead, attempt to overcome conflict through the above mentioned intuitive approach as well as through Confucian rituals, procedures and aesthetics.

Finally, the two traditions have radically different perceptions of the state of nature, the character of the international system and the actors that comprise it. The Western philosophies upon which neorealist concepts are built project the state of nature as one of anarchy, the absence of a central regulatory institution. The Confucian-influenced Chinese tradition assumes the existence of a preordained and hierarchical natural order among individuals. Establishing an analogy with the state of nature, neorealists portray the international system as an anarchical one that inevitably breeds conflict among the system's only consequential actors, sovereign nation-states. Confucianism displays a sino-centric vision of a global community based on virtue, the supremacy of the Middle Kingdom and a paternalistic-hierarchical interaction of cultures, rather than states.

By examining the differences between neorealism and Chinese philosophy I have not intended to judge the adequacy or usefulness of one stream of thought against the other. Rather, it was my objective to draw attention to the subjectivity and the foundationalist tendencies entailed in the neorealist approach to war and peace. This subjectivity is all the more striking considering that most key elements of one approach can also be found in the other one, albeit in a much less prominent role. The existence of 'realist' principles in Chinese philosophy has been mentioned briefly, particularly the elements of anarchy in Taoism and Mohism, the power politics of legalism and the rational-logical character of Sophist and later Mohist thought.

Several key elements of ancient Chinese philosophy are also recognizable in international relations theory and Western thought in general. Non-anarchical perceptions of the international system can be found in the pre-modern works of Dante and Thomas Aquinas, whose visions of a global harmony under either papal or imperial Christian authority bears many similarities with the hierarchical concept of the Middle Kingdom. The Chinese idea of peaceful interactions among societies, as opposed to antagonistic ones among states, can be seen in the ideas of early nineteenth-century liberals or in Karl Deutsch's concept of non-violent coexistence among regional pluralistic security communities.[63]

Even more similarities can be found between Chinese philosophy and the critical theoretical contribution to international theory. The role and limits of reason, already for long a subject of intense debates in Western philosophy, preoccupies now also analysts of international relations. The immanental Chinese view that structure is both constituted and constitutive has more than just superficial resemblance to the concept of 'duality of structure' expressed in Anthony Giddens' structuration theory.[64] Lao Tzu's reversal of priorities in chains of opposition finds its Western counterpart in Derridean poststructuralists, who attempt reconceptualization through the undoing of dualistic pairings and the reversal of hierarchies within existing dualistic concepts.[65] This mutual penetration of 'Western' and 'Eastern' methodologies, concepts and visions suggests that differences between neorealism and Chinese philosophy are neither a result of ignorance nor a matter of mere coincidence. They are at least partly the expression of deliberate choices and, more importantly, a reflection of subjective value patterns which were subconsciously diffused by a specific logo-cultural system.

Focusing on cultural influences is not meant to detract from the 'fact' that the powerful impact of anarchy requires attention and (realist) explanations. The continuous dissemination of Western values, practices and institutions has indeed transformed the European state system into a truly global one. This evolution partly supports the contention, implied throughout Waltz's treatise, that because each state is bound by the same official rules, systemic impacts on their foreign policy behaviour occur independently from – or at least parallel to – cultural influences.[66] However, this does not, as it is often asserted, make neorealist claims ahistoric and culturally neutral. It only shows that an ethnocentric theory may be able to account for one (systemic) source of conflict within a predominantly ethnocentric international system. Even in this narrow area, structural realism can only continue to be relevant as long as the international system is anarchical and culturally dominated by Western (realist) values.

If the critical theorist contention that discourses shape practices contains only one grain of truth, then realism must pay more attention to its reifying contents and open itself up to the emerging pluralism in international theory. Alternative discourses certainly cannot change immediately the international system or construct a more peaceful 'reality'. Yet if such ideas can break out of their conceptual confinement and challenge existing hegemonies, then they contain the potential to influence the behaviour of decision-makers and may even contribute to the avoidance of some conflicts. Thus, focusing our energies towards expanding or creating a new ahistoric and all encompassing theory would not greatly improve our understanding of conflict or the prospects for peace. Instead, greater awareness of unavoidable biases and the culturally conditioned construction of 'reality' would help international theory to become more effective in its search for the causes of war and its effort to overcome them.

ACKNOWLEDGEMENT

Support for this research was provided by the University of British Columbia, Department of Political Science and the Program on Nonviolent Sanctions, the Center for International Affairs, Harvard University. For comments on the earlier versions of the manuscript, I would like to thank Alex Asfour, Doug Bond, Beth Kier, Kal Holsti, Dave Hudnut, Yong-Joo Kim, Michelle Markley, Pete van Ness, and the editors of this book. Special thanks to Christine Sylvester for discussions on gender and other things.

NOTES

1. The bulk of this essay was originally written in autumn 1990. In late 1993 it was published in *Millennium's* special issue on 'Culture in International Relations'. Within the five years that have passed since bringing my thoughts to paper, my views have evolved. Yet a text takes off and becomes an object of appropriation over which the author inevitably loses control. Trying to halt this process is futile for, in Michel Foucault's words, 'writing unfolds like a game that invariably goes beyond its own rules and transgresses its limits' (M. Foucault, 'What is an Author?', in P. Rabinow (ed.), *The Foucault Reader* (New York: Pantheon Books, 1984, p. 102). While I have not added any substantial changes, I cannot refrain from drawing attention to what today I perceive to be an important but neglected dimension of the topic: the role of gender. Although I am primarily dealing with various cultural differences that exist between realist discourses and ancient Chinese philosophy, the two strains of thought also contain striking parallels that cannot be neglected. Both emerged out of a patriarchal context and are embedded in a strong masculine standpoint. Not only do both approaches to war and peace lack any substantial discussion of gender, but also they sustain discursive practices that entrench the exclusion of people called women from societal decision-making processes. The resulting far-reaching consequences are too complex and important to be addressed in footnotes or fleeting comments. Because of the above-mentioned separation between author and text, I am, at this point, limiting my remarks to the present comments and a few footnotes at points were the issue emerges in a particularly striking way.
2. F. Nietzsche, *The Joyful Wisdom* [Die Fröhliche Wissenschaft], trans. Thomas Common (London: T.N. Foulis, 1910), paragraph 57.
3. The standard reference to neorealist thought is K.N. Waltz, *Theory of International Politics*. (Reading, MA: Addison-Wesley, 1979). A selection of viewpoints presented by the paradigm's defenders, reformers, and critics is contained in R.O. Keohane (ed.), *Neorealism and its Critics* (New York: Columbia University Press, 1986).

4. See, for example, R.K. Ashley and R.B.J. Walker (eds), *Speaking the Language of Exile: Dissidence in International Studies*, special issue of *International Studies Quarterly* (Vol. 34, No. 3, 1990); R.W. Cox, 'Social Forces, States, and World Orders: Beyond International Relations Theory', *Millennium* (Vol. 10, No. 2, 1981), pp. 126-55; J. Der Derian and M. Shapiro (eds), *International/Intertextual Relations* (Lexington, MA: Lexington Books, 1989); Y.H. Ferguson and R.W. Mansbach, 'Between Celebration and Despair: Constructive Suggestions for Future International Theory', *International Studies Quarterly* (Vol. 35, No. 4, 1991), pp. 363-86; J. George, 'International Relations and the Search for Thinking Space: Another View of the Third Debate', *International Studies Quarterly* (Vol. 33, No. 3, 1989), pp. 269-80; A. Linklater, 'The Question of the Next Stage in International Relations Theory: A Critical-Theoretical Point of View', *Millennium* (Vol. 21, No. 1, 1992), pp. 77-98; and R.B.J. Walker, 'History and Structure in the Theory of International Relations', *Millennium* (Vol. 18, No. 2, 1989), pp. 163-83.
5. K.J. Holsti, *The Dividing Discipline: Hegemony and Diversity in International Theory* (Boston, MA: Unwin Hyman, 1985), p. 10.
6. Ibid., pp. 102-8.
7. A concise and helpful overview in English of the various influential opinions on the end or transformational capacities of contemporary philosophy is provided in K. Baynes, J. Bohmann and T. McCarthy (eds), *After Philosophy: End or Transformation?* (Cambridge, MA: The MIT Press, 1987).
8. See, for example, M. Foucault, *L'Archéologie du Savoir* [The Archeology of Knowledge] (Paris: Editions Gallimard, 1969); and J.F. Lyotard, *La Condition Postmoderne: Rapport sur le Savoir* [The Postmodern Condition] (Paris: Editions de Minuit, 1982).
9. J. Habermas, *Erkenntnis und Interesse* [Knowledge and Human Interest] (Frankfurt: Suhrkamp, 1973); K.O. Apel, *Diskurs und Verantwortung: Das Problem des Ubergangs zur Postkonventionellen Moral* (Frankfurt: Suhrkamp, 1988).
10. A concise exposition on the linguistic mediation of perceptions and behaviour can be found in B.L. Whorf, *Language, Thought, and Reality* (Cambridge, MA: Technology Press of MIT, 1956). Especially since Wittgenstein, questions related to language have occupied a key role in philosophical discourses. For a selection of classical essays on linguistic philosophy see R. Rorty (ed.), *The Linguistic Turn: Essays in Philosophical Method* (Chicago, IL: The University of Chicago Press, 1992). Languages, of course, also embed gender-related discriminations. The patterns of most Asian and Western grammatical structures reflect patriarchal practices and entrench as well as mask corresponding cultural values, role assignments and forms of oppression.
11. F. Nietzsche, *op. cit.*, in note 2, paragraph 380.
12. Giambattista Vico, quoted in Cox, *op. cit.*, in note 4, p. 132.
13. L. Walker, *The Multi-State System of Ancient China* (Hamden, CO: The Shoe String Press, 1953), pp. 73-9.

14. B.I. Schwartz, *The World of Thought in Ancient China* (Cambridge, MA: Harvard University Press, 1985), p. 63; R. Moritz, *Die Philosophie im Alten China* (Berlin: Deutscher Verlag der Wissenschaften, 1990), p. 49.
15. D.L. Hall and R.T. Ames, *Thinking Through Confucius* (Albany, NY: State University of New York Press, 1987), pp. 18–19.
16. Ibid., pp. 17–25. Lisa Raphals contrasts the two ways of thought in a similar way, but focuses on differences between theoretical and practical knowledge as well as on questions related to (metic) intelligence and language. See L. Raphals, *Knowing Words: Wisdom and Cunning in the Classical Traditions* of *China and Greece* (Ithaca, NY: Cornell University Press, 1992).
17. A.C. Graham, *Disputers of the Tao: Philosophical Argument in Ancient China* (La Salle: Open Court, 1989), p. 5.
18. Cox, *op. cit.*, in note 4, p. 128. See also R.W. Cox, 'Gramsci, Hegemony and International Relations: An Essay in Method', *Millennium* (Vol. 12, No. 2, 1983), pp. 162–75.
19. Cox, *op. cit.*, in note 4, p. 130.
20. M. Fischer, 'Feudal Europe, 800–1300: Communal Discourse and Conflictual Practices', *International Organization* (Vol. 46, No. 2, 1992), pp. 427–66.
21. C. von Clausewitz, *Vom Krieg* [On War] (Stuttgart: Reclam, 1980), pp. 329–38.
22. K.J. Holsti, *Peace and War: Armed Conflicts and International Order 1648–1989* (Cambridge: Cambridge University Press, 1991).
23. A. Wendt, 'Anarchy is What States Make of it: The Social Construction of Power Politics', *International Organization* (Vol. 46, No. 2, 1992), p. 395.
24. F. Nietzsche, *The Dawn* of *the Day* [Morgenröte: Gedanken über die Moralischen Vorurteile], trans. J.M. Kennedy, (London: T.N. Foulis, 1911), paragraph 44.
25. K.N. Waltz, *Man, the State and War* (New York, NY: Columbia University Press, 1959).
26. Waltz, *op. cit.,* in note 3, pp. 18–37.
27. M. Foucault, *L'Ordre du Discours* [The Discourse on Language] (Paris: Editions Gallimard, 1971), pp. 31–8.
28. Waltz, *op. cit.*, in note 3, p. 8.
29. Ibid.
30. See, for example, Chuang Tzu, 'The Chuang Tzu', trans. W.T. Chan, in *A Source Book in Chinese Philosophy* (Princeton, NJ: Princeton University Press, 1963), pp. 165–6.
31. A.B. Bozeman, *Politics and Culture in International History* (Princeton, NJ: Princeton University Press, 1969), p. 140; Graham, *op. cit.*, in note 16, p. 4; J.M. Koller, *Oriental Philosophies* (New York, NY: Charles Scribner's Sons, 1970), p. 197; Schwartz, *op. cit.*, in note 13, p. 414; H. Schleichert, *Klassische Chinesische Philosophie: Eine Einführung* (Frankfurt: Vittorio Klostermann, 1990), pp. 18–19.
32. M. Foucault, *Naissance de la Clinique* [The Birth of the Clinic] (Paris: Presses Universitaires de France, 1963).

33. T.J. Kaptchuk, *The Web That Has No Weaver: Understanding Chinese Medicine* (New York, NY: Congdon and Weed, 1983), pp. 1–33 and 256–66.
34. Ibid., pp. 34–5.
35. Chuang Tzu, *op. cit.*, in note 30, p. 190.
36. M. Weber, *Die Wirtschaftsethik der Weltreligionen: Konfuzianismus und Taoismus: Schriften 1915–1920, Gesammelte Schriften, Vol. 19,* ed. H. Schmidt-Glintzer (Tübingen: J.C.B. Mohr, 1989), pp. 309–13.
37. A.C. Graham, *Later Mohist Logic, Ethics and Science* (Hong Kong: The Chinese University Press, 1978); and J. Needham, *Science and Civilization in China* (Cambridge: Cambridge University Press, 1954).
38. Graham, *op. cit.*, in note 17, pp. 7–8, 75–94 and 137–42.
39. Chuang Tzu, *Chuang-tzu: The Inner Chapters*, translated by A.C. Graham (London: Unwin Paperbacks, 1986), pp. 48–61.
40. R. Gilpin, *War and Change in World Politics* (Cambridge: Cambridge University Press, 1981).
41. R.O. Keohane, 'Realism, Neorealism and the Study of World Politics', in R.O. Keohane (ed.), *op. cit.*, in note 3, p. 7. It should nevertheless be noted that a number of realist theorists, particularly the ones with a (neo)liberal outlook, are critical about certain aspects of reason. For example, the traditional liberal view emphasizes that rationality only applies to endeavour and not to outcome, or that various external and internal factors are responsible for decision-makers acting 'only' under bounded rationality. See R. Gilpin, *The Political Economy of International Relations* (Princeton, NJ: Princeton University Press, 1987), p. 28; and R.O. Keohane, *After Hegemony: Cooperation and Discord in the World Political Economy* (Princeton, NJ: Princeton University Press, 1984), pp. 111–14.
42. H.J. Morgenthau, *Politics among Nations: The Struggle for Power and Peace* (New York, NY: Alfred A. Knopf, 1978), p. 4.
43. Lao Tzu, *Tao Te Ching*, translated by D.C. Lau (Harmondsworth: Penguin Books, 1986), p. 117.
44. Waltz, *op. cit.*, in note 3, pp. 4–10.
45. Waltz, *op. cit.*, in note 25, p. 169. See also Gilpin, *op. cit.*, in note 40, p. 226.
46. M. Wight, *Power Politics*, ed. H. Bull and C. Holbraad (Leicester: Leicester University Press, 1978), p. 290.
47. W.B. Gallie, *Philosophers of Peace and War* (Cambridge: Cambridge University Press, 1978), pp. 28–9.
48. F.H. Hinsley, *Power and the Pursuit* of *Peace* (Cambridge: Cambridge University Press, 1963), p. 88.
49. Graham, *op. cit.*, in note 17, p. 30.
50. Chuang Tzu, *op. cit.*, in note 30, pp. 182–3.
51. Mo Tzu in Schwartz, *op. cit.*, in note 14, p. 142; T. Hobbes, *Leviathan*, ed. C.B. Macpherson (London: Penguin Books, 1968), p. 185; J. Locke, *Second Treatise* of *Government*, edited by R.H. Cox (North Arlington, IL: Harlan Davidson, 1982), pp. 3–10.
52. Confucius, 'The Analects', trans. in A *Source Book in Chinese Philosophy, op. cit.*, in note 30, p. 45.

53. J.J. Rousseau, *Discours sur l'Origine et les Fondements de l'Inegalité parmi les Hommes* [Discourse on the Origin of Inequality] (Paris: Gallimard, 1965), p. 49.
54. H. Bull, *The Anarchical Society* (New York, NY: Columbia University Press: 1977), p. 46; Waltz, *op. cit.*, in note 3, pp. 163–72; M. Wight, 'Western Values in International Relations', in H. Butterfield and M. Wight (eds), *Diplomatic Investigations: Essays in the Theory of International Politics* (London: George Allen & Unwin, 1969), pp. 102–3.
55. Schwartz, *op. cit.*, in note 14, p. 413.
56. Within the context of an all-embracing sino-centric vision of world order, the term 'international' is inappropriate since it suggests a system that consists of interacting national units. Being aware of its inadequacy, I am employing the term to facilitate a comparison with neo-realist arguments.
57. Schwartz, *op. cit.*, p. 141.
58. Ibid., p. 148. This concept evokes certain parallels with Plato's idea of a philosopher-king.
59. A. Waley, *Three Ways of Thought in Ancient China* (New York, NY: Doubleday Anchor Books, 1956), p. 177.
60. R. Aron, *Paix et Guerre entre les Nations* [Peace and War] (Paris: Calmann-Lévy, 1962), p. 103.
61. Bozeman, *op. cit.*, in note 31, p. 144.
62. Ibid., pp. 134–5. See also M. Haas, 'Asian Culture and International Relations', in J. Chay (ed.), *Culture and International Relations* (New York, NY: Praeger, 1990), p. 173; and J.K. Fairbank and S.Y. Teng, 'The Chinese Tradition of Diplomacy', in J. Larus (ed.), *Comparative World Politics: Readings in Western and Premodern Non-Western International Relations* (Belmont: Wadsworth Publishing Co, 1964), p. 192. The perception of the international system is also one of the areas in which both realism and Chinese philosophy display their strong masculine biases. The five-fold Confucian model of hierarchy is an example *par excellence* of a patriarchal system in which senior men control both junior men and women in order to consolidate a male dominated societal order. The extension of this domestic model of control to the realm of foreign policy accounts for a further entrenchment of patriarchy. Masculinity in Western approaches to war and peace is equally striking and amply documented. See, for example, J.B. Elshtain, *Women and War* (New York: Basic Books, 1987); C. Enloe, *The Morning After: Sexual Politics at the End of the Cold War* (Berkeley: University of California Press, 1993); Ch. Sylvester, *Feminist Theory and International Relations in a Postmodern Era* (Cambridge: Cambridge University Press, 1994); and J.A. Tickner, *Gender in International Relations: Feminist Perspectives on Achieving Global Security* (New York: Colombia University, 1992).
63. See K.J. Holsti, 'The Necrologists of International Relations', *Canadian Journal of Political Science* (Vol. XVIII, No. 4, 1985), p. 678; A. Lijphart, 'Karl W. Deutsch and the New Paradigm in International Relations', in R.L. Merritt and B.M. Russett (eds), *From National Development to Global Community* (London: George Allen & Unwin, 1981), p. 239; and D.J. Puchala and S.I. Fagen, 'International Politics in the

1970s: The Search for a Perspective', in R. Maghroori and B. Ramberg (eds), *Globalism versus Realism: International Relations' Third Debate* (Boulder, CO: Westview Press, 1982), p. 48.

64. A. Giddens, *The Constitution of Society: Outline of the Theory of Structuration* (Berkeley, CA: University of California Press, 1984).
65. See R.K. Ashley, 'Living on Border Lines: Man, Poststructuralism, and War', in J. Der Derian and M.J. Shapiro (eds), *op. cit.*, in note 4; J. Derrida, *A Derrida Reader: Between the Blinds*, ed. by P. Kamuf (New York, NY: Columbia University Press, 1991), pp. 259–76; Graham, *op. cit.*, in note 17, pp. 223–31; and R. Wiggershaus, *Die Frankfurter Schule: Geschichte, Theoretische Entwicklung, Politische Bedeutung* (München: Hauser, 1986), pp. 628–46.
66. See also R.B.J. Walker, 'World Politics and Western Reason: Universalism, Pluralism, Hegemony', in R.B.J. Walker (ed.), *Culture, Ideology, and World Order* (Boulder, CO: Westview Press, 1984), p. 205

6 Conflict Resolution across Cultures: Bridging the Gap
Raymond Cohen

INTRODUCTION

Conflict resolution in different societies reflects both particular and universal features. Specific understanding of and approaches to the disputing process are embedded within given cultural settings. This body of implicit, received truth is reflected both in actual behaviour and also in the language used by a society to talk about conflict. Every society has a vocabulary of specialized terms and expressions loaded with affective and metaphorical connotations. When conflict occurs across cultures, the ostensible issue under contention tends to be complicated by misunderstandings and procedural incompatibilities. Culturally grounded assumptions about conflict can be uncovered, in the first instance, by lexical analysis, and it is that convenient methodology that will be adopted here. Comparison of the meaning (and also, importantly, use) of relevant terms across cultures can then reveal potential sources both of dissonance and reconciliation. Identification of shared features of conflict resolution may then enable the parties to avoid pitfalls and construct bridging mechanisms. Two episodes in bridge-building, one international, the other inter-communal, will be analysed below and lessons drawn.

CULTURE AS MEANING

There are many possible perspectives on culture; the concept itself was invented by anthropologists to explain the astonishing variety of the human spectacle, the many answers that different societies have evolved to meet the same existential problems. No single characterization of culture possesses absolute validity. In recent years, however, culture has come to be seen as more about software than hardware, about the operating instructions for group life and not about behaviour or material artefacts as such. According to this view, particularly associated with the work of Clyde Kluckhohn (e.g. 1957), culture is made up of meanings, conventions and presuppositions. It is the syntax that governs the creation and use of symbols and signs, rather than some particular set of the same. As Avruch and Black point out, culture is not something tangible, a 'thing', it is not a commodity possessed uniformly by every member of a community (as in the misguided concept of 'national character'), nor is it a traditional way of behaving, a set of quaint customs to be learned before a trip abroad. Rather, it is to be thought of as the shared 'common sense', as Geertz puts it (1983: 73–93), 'the realm of the given and the undeniable' (ibid., 75), which is constitutive of a group's shared construction of reality, enabling it to live together and survive in a certain habitat. Indeed, culture is constitutive of the very community, because without it communication, co-ordinated activity, social life itself, would be impossible. Culture, in short, creates (intersubjective) meaning in the world and permits its members 'to perceive, interpret, evaluate, and act on and in both external and internal reality' (Avruch and Black, 1991: 27–30). Cultural analysis proceeds by examining the way symbolic systems work (Rubinstein, chapter 9, this volume). For present purposes – the comparative analysis of dispute practices – language is the most accessible and indicative symbolic system.

Agreement on the assumptions and conventions governing conflict and its resolution are a bedrock precondition for the existence of society. If conflict pits individuals and subgroups within a community against each other, holding out the threat of social disruption, violence and heightened vulnerability to external enemies, clearly there have to be accepted procedures for removing or at least containing that danger. Conflict resolution is posited on the assumption that disputants (and conciliators) concur on what a dispute is and what constitute reasonable grounds for its occurrence, how and to whom grievance is to be meaningfully articulated and the demand for redress framed, who is a legitimate party to the quarrel and its settlement, and what are the appropriate mechanisms by which the conflict is to be dealt with. Conflict resolution in different cultures may reflect similar surface motifs and procedures; the logical possibilities are limited to variations on the themes of arbitration, mediation, negotiation and litigation. But the set of underlying meanings governing these procedures and motifs can be shown to be culturally specific, having evolved to serve and protect the larger, axiomatic needs of the community. Such 'ethnoconflict theories', which 'undergird the techniques or processes of conflict resolution used indigenously' (Avruch and Black, 1994: 132), are lodged in the local language, and it is here that they can be investigated. Lexical analysis not only sheds light on current usage and practice, but also on the origins and historical development of key terms.

Grasp of the role of language is essential to understanding the connection between culture and conflict resolution. Without overlooking non-verbal forms of communication, the relation of language to culture is crucial, since it is the former that acts as the communal archive and conveyor belt by which shared meanings are stored and transmitted diachronically within human groups from one generation to the next. However, it is its remarkable capacity actively to imprint and purvey changing experience and shifting knowledge synchronically right across society that distinguishes language from more static and specialized symbolic systems. Language is a medium of evolution as well as of record. For the purposes of this chapter, though, the vernacular can best be thought of as the repository of that shared common sense constructing and governing the disputing process. It is the link between memory and practice. In its absence, it is hard to see how the meanings and conventions for defining and handling conflict could be preserved by the group, ready for translation into action at any time.

A LEXICAL APPROACH TO CULTURE AND CONFLICT RESOLUTION

'Symbols', Nader and Todd argue, 'lie at the very basis' of the disputing process (1978: 28). Symbolic representations, verbal and non-verbal, of aggression, claim, grievance, obligation, right, honour, shame, hurt, order, reconciliation, authority and compensation are the tokens with which the conflict resolution game is played. There is nothing deterministic about the game. Within societies a variety of procedures may be available to address a single kind of dispute without confusion, because people recognize that different circumstances require different expedients (ibid., 11). Contradictions arise when it becomes necessary to address disputes across communities 'characterized by social and cultural diversity'. In these cases the tendency is for the more powerful group simply to impose its norms and procedures on the weaker, as the British Raj imposed an alien system of law and courts on the indigenous Indian population. Conflict resolution then becomes a vehicle for perpetuating and legitimizing 'the dominance relations of some cultures or subcultures over others' (ibid., 20–1, 37). When coercion of the weaker party is not an available or desirable option, only a mechanism freely agreed to by the parties and expressing their equal status can satisfactorily bridge the gap between them. It is hardly surprising that in intercultural disputes the choice of procedure, usually thought of as secondary to substance, acquires crucial significance.

Because symbols and procedures matter deeply in these circumstances it is essential to engage in an open-minded cross-cultural analysis of the language involved in the disputing process. This kind of analysis has to be both connotative and denotative, in other words must address the implications and resonances of terms as well as their dictionary equivalents. It also has to be contrastive, opposing and comparing meanings and connotations across languages. A single-language analysis merely perpetuates the observer's unconscious ethnocentrism, the unreflective assumption that what is common sense within one cultural framework ('compromise is good') is equally meaningful in other cultures. Comparison, by confronting observers with dissonant preconceptions, helps to jolt them out of their intellectual complacency.

An exercise of the kind called for here has been very successfully carried out, albeit in a preliminary way, by the critical Assyriologist Mario Liverani in his study of the political lexicon and ideology of the mid-fourteenth century BCE Amarna letters (1993: 41–56). These letters are of particular interest from the point of view of cross-cultural analysis because they consist of political and diplomatic exchanges between the Pharaonic court and its Canaanite vassals and the other great powers, such as Babylon, Mittani and Hatti. While the despatches for delivery were written in Akkadian, the *lingua franca* of the age, the original drafts or royal instructions would have been in the correspondents' native languages, whether Egyptian, Canaanite or whatever.

Liverani demonstrates how misunderstanding and confusion arose in the translation of a term from Egyptian, via Akkadian, to Canaanite, and vice versa. The 'act of translating', Liverani argues, 'is unavoidably forced or approximate' because the 'semantic fields' of equivalent terms in different languages may overlap but not coincide precisely. An expression chosen in the target language to translate a word or phrase in the original language 'cannot express all the nuances . . . nor can it avoid adding improper nuances' (ibid., 45). Let us assume that a Canaanite correspondent wishes to convey meaning A, but the word for A also carries the sense of B in Canaanite; its semantic field is A–B. That it possesses this dual association is of no special significance to the native speaker; that it should do so is Canaanite common sense. The Canaanite scribe writes to Pharaoh using the appropriate Akkadian word; however, the term only covers the semantic field B. In Egyptian the translated equivalent of B also carries the connotation C; its semantic field is B–C; this *double-entendre* is Egyptian common sense. Thus not only will Egyptian readers of the Akkadian despatch fail to extract meaning A from the correspondence, they are also likely to pick up the unintended and erroneous sense of C. Liverani sums up the confusion: 'The semantic equivocality proceeding from inadequate translation is generally unconscious: each of the two different lexical systems is so deeply imbedded in the "world view" of its bearer that he cannot even perceive that the lexical system and world view of his dialogue-partner are different' (ibid.). Liverani's method is directed to the use of a *lingua franca* mediating between two other languages, but works equally well for bilingual situations.

THE CASE OF THE 'RECALCITRANT' PRIME MINISTER

Disputes over words – concealing deeper antinomies – are at the heart of intercultural conflict. They reveal, exacerbate and perpetuate hurt, and prevent its mitigation. A case in point occurred not long ago in Australian–Malaysian relations. The background to the affair was the redrawing of the map of regional relationships underway in the Pacific region since the downfall of communism. On the one hand Australia sought to redefine its international identity, realigning itself away from Europe to Asia. On the other hand Malaysia feared being dominated by a powerful and culturally alien neighbour whose real orientation was to the Western world. The occasion for the incident was the refusal by Prime Minister Mahathir Mohamad of Malaysia to attend a trade summit in Seattle in November 1993 of the Asia-Pacific Economic Cooperation organization [APEC] (*New York Times*, 9 December, 1993). Mahathir explained his decision on the grounds that the United States and its partners had been unenthusiastic about the idea of an ASEAN-type trading group.[1] Reserved for Asians only, such a body would have excluded Western states such as Australia, Canada and the United States, and would have allowed Malaysia to play a central regional role. Mahathir had championed the proposal as his special cause. Asked in Seattle about the Malaysian prime minister's absence, Australian Prime Minister Paul Keating gave the following reply:

I don't know and I don't care. I am sick of asking [*sic*] questions about Dr. Mahathir. Everyone has a chance to come here. If he didn't come, that's his business. The thing about it was there was just a very historic meeting. Please don't ask me any more questions about Dr. Mahathir. I couldn't care less, frankly, whether he comes or not. APEC is bigger than all of us – Australia, the US, and Malaysia, and Dr. Mahathir and any other *recalcitrants*. (*FBIS*, 23 November, 1993; my italics)

These remarks infuriated the Malaysian government, drawing bitter recriminations and sanctions in their wake. The subsequent diplomatic crisis dragged on for almost three weeks and threatened a dislocation of relations and full-scale trade war.

The immediate response of the Malaysian government was that the kind of outspoken language acceptable in Australian society was utterly out of place in Asia. Prime Minister Mahathir said that 'Australians do not have the values of respect and manners that Asians do.' Therefore, Australia's claim that it was an Asian country was meaningless (*FBIS*, 24 and 26 November, 1993). Information Minister Mohamed Rahmat added: 'In the Australian context it is all right to be blunt but when you deal with Asians you have to be extra careful. If you want to be part of Asia you have to be sensitive to the Asian way of life and Asian culture' (*The Age*, 13 December, 1993).

At one level the dispute was clearly a classic cross-cultural clash between high- and low-context cultures, the former indirect, allusive and sometimes tacit, the latter explicit, blunt and very verbal (Hall, 1976: 85–103; Cohen, 1991: 19–32). High-context articulation, in which much of the burden of meaning is contained in the situation itself and accompanying non-verbal cues, is typical of societies in which obligations to the group are paramount, honour and face are all-important, and great effort is made to avoid offence. Low-context articulation, of which Australian speech is a striking example, is characterized by an emphasis on words rather than accompanying hints, and is typical of cultures in which individual rights are given more weight than affiliation to an extended family. Immigrant countries such as the United States, Australia and Israel tend to be particularly low-context, with speech lacking the subtle references and allusions of more homogeneous, traditional societies. It is worth adding that in Geert Hofstede's work on cultural differences, Malaysia and Australia are shown to be virtually polar opposites in their ranking on two central cultural dimensions: 'individualism' (contrasted with 'collectivism'), and 'power distance', defined as the acceptability of inequalities in society (Hofstede, 1982: 40).

If overall cultural dissonances in the Australian–Malaysian relationship provide fertile ground for misunderstanding, the episode in question also exemplifies the potential for abrasion when loaded terms are translated from one language and cultural context to another. The word 'recalcitrant', which so offended Dr Mahathir, means according to *The Oxford English Dictionary* '"kicking" against constraint or restriction; obstinately disobedient or refractory'. It is not a complimentary word, certainly, but neither does it sound particularly abusive to the Anglo-Saxon ear; indeed, it can possess a wry flavour of grudging admiration. Like other words referring to wilful behaviour such as 'stubborn', 'hard-nosed' or 'aggressive', it has come to acquire the added sense of standing up for yourself in a competitive world, where it is 'each man for himself'. These individualist tones, however, were entirely absent from Malaysian equivalents of 'recalcitrant'. Two expressions were used to translate the term: *kurang ajar* and *keras kepala*. The semantic fields they cover include an entire area of denigration entirely absent from the original English. *Kurang ajar* means not just disobedient in Malaysian, but also ill-educated. In Malaysia's collectivist, family-oriented society, where the reputation of the individual casts shame or honour on his kinship group, such an implication carried a grave imputation. This disobedient person, it suggested, the prime minister of the country no less, had not been brought up properly; his conduct brought discredit on his family and community (*FBIS*, 7 December, 1993). Similar pejorative connotations were attached to *keras kepala*. Seen in this light it is less surprising than appears at first sight that Information Minister Rahmat might conclude that Keating's comments 'had humiliated Dr. Mahathir and the Malaysian nation' (*FBIS*, 26 November, 1993).

The sort of behaviour expected of an ASEAN member is described by Thambipillai and Saravanamuttu (1985: 10–17). Relations within ASEAN, they argue, are modelled on the system of consensual decision-making through discussion and consultation (*musyawarah*) found in village politics in Indonesia, Malaysia and the Philippines. Since open disagreement and controversy must be avoided at all costs in the intimate face-to-face society of the village – as potentially disruptive of communal life – an elaborate system of prior consultation, mutual adjustment and synthesis has become ingrained, intended to lead eventually to a unanimous decision known as *mufakat*. The effective leader is one who is able to meld together contrasting viewpoints into a single, generally accepted conception. Projected onto the international arena, *musyawarah* requires that negotiations be conducted in a face-saving manner that ensures continuing harmony among the participants. Confrontation is avoided at all costs; rather than register a blunt contradiction of others' positions, postponement and further attempts at conciliation are preferred. Courtesy, due form, gracious behaviour and humility are of the essence. Aggressive, arrogant conduct, outspokenness and crude directness are abhorred. Unfortunately, these were precisely the qualities displayed by Australian Prime Minister Keating in his 'recalcitrants' outburst. In this he was doing no more than acting in conformity with the accepted, low-context norms of Australian public life.

It proved extraordinarily difficult to retrieve the situation following the Seattle incident. Just as Keating had stumbled unawares into a trap for which sound Australian common sense hardly prepared him, so did his cultural conditioning deprive him of the tools of reparation obvious to Malaysians: As far as Mahathir was concerned, the appropriate remedy for insult was a *public apology*, and this was soon made clear by the Malaysian government and media (*FBIS*, 26 and 27 November, 1993). For a time Keating rejected this out of hand, going so far as to suggest that it was Australia that was the injured party (ibid., 2 December, 1993). Following warnings and a verbal protest from Kuala Lumpur, Keating then wrote a letter to Mahathir putting the incident 'in some sort of context' and claiming 'that what I said was not calculated to offend him'. The issue had been blown out of proportion, it was not in the long-term interests of either party for it to continue, and they should put it behind them (*The Age*, 3 December, 1993). Mahathir's reaction was that the letter was 'not in the least ... an apology', and did 'not even appear conciliatory'. Though Keating's words 'were not meant to be offensive ... they cannot but be interpreted as being offensive.' The Malaysian Foreign Minister concluded that the letter had actually made things worse. 'The letter sent by Keating to Dr. Mahathir Mohamad does not come from a person who appears to be sorry and regrets what happened as a result of his own remarks which went beyond extreme [sic] ... what disappoints us most is that his letter neither offers an apology nor shows any interest to be friendly' (ibid.). There were implied threats of trade sanctions and a downgrading of relations (*FBIS*, 6 December, 1993).

Only now did Keating take the step called for all along. Appearing on television on 5 December, the Australian prime minister stated: 'If my remarks were not intended to offend him and he has taken offence, naturally one would regret that.' This albeit backhanded apology was repeated by Foreign Minister Gareth Evans in Parliament and by Federal Trade Minister Peter Cook on a mission to Kuala Lumpur (ibid., 7 December, 1993). Mahathir quickly pronounced himself satisfied with Keating's expression of regret and declared the quarrel at an end (ibid., 9 December, 1993).

One does not need to be a conflict resolution expert to see that some kind of apology was the fitting antidote for the insult to Dr Mahathir, whether real or imagined. Why, then, was the Australian government unable to arrive at an elegant solution much sooner? Partly the responsibility must lie with Mr Keating personally. In the end he was the truly 'recalcitrant' prime minister. But it is also possible to interpret the affair as a cross-cultural misunderstanding over the form apology should take. *The Oxford English Dictionary* defines 'apologize' as 'To speak in, or serve as, justification, explanation, or palliation of a fault, failure, or anything that may cause dissatisfaction; to offer defensive arguments; to make excuses.' As the dictionary definition makes clear, it is an act undertaken by the wrongdoer; something that the one who apologizes bestows on the aggrieved party. It would probably not be considered appropriate for remedying a serious grievance, but rather seen as a supplementary device or one used for making rather minor amends.

Within societies – like Malaysia – organized on hierarchical, kin-based lines, apology is an important way of disposing of a dispute. When a conflict occurs that threatens relationships within the community apology, taking an elaborate, stylized form of entreaty and deference, enacts the humble status of the petitioner and the superior status of the forgiver. Thus honour is requited and hierarchy reaffirmed. Anger cannot be maintained and retribution inflicted when the injured party's superior rank has been recognized and mercy requested (Hickson, 1986: 285–7). A lexical analysis may further clarify the difference between Malay and Anglo-Saxon sensibilities: Malay has no exact words to denote 'apology' or 'apologize'. The expressions commonly used are *meminta maaf*, *menuntut maaf* or *meminta ampun*, meaning to ask or pursue forgiveness or pardon from someone who has been wronged. Unlike English, where apology is framed as an action taken by the apologizer, Malay places the onus on the aggrieved party to absolve the offender as an act of grace. The Malay does not 'apologize', he begs for pardon.

Since Mahathir felt that he had been slighted in public and his family background impugned, it was natural for him to expect a public acknowledgement of contrition on Keating's part, accompanied by an appeal for forgiveness. At first, Keating completely failed to grasp the unavoidable need to express regret in order to restore communal harmony, and clumsily transformed the dispute into an irrelevant contest of wills, in the polemical, confrontationary tradition. When he finally understood the need to apologize he did so in the exact manner surrounding the usage of the term in English: He *explained* what had gone wrong, shifting the blame on extenuating circumstances ('putting it in some sort of context'), and even suggested that the ostensibly injured party was partly responsible in that he had misunderstood remarks that were not intended to offend (ibid., 291). It should be noted that it was just this parade of excuses and claim to have been misinterpreted that so annoyed Mahathir. If Keating absolved himself of all responsibility there could be no true appeal for forgiveness. 'Intention alone will not suffice', the Malay leader complained. 'If our intention is good but we utter bad words, people will only remember our words and not our intentions' (*FBIS*, 6 December 1993).

In the end the message that Malaysian diplomacy had been hammering home for almost two weeks finally got through and Keating used the magic word 'regret' on television, a public apology. Mahathir, his superior status symbolically acknowledged, could now graciously grant pardon, cancelling planned punitive action against Australia. 'The Government is of the view that the matter has brought about greater Australian appreciation of the sensitivities of Malaysians, which should help prevent similar incidents in the future' (*The Age*, 13 December 1993).

CONFLICT RESOLUTION IN ISRAELI AND PALESTINIAN SOCIETIES

The combination of semantic and procedural dissonance observed in Australian–Malaysian relations is also a feature of Israeli–Palestinian ties. Jews and Arabs have long-established, sophisticated systems of conflict resolution which have evolved in very different ways to meet the special circumstances and needs of each society. Take the important concept of 'mediator', conventionally translated into Arabic as *wasta* and Hebrew as *metavekh*. In English 'mediator' has acquired both beneficent and professional associations; doing good by helping disputants arrange their differences, in line with fiduciary expectations of competence, disinterest and objectivity. Mediators in the English-speaking world are supposed to be impartial, trained professionals, often with a legal background, assisting the protagonists in labour and other disputes to communicate, and suggesting alternative options to them. As litigation has become more protracted and expensive, mediation has become increasingly attractive as a technique of *alternative dispute resolution*.

In Jewish and Arab cultures the semantic fields covered by the various terms for mediator evoke different affective and functional associations. In Arabic, *wasta* or *wasit*, meaning literally 'the middle', connotes an influence broker, a source of *proteksia* in the Russian sense of 'pull' or special treatment (see Cunningham and Sarayrah, 1993). As such he – for women do not qualify – is a central figure, indispensable in lubricating contacts and conducting business in the family-centred, hierarchical, honour-based societies of the Arab world. Where authority is highly personalized and yet access to it limited and dependent on connections, intermediaries play a crucial role in every walk of life from initiating a contact, cutting a deal, intervening with dignitaries and the bureaucracy, negotiating the terms of marriage, and placing people in employment.

The services of the *wasta* (or his functional equivalent, since terms vary) are also essential in mediating local disputes. This particularly applies in matters that threaten to disrupt communal harmony by setting off a blood feud between contending clans, such as murder or manslaughter, family honour, the virtue of women and property. *Wastas* in the resolution of conflict are chosen from prominent, honoured members of disputing groups. They are expected to shuttle between rival groups, negotiate a truce (*hudne*), scrupulously protect the honour of disputants, restore equilibrium between them (if necessary by preferring the claims of the weaker party), negotiate compensation, organize the reconciliation ceremony of the *sulkha*, and act as guarantors for the settlement. Their strongest appeal is not to ethics, but to the good of the community; the settlement is expected to reflect an honourable balance of advantage rather than some abstract concept of justice. The actual process of conflict resolution via mediation is known as *atwah* or *sulh asha'iry*, and consists of a series of established, ritualized procedures, visits and ceremonies (Qleibo, 1993). If the term *wasta* as influence broker has the connotation of favouritism, the sense of even-handedness in conflict resolution can be conveyed by the term *wasata*, while the additional idea of the auspices or good offices of a dignitary is given by the expression *rai elmutamar*.

In Jewish culture mediation evolved to meet an assortment of peculiar environmental and social needs, and this is reflected in the vocabulary. Unlike traditional Palestinian society, Jewish communities in the Diaspora were usually located in urban settlements rather than villages. Excluded from citizenship and land ownership by the Christian or Moslem majority, the major imperative was confessional solidarity rather than loyalty to some clan. No sub-group intervenes between the nuclear family and the wider community of the faithful. Common denominators were religion and the shared fate of a vulnerable minority. Social cohesion was maintained by external pressures and autonomous courts granted by host rulers. The sort of lineage divisions and social inequalities that necessitate pervasive *wasta*-type figures were absent. In their place Jewish culture evolved a selection of specialized intermediary roles. *Shadkhan* is the broker who arranges marriages. *Metavekh* is primarily a mediator in the sense of broker or middleman in commercial transactions. In modern Hebrew *metavekh* frequently refers to estate agent, realtor in American English. It is also the commonly accepted translation of 'mediator' and is used, for example, to refer to *professional* (invariably) *American diplomats* mediating between Israel and her Arab neighbours. Still, *metavekh* lacks the beneficent associations of the English word. (Note that the significant political/religious *double-entendre* in the English term 'diplomatic *mission*' is also absent from the Hebrew.) A third term, *shtadlan*, lobbyist, has (slightly pejorative) echoes of the go-between acting on behalf of the Diaspora Jewish community at the court of the *poritz*, the local nobleman upon whose benevolence the Jews of Christian Europe depended for their survival and sustenance.

Strong connotations of conciliation in Israeli culture are reserved for the *borer*, an individual – often a rabbi – who arbitrates between the parties, attempting to arrive at a fair settlement (known as *peshara*, literally compromise). The role of *borer* is steeped in history and tradition and can be traced back at least to the second century CE (*Encyclopedia Judaica*, 1971, 3: 294–300). The rules governing arbitration (*borerut*) are exhaustively treated in the *Talmud* (second–fifth centuries CE) and have greatly influenced dispute resolution in modern Israel. Current practice is regulated by the Arbitration Law, 5728/1968, which recognizes arbitration freely entered into according to certain procedures as legally binding. Nevertheless, resort to litigation is as pervasive in modern Israel as it is in the United States, and the courts are gravely over-burdened with a backlog of work. Where appropriate a judge may offer his services as arbitrator rather than adjudicator. To date, attempts to develop alternative dispute resolution techniques based upon the work of trained mediators have had mixed success (Matz, 1991: 11–16).

As long as Arabs and Jews lived quite separate communal lives differences between their respective dispute management traditions remained moot. Before 1967 Arab citizens of Israel preferred, on the whole, to resolve conflicts within their own community according to traditional practices (Cohen, 1965). Disputes between Jews and Arabs were subject to the law of the land, as they had been under the British Mandate (1922–48). After 1967, and the capture of the West Bank of the Jordan by Israel, Israelis and Palestinians found themselves linked by a growing range of commercial, professional and neighbourly ties, particularly in the Jerusalem area. Formally, disputes were to be brought before the Israeli courts, but Palestinians usually shrank from this resort, rightly or wrongly doubting the impartiality of Israeli justice between Jew and Arab. With the outbreak of the *intifadah* in 1987 this situation was accentuated.

A number of innovative attempts have been and are being made to develop mechanisms for resolving conflicts between the communities. One important and suggestive experiment in building bridges has been underway for several years under the auspices of The Jerusalem Institute for Arbitration (Zilberman, 1994; 1995). Headed by lawyer Hiba Husseini of the Arab Studies Society and anthropologist Ifrah Zilberman of the Hebrew University of Jerusalem, this is an inter-communal organization providing conciliation services (Hebrew, *pishur*; Arabic, *takhkim*) in mixed disputes. The basis for the work of the organization is two-fold: the fundamental assumption that justice is universal, and compatible customs of arbitration. The Jewish tradition of arbitration, enshrined in the 1968 Arbitration Law, has already been mentioned. The Arab pillar of the structure is a system of local customary law, '*arf*, originating within a powerful alliance of Hebronite kinship groups headed by the Ja'abari clan, and spread by migration from Hebron to Jerusalem and Amman in the 1930s. '*Arf* is not a fixed body of rules, but a flexible set of arbitral expedients calibrated to the nature of the offence. Unlike the conventional system of mediation and reconciliation between rival clans it draws its efficacy from the persuasive and coercive power of an integrated, co-liability association (Zilberman, 1991).

The service provided by The Jerusalem Institute for Arbitration rests on both Israeli and Palestinian traditions, but its graduated set of expedients most resembles '*arf*. Stage one is a form of non-compulsory conciliation between neighbours involving minor squabbles or small sums of money. Zilberman calls this *tivukh l'kiruv levavot*, 'mediation to draw hearts together'. Stage two is mediation without a binding document of arbitration and deals with more serious disputes involving a degree of honour and shame. The conciliators may invite witnesses, but their objective is to reconcile the parties using some resort to social pressure. Stage three is full-blown arbitration of weighty issues. Disputants enter the process quite voluntarily, but accept its irreversible force in a legal document recognized by the Israeli courts as binding. Arbitrators are not necessarily jurists, but they must have a sound knowledge of technical and customary aspects of the issue under contention. The number of arbitrators ranges from one to three and the selection procedure is very flexible, though arbitrators must be of impeccable reputation. Each disputant may bring his or her own arbitrator, one Jewish, one Arab, agree to a common arbitrator, or select names from a list provided by the institute. If there are two arbitrators they may, if they wish, together agree on a third arbitrator (a practice found among both Jews and Arabs). Zilberman accepts that deep cultural divisions may hinder the work of arbitration, but a shared sense of natural justice provides a compass.

For both Jews and Arabs the institute offers a more attractive alternative than expensive and drawn-out litigation. Most important, it promises an equitable, non-zero sum outcome. Both parties recognize its procedures to be familiar and fair: Arabs, because of its resemblance to *'arf*; Jews – particularly those of Sephardic origin and long-established residents of Jerusalem – according to Dr Zilberman, because of their intuitive grasp of the institutions of *wasta* and *sulkha*, and possibly memories of pre-1948 inter-communal methods of dispute resolution. It is worth remarking that the Israeli police to this day use mediation methods in their work with Arabs developed in the Ottoman and Mandatory periods.

CONCLUSION

The two cases discussed here of conflict resolution across cultures are clearly in no sense representative and permit no general conclusions. Rather, they illustrate significant features of the problem and provide hints at possible solutions. They graphically portray different approaches to the disputing process: In the Malaysia–Australia case the dispute arose from a classic dialogue of the deaf (Cohen, 1990). Group-oriented and individualistic cultures clashed over the hidden associations of a word, the semantic debate setting off deeper resentments and sensitivities. To restore face lost by the perceived slur it was obvious to the government of Malaysia that there would have to be an apology – a publicized display of contrition enacting Malaysian moral superiority. The significance and choreography of such an act was not at first obvious to the low-context Australians, who initially modelled the incident as a contest of wills. What could, if performed at once, have been a relatively painless acknowledgment of error, acquired with the passage of time the flavour of an undignified Australian climb-down. The episode is a reminder of the salience of apology as a primary restorative device in hierarchical, shame societies.

Palestinian and Israeli societies display profound dissonances on many dimensions, reflected in their contacts and relations at both the individual and political level. The blood-feud, still ubiquitous among Palestinian clans, was abandoned by Ancient Israel when tribal loyalty was replaced by an overarching national and cultic affiliation. For years, acts of violence followed by revenge locked Jews and Arabs into a seemingly never-ending conflict. A comparison of their respective philosophies of conflict resolution reveals the emphasis in the former on mediation, in the latter on litigation and arbitration. Whereas Palestinians seek to insulate disputants from each other through a third party, lest personal friction ignite a conflagration between lineage groups, Jews pursue social harmony by placing their differences before the learned judgment of an authority figure. However, as Husseini and Zilberman have discovered, it is possible to establish a bridging mechanism for the resolution of disputes across cultures by selecting compatible features of both traditions. In effect, Israelis resorting to the good offices of The Jerusalem Institute for Arbitration are being co-opted into the framework of *'arf*, Palestinian customary law. Fortuitously, this system of conflict resolution, pervasive in the Jerusalem area, conforms to the Jewish requirements of third-party judgment while simultaneously answering the Arab need for a buffer separating opponents.

In conflicts across cultures one possible paradigm is the Camp David strategy employed by President Jimmy Carter of the United States in 1978: intervention of a respected mediator from a prestigious third culture. This has been the principle behind much private (Quaker, Mennonite) and official American involvement in the Arab–Israeli conflict over the years. This approach has clearly had several notable successes, but it demands an onerous commitment of time and resources on the part of the mediator and is hardly a long-term answer to a permanent structural problem. The parties have to learn to get along by themselves without nanny. Another strategy is to train Jews and

Arabs in conflict resolution techniques developed and perfected elsewhere, particularly in North America. This is the philosophy of various distinguished bodies and individuals such as the Washington Institute of Multitrack Diplomacy, Herb Kelman, Jay Rothman, Pyotr Patrushev and others (e.g. Rothman, 1993). The problem here is that Jews and Arabs may behave themselves only so long as the trainer is present and such initiatives tend to peter out. Moreover, methods taught may not meet the special culturally grounded expectations of the parties. Describing a training project in the Middle East, Pyotr Patrushev acknowledges the resistance to his ideas of the participants and correctly concludes that conventional Western conflict resolution techniques have to be re-evaluated in the light of local 'cultural beliefs and values' (Patrushev, 1994: 17).

The approach that worked in the Malaysian–Australian and Palestinian–Israeli cases involved the protagonists working out a solution of their problem *on their own* more or less by a process of trial and error. Keating's apology took a little while, but was the result of effective consultation between officials of both governments genuinely concerned to dispose of a sterile dispute that was in nobody's interest. The Australians deserve credit for actually listening to their Malaysian counterparts. Similarly, Husseini and Zilberman have arrived at their solution after much thought, observation, analysis, and lifetimes of experience of Arab–Jewish conflict. So the source of joint solutions is dialogue and co-operation between serious, dedicated people from both sides of the cultural divide. No outsider could have made the match between *'arf* and *borerut*, especially as it is tailor-made for the special historical-cultural circumstances of the Jerusalem area.

A final point is worth noting. Both Australians and Israelis – the stronger parties in their respective disputes – made the important, conciliatory gesture of adjusting themselves to the conflict resolution procedure of the weaker partner. Instead of insisting on the priority of their own method in the tradition of the British Raj they had the insight to realize that the first step in conflict resolution across cultures is to establish an honourable equilibrium between the parties.

ACKNOWLEDGEMENT

The author wishes to thanks Jacob Bercovitch, Uthman Na'amena, Avraham Sela and Itzhak Zilberman for their kind help.

NOTES

1. ASEAN, the Association of Southeast Asian Nations, established in 1967, consists of Indonesia, Malaysia, the Philippines, Singapore and Thailand.

BIBLIOGRAPHY AND REFERENCES

Avruch, K. and Black, Peter W. (1989) 'Some Issues in Thinking about Culture and the Resolution of Conflict', *Humanity & Society* 13: 187–94.
—— (1991) 'The Culture Question and Conflict Resolution', *Peace & Change* 16: 22–45.
—— (1994) 'Conflict Resolution in Intercultural Settings: Problems and Prospects', in *Conflict Resolution Theory and Practice*, Dennis J.D. Sandole and Hugo van der Merwe (eds), Manchester: Manchester University Press.
Cohen, Abner (1965) *Arab Border Villages in Israel*. Manchester: Manchester University Press.
Cohen, Raymond (1990) *Culture and Conflict in Egyptian–Israeli Relations: a Dialogue of the Deaf*. Bloomington: Indiana University Press.
—— (1991). *Negotiating across Cultures*. Washington: United States Institute of Peace Press.
Cunningham, Robert B. and Sarayrah, Yasin K. (1993) *Wasta*. Westport: Praeger.
Encyclopedia Judaica (1971) Jerusalem: Keter.
Foreign Broadcast Information Service (*FBIS*), Southeast Asia, November–December 1993.
Geertz, Clifford (1983) *The Interpretation of Cultures*. New York: Basic Books.
Hall, Edward T. (1976) *Beyond Culture*. New York: Doubleday.
Hickson, Letitia (1986) 'The Social Contexts of Apology in Dispute Settlement: a Cross-Cultural Study', *Ethnology*, 25: 283–94.
Hofstede, Geert (1982) 'Lessons for Europeans in Asia', *Euro-Asia Business Review* 1: 37–41.
Kluckhohn, Clyde (1957) *Mirror for Man*. New York: Fawcett.
Liverani, Mario (1993) *Akkad, the First World Empire: Structure, Ideology, Traditions*. Padova: Sargon.
Matz, David (1991) 'ADR and Life in Israel', *Negotiation Journal* 7: 11–16.
Nader, Laura and Todd, Harry F. Jr (eds) (1978) *The Disputing Process – Law In Ten Societies*. New York: Columbia University Press.
New York Times, December 1993.
Patrushev, Pyotr (1994) 'Psychological Anthropology and Developmental Psychology: Implications for Conflict Resolution Theory and Practice', *Conflict Resolution Network News* (Australia) September: 16–17.
Qleibo, Ali H. (1993) 'Tribal Methods of Conflict Resolution – The Palestinian Model: *Atwah* or *Sulh Asha'iry*', pp. 57–61, in *Practicing Conflict Resolution in Divided Societies*, Jay Rothman (ed.). Jerusalem: The Leonard Davis Institute.
Rothman, Jay (1993) 'Bringing Conflict Resolution to Israel: Model-Building, Training, and Institutionalization', pp. 1–15 in *Practicing Conflict Reso-*

lution in Divided Societies, Jay Rothman (ed.). Jerusalem: The Leonard Davis Institute.
Simpson, J.J. and Weiner, E.S.C. (1989) *The Oxford English Dictionary*. Oxford: Clarendon Press.
Thambipillai, Pushpa and Saravanamuttu, J. (1985) *ASEAN Negotiations: Two Insights*. Singapore: Institute of Southeast Asian Studies.
The Age (Melbourne), December 1993.
Zilberman, Ifrah (1991) 'Customary Law as a Social System in the Jerusalem Area' (Hebrew). *The New East* (Israel) 33: 70–93.
—— (1995) Interview with author, 11 June.
—— and Husseini, Hiba (1994) 'Bridges to Peace – A New Approach to Mediation and Arbitration in Jerusalem'. Lectures at a seminar on 'Conflict Resolution in Israel, the West Bank and Gaza – Realities and Potential', the Leonard Davis Institute, the Hebrew University of Jerusalem, 7 December.

7 The Bounds of 'Race' in International Relations[1]
Roxanne Lynn Doty

INTRODUCTION

Two sets of observations motivate the concerns expressed in this chapter. The first involves the increasingly widespread incidents worldwide with racial overtones which have occurred in recent years. I will mention just a few. In 1988, in part due to the rapidly increasing 'Third World' immigrant population and the ensuing violence against them, racism became a national issue in Italy. In June 1991, the Mayor of Paris, Jacques Chirac, suggested that French workingmen had had an overdose of polygamous North African welfare scroungers. In September 1992, former French President Valéry Giscard d'Estaing suggested that the country was facing an invasion of dark-skinned immigrants and suggested that the 'right of blood' be instilled into citizenship legislation. Conservative figures reported to Britain's Home Office suggest that there were 7780 racially motivated attacks in 1992. Meanwhile, special committees of the European Parliament have twice looked at the increase in racist and xenophobic activity throughout Europe and concluded that it is getting worse.[2] In May 1992, riots in south central Los Angeles provided the world with a stark and painful reminder that race remains a salient issue in the United States.

It is obvious from these examples that race still figures prominently in the domestic societies of Western democracies. Nor are non-Western societies immune from racial tensions. South Africa is the most obvious but certainly not the only example. African students in China have been systematically attacked. Indians in Fiji have been victims of racism, as have Tamils in Sri Lanka.[3] While the prevalence of racial problems in national societies does not necessarily imply the relevance of race to the international realm, it does suggest that the issue of race touches an extremely diverse array of societies and leads one to suspect the possibility that race and racism may be relevant to global relations.

The second set of observations involves scholarly attention to the issue of race. When one steps outside the bounds of orthodox International Relations (IR), one can note a marked proliferation in the literature on race in several academic disciplines. This includes the fields of comparative literature, philosophy, feminist theory, cultural studies and British sociology.[4] Again, this should not lead one automatically to assume that race should also be relevant to IR. It should, however, raise that possibility, especially given that much of the work on race deals with issues that are not neatly framed within a domestic/international dichotomy. A careful reading of this literature suggests ways in which race is relevant to IR.

What then can one say or ask about race in the international realm? To pose this question raises issues that go to the heart of some of the current controversies and debates within the discipline. While the purpose of this chapter is not to engage in a full-blown discussion of these controversies, the question of race in international relations cannot be addressed without at least touching upon them. I do this by way of focusing on a particular issue that cuts across many of the current controversies in IR. This is the issue of identity and difference. How do particular understandings of identity and difference frame the way we define and approach our subject matter and our constructs? Who are 'we'? Who are 'they' to whom we relate? How do 'we' relate to 'them'? How are the identities of 'us' and 'them' constituted? How does 'race' figure in identity and how is this relevant to international relations?

In international relations theory and practice, these questions have been resolved in historically specific ways. In many cases race has been a constitutive element of these resolutions. Those who regard race as solely a domestic issue ignore and arguably obscure the processes by which these resolutions have taken place. They also presume an unproblematic inside/outside dichotomy between the domestic and the international, a dichotomy which is itself constructed within the terms of these resolutions. It is possible that race has and continues to be an important organizing principle, especially in that aspect of international relations known as North–South relations. This is a matter that at the very least deserves careful consideration and investigation. It is thus not just a matter of adding race to the International Relations agenda. Rather, it is a matter of discerning how race has worked in the past in constructing various aspects of global politics, the various transformations it has undergone, and if and how it continues to work today.

Before proceeding, I wish to acknowledge that it would be arrogant as well as inaccurate to suggest that I am voicing a completely new concern. IR scholars in the late 1960s and early 1970s raised the issue of race in international relations and offered some fruitful directions in which to proceed. These are discussed further below. Yet, interest in race was not sustained and never did cut to the heart of IR as an academic discipline. One need only survey the mainstream IR journals over the past 50 years to confirm the marginalization of race. This author's survey of *World Politics, International Studies Quarterly, International Organization, Journal of Conflict Resolution* and *Review of International Studies* for the period 1945–93 revealed only one article with the word race in the title, four with the term minorities and 13 with the term ethnicity.

Below I discuss earlier efforts to bring race into the IR agenda. I then explore some tensions in this literature suggesting that a particular understanding of identity has been privileged and that this has limited the way race can be conceptualized and studied. I then discuss an alternative understanding of identity that permits a reconceptualization of race. Finally, I suggest how this reconceptualization can usefully inform our research on race and international relations.

RACE IN INTERNATIONAL RELATIONS: VOICES FROM THE RECENT PAST

Over 20 years ago a handful of scholars were concerned to include race in the IR research agenda. Interestingly this coincided with racial tensions and black power movements in the United States (US). Findings of the Kerner Commission's Report on Civil Disorder that racial cleavage and white racism were an integral part of the American political system prompted scholars to ask why one should assume that politics becomes non-racial when one moves from the domestic to the international realm.[5] Some scholars suggested that there would be worldwide demonstration effects based upon how countries such as the US, Britain, France and the Soviet Union handled their own race relations. These effects would involve alignment choices regarding support for black Africa in its confrontation with Southern Rhodesia (now Zimbabwe) and South Africa.[6]

Concern with race in international relations also coincided with the increased prominence of 'Third World' countries in the United Nations. Some took this as evidence of increased racial equality in international society.[7] Others raised concerns about the possibility of arms races and wars between racial groups. Karl Deutsch assumed that towards the end of the twentieth century the world's non-white people would achieve nuclear parity with the world's white people and would have enough weapons to kill all the whites in the world.[8] Others regarded the increased number of non-white members of the United Nations as merely a nuisance that served to distract statesmen from other, more important, matters. Reflecting this latter position, Adlai Stevenson complained that he was impatiently waiting for the time 'when the last black-faced comedian has quit preaching about colonialism so the United Nations could move on to the more crucial issues like disarmament'.[9] Despite Stevenson's rather crude assessment, some IR scholars felt that disarmament was not the only important topic to address, or that race might be related in some ways to disarmament, as well as to other important issues. These scholars sought to develop frameworks within which to study its impact on international relations.

One of the most concerted efforts was undertaken by the Center on International Race Relations at the University of Denver which published a number of monographs. In 1970, *Race among Nations: a Conceptual Approach*, a major effort to gain wider recognition of the role of race in international affairs, was edited by George W. Shepherd, Jr and Tilden J. LeMelle and published for the Center. In this volume, Shepherd and others raised several important issues, two of which are of lingering importance and highlight both the salience of race and the difficulty of studying it. I pursue these two issues in detail below. Let me just mention briefly that the first has to do with the 'uncertainty regarding the concept of race' and the second with the 'distinction between foreign and domestic issues'.[10] These issues surface, at least implicitly, in much of the literature on race and international relations, which I examine briefly below.

Rosenau articulated the difficulty involved in dealing with race in international relations when he suggested that '[t]he more one ponders the task of assessing the role of race in world politics, the more staggering does it become'. Nevertheless, he developed a conceptual framework which included three elements: (1) persons or groups whose behaviour brings consciousness of physical characteristics into the international arena; (2) sources of behaviour that infuse it with racial consciousness; and (3) types of behaviour that reflect racial consciousness. Drawing upon the analytic scheme suggested earlier in his pre-theory of foreign policy, Rosenau posited five basic clusters of variables (individual, role, governmental, societal and systemic) from which to derive racial and race-susceptible variables. Such a scheme would enable one to analyse the role of race in the external conflict behaviour of those who acted on behalf of national societies.[11]

Others suggested that Rosenau's issue-area concept could show how race, in its cross-national manifestations, was pulled into American foreign policy. Shepherd believed that this conceptual framework could be used for analysing 'pan-Negro civil rights movements' and could show 'how American Negroes seek to project their own aspirations through American foreign policy, e.g., in South Africa'.[12]

Drawing on his work in communication theory, Karl Deutsch suggested that race was a built-in, rapid, inexpensive and reliable signalling device which is added to other variables including economics, ethnicity, stratification and culture. The addition of race to these other items permitted the identification of a group of persons on the basis of some physical characteristic, very quickly, cheaply and reliably, without elaborate procedures for verification. Deustch believed that this labelling, which was not necessarily a conscious act, was inescapable. A person was so labelled from birth to death.[13]

Drawing upon Deutsch and Nye's systems integration theory, George Shepherd Jr suggested that race acts as an independent variable, intensifying the ethnic economic rivalries between sub-systems in the international system. Race gives a visible dimension to hierarchy in white dominance systems in which white groups control the reward system and exercise discrimination. Shepherd suggested that comparative analysis could yield results that would contribute to a rational assessment of the extent to which racism deprives a nation of the capacity for objective self-knowledge and social control. Nye demonstrated the importance of ethnic and racial cohesion for regional integration.[14]

Nakanishi conceptualized race as individual self-identification with a racial and/or ethnic group. Race, according to Nakanishi, was a transnational issue rather than one to be studied comparatively. He suggested that minority groups are transnational and engage in actions which transcend domestic political systems.[15]

Taken as a whole, this literature contains two important tensions that hearken back to the two issues mentioned earlier, i.e. the uncertainty over the concept of race itself and the uneasiness with assuming an unproblematic separation between domestic and foreign/international issues and policy. These tensions if more fully explored may provide us with openings for new ways of thinking about race in international relations. The first concerns the tension between the, at least implicit, recognition that race is more than merely a physical marker and the theoretical/methodological imperative to have clear and unambiguous definitions of concepts. This tension is evident to some degree in all positivist approaches to social issues. Scholars working within positivist approaches do, of course, recognize the problems inherent in the process of moving from a concept or construct to an operational definition which specifies how that construct is to be measured. Like 'post-positivists', positivists recognize that the constructed nature of all social science concepts makes it ultimately impossible to reach closure regarding the 'real' meaning of terms. Positivists, however, solve the problem through the use of methodological measurement criteria such as reliability and validity tests.

For those who reject positivist approaches, the very process of conceptualization, i.e. moving from construct to operational definition, is itself a political practice that is implicated in creating meanings. Most importantly, this process is not neutral. The concept of 'race' is a particularly pertinent example of how studying a concept in a certain way can perpetuate a particular way of thinking and in an important sense 'naturalize' that way of thinking. As Husband points out, an essential part of race thinking is the common sense assumption that 'race' is a real and self-evidently neutral fact, not to be confused with racism which is a special condition of a few bigots. Once the conceptual language of 'race' is used, all sorts of other images are invoked, e.g. superior/inferior, light/dark, good/evil.

Shepherd expressed misgivings about measuring and quantifying, but did not extend these misgivings to defining race itself. Deutsch recognized that the 'simplifying device of a dark coloring lumps into one category very different individuals, thereby implicitly calling attention to the problematic nature of race'.[16] Culture, as a distinct concept however, enabled Deutsch to explain differences within one race, rather than calling race itself into question. Several studies never explicitly define race, the presumption being that we already know what it is. In other words, race is taken as given, a real and self-evidently neutral fact. When race is defined, it is as an independent variable that interacts with other variables to produce certain outcomes, e.g. discrimination and stratification patterns.

The problem with the understanding of race illustrated in these and other studies is that the political nature of race itself is obscured. The historical and social practices which construct race cannot be the subject of analysis. Rather, an understanding is promoted of race as a neutral category with no clear notion of politics, exclusion and power being at the heart of the concept itself. This is not to suggest that it was not recognized that situations of racial conflict often involved exclusions and power. What I mean is that the very notion of race as a category is inherently linked to practices of exclusion and power. The problem is in the concept itself and how it is generally defined and applied. 'The evil that is done is done by the concept and by the easy yet impossible assumption as to its application.'[17] These issues are discussed in greater detail in the following section.

The second tension that is evident in this literature concerns boundaries. Many of the scholars dealing with race suggest its importance in drawing and redrawing political maps.[18] The work on subsystem integration and the importance of race in this regard especially call our attention to the relevance of race in constructing boundaries. We also find support for the notion that race exceeds domestic boundaries in the suggestion that race can potentially lead to identities that transcend that of a national identity, e.g. the internationalization of black power movements or pan-Africanism. If this implicit problematization of boundaries were further pursued in conjunction with a problematization of the category of race itself, one could fathom the possibility that race not only exceeds, but might itself be, a site where such boundaries have been constituted.

These two tensions, while potentially quite rich and suggestive, are nonetheless suppressed. This suppression, I suggest, can be understood in terms of a particular understanding of identity and difference which frames our understandings of what race is, how we can study it and the ways in which it can be relevant to global politics. Each of these tensions is discussed in the following two sections within the context of alternative understandings of identity and difference.

CONCEPTUALIZING RACE

As suggested above, race is not an unproblematic construct. When the term race is used, it connotes much more than the presence of a physical marker(s). Just as gender has signified more than anatomical difference, race has signified more than physical difference. To limit one's definition of race to physical/morphological markers such as skin colour, hair texture, and so on is to obscure the fact that other elements have been inextricably linked with these physical markers to construct race itself. Race does not follow from colour in any direct way. Human variation and difference have not been experienced as they 'really are' but by and through metaphorical systems that structure the experience and understanding of difference.[19]

However, at the same time, it is not possible to say *a priori* across time and space precisely what these metaphorical systems and the elements they contain are. If one seeks a more encompassing definition of race, i.e. that goes beyond physical markers, one then runs the risk of reifying the cluster of elements that have been linked with physical markers and called race, and thus reifying race itself. While the literature on race and international relations does not conceptualize race as biological, the reliance on physical difference ultimately works its way back to biology/genetics. To conceptualize race as an independent variable, as all of this literature does, permits biology/genetics to re-enter through the back door. The presumption must be made that physical characteristics such as skin colour and hair texture stand for real and more subtle differences. At the same time, if one tries to name those other differences, then race becomes a very slippery and unmanageable concept because those other differences are not the same across time and space and are themselves socially constructed. Appiah makes a similar kind of argument in his analysis of the writings of W.E.B. Du Bois, suggesting that Du Bois, who 'thought longer, more engagedly, and more publicly about race than any other social theorist in our century', was never able to escape from the concept of race and its biological roots.[20]

It seems then that one is faced with the impossible task of providing a sense of what is meant when one speaks of race and at the same time eschewing definitions of race that bear any resemblance to scientific racism. This, I want to suggest, is only a problem if one adheres to a particular understanding of identity and difference that is prevalent in International Relations and social science more generally, but that is increasingly being called into question by critical scholars in a wide array of disciplinary fields. As Connolly points out, contemporary IR theory recognizes that reality always exceeds the terms of theory. Difference always haunts any attempt to securely identify the terms, i.e. concepts, categories, of any theory. At the same time, though, orthodox theory dissolves issues of identity and difference into its categories of theory, evidence, rationality, sovereignty and utility.[21] This is analogous to studies of race, which implicitly recognize that it exceeds physical markers of difference, but nonetheless define it in these terms.

Connolly refers to this resolution of identity and difference as epistemic realism or an epistemology of representation whereby a theory seeks to mirror a fixed reality that precedes representation of it. This can be likened to conceptions of identity that others have referred to as foundationalist or essentialist.[22] According to this understanding, the identity of a person, group, object, concept, category, nation, state is based upon an essence which determines its identity. This essence provides for unity within a category. Difference(s) are presumed to lie outside the category in other categories which are also defined by an essence. Identity and unity lie within. Difference lies without. This understanding of identity and difference is evident in the theoretical/methodological imperative to provide precise and unproblematic definitions to the concepts we use, most notably in quantitative research, but certainly by no means limited to this. The problem is that race (and many other concepts such as gender) do not readily lend themselves to precise definitions. Indeed, the very power of these constructs may lay precisely in this fact.

How, then, does one proceed in light of this dilemma? A useful beginning is to defamiliarize race, to recognize the problematic and socially/discursively constructed nature of racial identity, indeed to reconceptualize identity itself. As a preliminary task it might be useful to attempt a differentiation between the way race and ethnicity are generally understood. Though I would suggest that distinctions between race and ethnicity can only ultimately be determined (if at all) in specific historical settings, it is useful at this point to highlight some distinctions that have been made in the literature. This will help to clarify what I am not doing in this chapter: I am not addressing self-identification with a group, what is generally thought of as ethnic identity. In making this distinction I do not mean to imply that ethnicity is somehow a 'natural' category of identity while race is socially constructed. As will be discussed in greater detail below, I suggest that all identities are socially constructed. My purpose in discussing the distinction between race and ethnicity here is rather to differentiate what I am referring to as race from what others have referred to as ethnicity.

Ethnicity is generally regarded as entailing a sense of collective self-identity. For example, Horowitz suggests that ethnicity consists of an interplay between self-definition and the definition of other groups. Similarly, Issaac attributes to ethnicity a sense of belongingness and attachment. Glazer and Moynihan suggest that ethnic groups be thought of in terms of interest groups. Patterson stresses that an ethnic group only exists where members consider themselves to belong to such a group. Ethnicity, Patterson emphasizes, is a chosen form of identification. A conscious sense of belonging is critical in the conception of ethnicity. Cashmore and Troyna also suggest that ethnicity entails a subjective element, a sense of shared identity among a group.[23]

It would be difficult to attribute the same qualities to race. While not denying that race can and has in certain circumstances entailed a sense of belonging, shared purpose and identity (as with black power movements in the US, pan-Africanism and black cultural politics today in Britain), historically race has usually been imposed from the outside. This distinction is consistent with that offered by others. For example, Lyon suggests that a racial category is the consequence of categorization from the outside. Cashmore and Troyna also suggest that racial labels have been stuck on collections of people by others who feel themselves to be different.[24] Historically, the modern use of the term race evolved around explicit doctrines of inequality and in contexts in which these doctrines justified exclusionary practices. Race in the Western world is intimately connected with slavery and imperialism. If one could point to a relatively constant element of race in the modern age, it would in fact be the use of a physical marker(s), generally skin colour, to set off self from the racial other. However, the characteristics that are linked to physical markers and the processes by which they become so linked and thereby constitute race are extremely variable across time and space. What is more, these processes have been inextricably linked with relations of power and knowledge. What race means today is not what it meant in the nineteenth century, and what it meant in the nineteenth century is not what it meant in the seventeenth and eighteenth centuries. As Gilroy points out, race is a political category that can accommodate various meanings.[25]

In saying that race is other defined, I do not mean to suggest that groups whose identities have been defined from the outside never form a sense of collective identity based upon shared experiences such as exploitation, or never resist the imposed identity. Rather, I am suggesting that oppression, domination and power are at the very core of the concept of race. Race and inequality are intimately connected. This is useful in making a further distinction between race and ethnicity which, as discussed above, implies a self-conscious group identification and does not necessarily involve an exploitative relationship. This is not to suggest that there cannot be domination, inequality and oppression between/among ethnic groups. However, this is not a defining feature.

Conceptual, theoretical and analytic implications follow from the above discussion. In order to study race in international relations we cannot begin by presuming that we know precisely what race is. Rather, we must examine the practices that construct and reconstruct race, i.e. racial categories, racial difference. Omi and Winant use the term radicalization to 'signify the extension of racial meaning to a previously racially unclassified relationship, social practice or group'. They suggest that racialization is an historically specific, ideological process which draws upon pre-existing discursive elements and emerges from struggles of competing political projects and ideas. Their use of the term racial formation emphasizes the social nature of race, the absence of any essential racial characteristics and the historical flexibility of racial meanings and categories.[26]

Others have also suggested that race has no fixed and objective properties, no essential empirical referents. Indeed, one could speculate that the very power, persistence and dynamism of race and racism(s) derive from this lack of essence and specificity. It has been suggested that 'racial codes' have facilitated the rearticulation of racism disguised with ostensibly non-racist rhetoric. Domestically, racial codes might be found in discourses on welfare reform, affirmative action and the urban underclass. Internationally, racial codes can be found in development discourses which draw upon particular conceptions of 'modernization' and/or which suggest that 'culture' plays a significant role in explaining development or the lack thereof. My own conceptualization is to regard race (i.e. racial identity and difference) as a site: a social, political and discursive location where questions of identity and difference, self and other, are resolved though always in a contingent, unstable and tentative way. It is at this site(s) that racial difference is constructed. I am borrowing here from Butler's ideas on gender.[27] Race does not denote a substantive being, but a relative point of convergence among culturally and historically specific sets of relations. This implies a radically different understanding of identity itself and has implications for how we sudy race in International Relations.

Some feminist scholars, in trying to come to terms with gendered identity, have suggested an anti-foundationalist or discursive understanding of identity. Rather than depending upon some notion of foundational categories of identity or an inner psychological self, identity is reconceptualized as simultaneously a practice and an effect that is always in the process of being 'written' or constructed. Identity and difference are not mutually exclusive. Rather, '[i]dentity always contains the specter of non-identity within it, the subject is always divided and identity is always purchased at the price of the exclusion of the other.'[28]

This conceptualization of identity and difference has been suggested by poststructuralists such as Derrida, Foucault and Lacan and has increasingly found its way into critical IR literature.[29] Identity is not based upon some foundational feature such as biological sex (i.e. the body, race, an inner psychological core) but must be continually constructed through practices which suppress differences and inconsistencies. It is not just the case that identities are relational and dependent upon collective understandings; identity itself is contingent and exists only by virtue of strategies which expel the surplus meanings that would expose the failure of identity. 'Exclusions and repressions support the seeming homogeneity, stability and self-evidence of "white identity" which is derived from and dependent on the marginalisation of differences within as well as without.'[30]

The importance of this understanding of identity is that it permits inquiry into the enabling conditions for the assertion of identity itself, e.g. for asserting that 'I am a man' or 'I am an American' or 'I am a sovereign nation-state'. It also permits inquiry into the enabling conditions for taking on specific roles which are often associated with or seen as synonymous with identity. These enabling conditions are provided by practices of signification that produce the codes that condition and limit the terms of intelligibility which permit the assertion of agency. This suggests that one cannot say just anything and have it be taken seriously. One must speak within the terms of intelligibility available within a social formation. This points to one of the problems with assuming that identity is basically like taking on roles. Subjects cannot just freely decide to take on any role. Rather, the taking on of certain roles becomes possible within a larger social context wherein identities are discursively constructed. For example, gendered identity has enabled and disabled subjects from assuming certain roles. This is not to suggest that this is a closed system, however. The very nature of language and signification is inherently incomplete and open so that spaces for variation and disruption exist.

The dominant understandings of theory and explanation in International Relations have generally precluded such a conceptualization of identity, with the result being the marginalization of complex issues/concepts such as race, or the forcing of these into constraining modes of conceptualization and explanation. Incorporating race into the IR agenda is not just a matter of studying how race affects international relations, but rather, interrogating race itself, how it is constructed and how it functions in historically and spatially specific locales. The conceptualization of race I have offered above can facilitate this. This is further explored below.

IDENTITY AND THE BOUNDS OF RACE IN INTERNATIONAL RELATIONS

In this section I discuss how a discursive understanding of identity and the reconceptualization of race suggested above leads to the posing of different kinds of questions regarding race and international relations, questions that are intended to get at race as constitutive of aspects of international relations. A focus on the issue of boundaries provides an entry point for this discussion. As discussed above, the earlier literature on race and international relations implicitly called our attention to the relevance of race in constituting or exceeding boundaries. This was mainly in the form of understanding race as a transnational issue and also of recognizing the role it plays in sub-system integration. In this section I would like to pursue further the relationship between race and boundary construction, keeping in mind the reconceptualization of race I offered above.

Boundaries in international relations are generally associated with territoriality. The most obvious one involves the separation among the individual states that together constitute international society. However, not all boundaries are territorial. For example, Ruggie refers to the unbundling of territoriality or 'nonterritorial functional space' as a place wherein international society is anchored. The doctrine of extra-territoriality is a prime example of such functional space.[31] Other boundaries such as those separating the 'core' from the 'periphery' or the 'First World' from the 'Third World', while related to territory, are also premised upon differentiations more profound than that of geographical space, or even functional requirements. This is also true for the conceptual boundaries previously separating the 'free world' of the West from the communist world of the East. While ostensibly attached to territory, these spatial differentiations depended upon and were/are made possible by a series of oppositional constructs that are quite familiar to us, e.g. traditional/modern, backward/advanced, democratic/totalitarian, and so on. Inextricably linked with space then are socially embedded interpretative possibilities which make identities possible.

The anti-foundationalist understanding of identity discussed above is premised upon recognition of the problematic nature of boundaries as well as the binary oppositions that often undergird them. This is because identity and difference are not mutually exclusive. The presence of difference always threatens claims to identity. Identity, then, is not solely a matter of self-presence or a self-defined identity. Rather it is dependent upon the constant work of excluding difference(s) that would call identity into question. This being the case, the boundaries between inclusions and exclusions and the oppositions they depend upon are always in the process of being constructed. It is through discursive practices, practices of signification and the repetition of these practices that these constructions take place and become socially embedded.

To regard race as a site where issues of identity and difference, self and other, inclusion and exclusion are resolved highlights the importance of radicalization as a dynamic process through which the identities of social groups can be defined and bound. This, of course, is not to suggest that radicalization is the only such process by which identities are constructed and boundaries drawn. It is, however, to suggest that radicalization is an inherently social and cultural process that interacts with and overlaps other social and cultural processes that have been important in constructing identities and drawing boundaries.

Critical IR scholars have long argued for the importance of the social episteme in understanding international life and international theory.[32] Recently, John Ruggie has argued for the relative autonomy for the realm of social epistemology in explaining the social construction of the modern system of states. Continuity and transformations can be explained in part by examining changes in the 'social episteme'.[33] Discursive practices and the regularities in those practices are at the core of the concept of an episteme. Foucault defines an episteme as the discursive practices that give rise to epistemological figures, sciences and formalized systems. An episteme is what makes possible the existence of epistemological figures and science. It provides a grid of intelligibility whereby one 'knows' the world and the subjects and objects that constitute that world.[34] Certainly the ways in which identity and difference, self and other are resolved are important aspects of an episteme. By extension, then, prevailing configurations of racial difference become quite relevant.

The construction and expansion of the modern state-system entailed historically specific resolutions to questions about political identity.[35] Some of these resolutions coincided with the construction of boundaries and oppositions that were attached to and differentiated peoples and geographic space and that functioned as a way of distinguishing self from other. Race was a prominent part of the modern episteme that accompanied the rise and expansion of the modern state system. The project of modernity entailed the development of rational modes of thought which it was believed promised liberation from the irrationalities of myth, religion and superstition, and a release from the dark side of human nature.[36] Efforts to develop objective science and modes of classification facilitated the development of a 'science' of race and scientific racism. It has been widely recognized that ideas about race were an intrinsic part of the rise of the West. Similarly, the relevance of race in the transition from a European to a global international order has been discussed in several historical accounts by International Relations scholars.[37]

However, in acknowledging this recognition, we must return to the issue raised in the previous section, i.e. of conceptualizing race. The appreciation of the relevance of race has not been accompanied by a problematization of race itself. Thus, it can be suggested that the current relevance of race to international relations is much exaggerated and stems mainly from its propagandistic value, since racial equality is now an international norm.[38] Indeed, it has been argued that 'racial sovereignty' has become a new principle of international legitimacy.[39] While it is certainly not incorrect to argue that racial equality is an international norm and a principle of international legitimacy, the conclusion that race is no longer relevant to international relations or relevant mainly as a propaganda tool does not follow. The failure to interrogate race itself in the process of studying it is dangerous because it narrows the possibilities of the ways in which we can imagine that race 'works'. The conceptualization of racism becomes mainly one which is manifest in discriminatory behaviour or professions of overtly racist attitudes and doctrines.

My conceptualization of race moves us away from historical accounts of how race has been relevant in international relations to a critical genealogy of the sites where racial differences have been constructed. Such a study or studies would not begin with the presumption of boundaries, e.g. domestic/international boundaries, boundaries separating human beings into different races, but would regard these and other boundaries as always in the process of being constructed. Race does not just cross boundaries but becomes a site where boundaries are produced. Thus, for example, instead of an historical account of how race justified certain practices (which is not unimportant but has been amply studied), we need accounts of how race itself was constructed by these practices and how in the process boundaries were drawn, boundaries between/among human beings, territory and sociopolitical space. For example, it is relatively unremarkable to suggest that race justified European and US imperialism. What needs to be done is to examine the discursive practices in specific historical instances of imperial expansion (as well as other events) to see how issues of identity and difference, self and other were articulated in terms of racial frames of reference and with what consequences. Posing and examining this 'how' question would not only permit a deconstruction of race but might enable us to account for its continuing efficacy by juxtaposing different situations in different locales and across different time periods. It is possible that we might find that resolutions to issues of identity and difference, self and other, are not always in terms of superior/inferior but retain racial frames in other guises, e.g. that of 'cultural difference'.

It would also be fruitful to examine the discursive practices surrounding international efforts to reduce racial discrimination to see how race was constructed in these discourses. An important question would be, what permitted the continued unequal treatment despite international agreements on the principles of humanity and justice. For example, paradoxically, prohibitions against the slave trade in the early 1800s gave rise to even greater British encroachment and control in Africa.[40] The continued and increased exploitation of Africa despite official proclamations and international agreements may not have been due solely to shortcomings in the agreements themselves or individual states' refusal to cooperate. On the contrary, it could be that the discourse instantiated in agreements constructed identities such that one form of interference could easily be replaced by another. In other words, the same system that gave official protection to black Africans in the form of prohibitions on slavery also constructed particular identities for those same subjects that made other forms of unequal treatment possible. In this regard we can learn from literature outside of IR. For example, Brantlinger suggests that abolitionism contained the seeds of empire and that humanitarianism applied to Africa pointed insistently to imperialism. He reaches this conclusion from a reading of anti-slavery writing.[41] This points to the need to broaden our understanding of what is relevant in understanding international relations, e.g. literature, art and other items generally relegated to the realm of 'culture' and summarily dismissed.

Additionally, one might examine the shifting sites of racial construction and how this has coincided with various other globally relevant issues. For example, it is interesting to note that race was at one time predominantly an international issue. During the age of European explorations, expansion and colonialism race relations were global relations. Concern with the issue of race coincided with curiosity about human beings in different geographic locales. Along with decolonization after the Second World War (approximately from 1945 to 1970) one finds a displacement of race relations from the global realm to domestic societies. Decolonization coincided with mass movements of former colonial subjects into urban centres of the West creating what we now refer to as multicultural societies. These changes, of course, coincided with changes in the global economy, e.g. the rise of the US as a hegemon, tremendous postwar economic growth in Western Europe, and an increase in international interdependence. Put this way, race becomes a relevant issue when discussing global transformation. This places the specific racial incidents mentioned at the beginning of this article in a global context. Race is simultaneously relevant in configuring domestic and international society. The resolution of identity and difference, self and other within racial frames occurs both globally and domestically. Racial identity becomes an important element in the construction of national identity, e.g. in terms of North/South distinctions. Simultaneously, however, racial difference itself is constructed in domestic societies in the West that must now accommodate large numbers of 'Third World' peoples within their national borders.

Here, one should note the significance of the EU's influence in setting the criteria for national identity and citizenship in its member countries which has resulted in the construction of separate categories for non-white, former colonial subjects in an effort to prevent them having the freedom of movement among EU countries that will be granted to each member's citizens. This is a potentially fruitful area of research, i.e. an international organization such as the EU having influence in how a nation-state defines its own citizenry. This points to a realm of 'North/South' relations that calls into question our traditional ways of thinking about the boundaries separating these two realms, i.e. an aspect of North/South relations that is constituted within the geographic territory of the North itself and in which race figures prominently if often silently.

Related to the above is the question of the relationship between race and nationalism. This becomes especially important today when issues of inclusion and exclusion are constantly being raised by the disintegration of old boundaries and the construction of new ones, e.g. the former Soviet Union, the former Yugoslavia and continuing conflicts throughout Africa. No less important is the continual construction of both internal and external boundaries in Western democracies, through the use of categories such as the 'illegal alien', the 'refugee' and the 'migrant worker'. These and other categories have historically been created within a frame of racial difference, have been operative in the construction of 'homogeneous' national identities and have involved exclusionary practices.[42] This has important implications for our understanding of political community, democracy and citizenship.

CONCLUSION

The theoretical/conceptual moves I am suggesting here would take us towards a more complex understanding of race and how it has worked internationally and how it persists. This would move away from the notion of racism as always entailing explicit or implicit assumptions of superiority and inferiority and towards other manifestations. For example, Martin Barker uses the term the 'new racism' to refer to situations in which there is no reference to race but the key notion is that a way of life is being threatened by 'outsiders' carrying with it the policy implication of imposing boundaries. Similarly, Cashmore and Troyna suggest that racism today makes no necessary assumptions about inferiority, but is rather a relationship between insiders and outsiders. Joel Kovel refers to 'meta-racism' as impersonal and exteriorized violence which entails few traces of a commitment to race superiority but which operates through economic and technocratic means. What is common to these efforts to come to grips with race and racism in the late twentieth century is the notion that race itself is problematic.[43]

Making race itself problematic and a subject of analysis would have several important consequences. For one, it would extend the notion of what is political by permitting one to locate the play of power and politics in the discursive practices that construct the categories of identity. No matter how critical the intent of an analysis is, if one accepts categories of identity such as race as foundational the critical edge is blunted and the analyst becomes complicit in the very construction/reconstruction of those categories. Focusing on the practices that construct categories of identity also leads to a more dynamic kind of analysis in that the emphasis is truly always focused on practice, the doing rather than the doer, on pre-existing subjects.

Important consequences also follow for how we think about and understand agency. It has recently been suggested that any new agenda in International Relations must address the issue of agency in international affairs.[44] A discursive understanding of identity does not deny the possibility of agency. Rather, it shifts the location of agency away from that associated with subjects understood as having relatively stable core identities prior to their encounter and interaction with society to the discursive practices and the possibilities for agency that they create or deny. Thus, analyses of signifying practices can tell us how agency comes to be associated with some kinds of identities but not with others. Relative to international politics we might ask what practices of signification are replicated in a variety of locales and situations. For example, the signifying practices present in discourses that denied agency to colonial subjects may be replicated in a wide variety of other situations, e.g. development discourses, intervention discourses.

The lines of inquiry being suggested here are intended to be critical in two senses. First, they would open up spaces for addressing an issue heretofore not explored in the way I have suggested it could fruitfully be approached. Second, they would require the field of international relations to broaden its understanding and acceptance of how we can legitimately theorize, conceptualize and offer explanations. This is not to suggest that we now discard all other perspectives and address everything of global relevance as a discursive construction. It is rather to suggest that some subjects, and I have argued that race is one of them, are extremely problematic and require a radical move to more nontraditional and critically oriented approaches.

NOTES

1. I would like to thank the following people for commenting on this chapter at various stages of its development: Suresht Bald, Steve Bataldan, David Jacobson, Pat McGowan, Mike Mitchell, George Thomas, R.B.J. Walker and Steve Walker. A version of this chapter was presented at the 1993 International Studies Association meeting in Acapulco, Mexico.
2. *The Atlantic*, February 1992; April 1992; *The Economist*, 5–11 December 1992.
3. E. Cashmore and B. Troyna, *Introduction to Race Relations* (London and New York: The Falmer Press, 1990), p. 3.
4. D. Goldberg (ed.), *Anatomy of Racism* (Minneapolis, MN: University of Minnesota Press, 1990); D. Goldberg, *Racist Culture: Philosophy and the Politics of Meaning* (Oxford: Basil Blackwell, 1993); D. LaCapra (ed.), *The Bounds of Race: Perspectives on Hegemony and Resistance* (Ithaca and London: Cornell University Press, 1991); P. Gilroy, *There Ain't No Black in the Union Jack: The Cultural Politics of Race and Nation* (Chicago, IL: University of Chicago Press, 1987); C. Husband, *'Race' in Britain: Continuity and Changes* (London: Hutchinson, 1984); P. Jackson,

Race and Racism: Essays in Social Geography (London: Allen and Unwin, 1987); H.L. Gates Jr, *'Race', Writing and Difference* (Chicago, IL: University of Chicago Press, 1985); D. Fuss, *Essentially Speaking: Feminism, Nature, and Difference* (New York and London: Routledge, 1989), ch. 2. Works more directly related to international relations include E. Balibar, 'Racism and Politics in Europe Today', *New Left Review* (No. 186, 1991), pp. 5–19; E. Balibar and I. Wallerstein, *Race, Nation, Class: Ambiguous Identities* (New York: Verso, 1991); M. Hunt, *Ideology and US Foreign Policy* (New Haven and London: Yale University Press, 1987); P.G. Lauren, *Power and Prejudice: The Politics and Diplomacy of Racial Discrimination* (Boulder and London: Westview Press, 1988); R. Miles, *Racism and Migrant Labour* (London: Routledge and Kegan Paul, 1982); H. Tinker, *Race, Conflict, and the International Order: From Empire to United Nations* (New York: St. Martin's Press, 1977); and R. Francis Weston, *Racism in US Imperialism: The Influence of Racial Assumptions on American Foreign Policy 1893–1946* (Columbia, SC: University of South Carolina Press, 1972).

5. G. Shepherd Jr. and T.J. LeMelle (eds), *Race among Nations: a Conceptual Approach* (Lexington, MA: D.C. Heath and Co., 1970).
6. K. Deutsch, 'Research Problems in Intranational and International Relations', in Shepherd and LeMelle (eds), *op. cit.*, in note 5, p. 147.
7. R.J. Vincent, 'Racial Equality', in H. Bull and A. Watson (eds), *The Expansion of International Society* (Oxford: Clarendon Press, 1984), pp. 239–54; Lauren, *op. cit.*, in note 4.
8. Deutsch, *op. cit.*, in note 6, p. 149.
9. Quoted in T.J. Noer, *Cold War and Black Liberation The United States Rule in Africa, 1948–1968*, (Columbia, MI: University of Missouri Press, 1985), p. 84.
10. G. Shepherd Jr, *The Study of Race in American Foreign Policy and International Relations* (Denver, CO: University of Denver monograph series, 1970), pp. 2–3.
11. J.N. Rosenau, 'Race in International Politics: a Dialogue in Five Parts', in Shepherd and LeMelle (eds), *op. cit.*, in note 5, pp. 61–122.
12. Shepherd, *op. cit.*, in note 10, 1970.
13. Deutsch, *op. cit.*, in note 6, p. 124.
14. G. Shepherd Jr, *Non-Aligned Africa: an International Subsystem* (Lexington, KY: Heath Lexington, 1970; and J. Nye, *Pan-Africanism and East African Integration* (Cambridge, MA: Harvard University Press, 1965).
15. D.T. Nakanishi, *In Search of a New Paradigm* (Denver, CO: University of Denver monograph series, 1974).
16. Deutsch, *op. cit.*, in note 6, p. 15.
17. K.A. Appiah, 'The Uncompleted Argument: DuBois and the Illusion of Race', in Gates (ed.), *op. cit.*, in note 4, pp. 21–37.
18. J.D. Grove, *The Race vs. Ethnic Debate: A Cross-National Analysis of Two Theoretical Approaches* (Denver, CO: University of Denver Monograph series, 1973).
19. N.L. Stepan, 'Race and Gender: the Role of Analogy in Science', in Goldberg (ed.), *op. cit.*, in note 4.

20. Appiah, *op. cit.*, in note 17, p. 25.
21. W.E. Connolly, *Identity and Difference: Democratic Negotiation of Political Paradox* (Ithaca and New York: Cornell University Press, 1991).
22. J. Butler, *Gender Trouble: Feminism and the Subversion of Identity* (New York, NY: Routledge, 1990); D. Fuss, *Essentially Speaking Feminism, Nature, and Difference* (New York and London: Routledge, 1989); and I.M. Young, *Justice and the Politics of Difference* (Princeton, NJ: Princeton University Press, 1990).
23. Cashmore and Troyna, *op. cit.*, in note 3; N. Glazer and D. Moynihan, *Ethnicity Theory and Experience* (Cambridge, MA: Harvard University Press, 1975); D. Horowitz, 'Ethnic Identity', in Glazer and Moynihan, ibid.; H.R. Issaac, 'Basic Group Identity: the Idols of the Tribe', in Glazer and Moynihan, ibid.; and O. Patterson, 'Context and Choice in Ethnic Allegiance: a Theoretical Framework and Caribbean Case Study', in Glazer and Moynihan, ibid.
24. M. Lyon, 'Race and Ethnicity in Plural Societies', *New Community* (Vol. 1, No. 3, 1972), pp. 256–62; and Cashmore and Troyna, *op. cit.*, in note 3, p. 28.
25. Gilroy, *op. cit.*, in note 4, p. 38.
26. M. Omi and H. Winant, *Racial Formation in the United States From the 1960s to the 1980s* (New York and London: Routledge, 1986).
27. Butler, *op. cit.*, in note 22, pp. 3–10.
28. Fuss, *op. cit.*, in note 4, p. 103.
29. For example in the works of R.K. Ashley, D. Campbell, J. Der Derian, J. George, B. Klein, M. Shapiro, R.B.J. Walker and C. Weber, to mention just a few.
30. B. Martin and C. Mohanty, 'Feminist Politics: What's Home Got to Do With It?', in T. de Lauretis (ed.), *Feminist Studies/Critical Studies* (Bloomington, ID: Indiana University Press, 1986).
31. J.G. Ruggie, 'Territoriality and Beyond', *International Organization* (Vol. 47, No. 1, 1993), pp. 139–74.
32. For example, R.K. Ashley, 'The Geopolitics of Geopolitical Space: Towards a Critical Theory of International Politics', *Alternatives* (Vol. 12, No. 3, 1987), pp. 403–34; R.K. Ashley, 'Living on Border Lines: Man, Poststructuralism and War', in J. DerDerian and M. Shapiro (eds), *International/Intertextual Relations: Postmodern Readings of World Politics* (Lexington, MA: Lexington Books, 1989); R.K Ashley and R.B.J. Walker, 'Reading/Writing the Discipline: Crisis and the Question of Sovereignty in International Studies', *International Studies Quarterly*, (Vol. 34, No. 3, 1990), pp. 367–416; J. George and D. Campbell, 'Critical Social Theory and International Relations', *International Studies Quarterly* (Vol. 34, No. 3, 1990), pp. 269–94; R.B.J. Walker, 'Realism, Change, and International Political Theory', *International Studies Quarterly* (Vol. 31, No. 1, 1987), pp. 65–86; R.B.J. Walker, 'History and Structure in the Theory of International Relations', *Millennium* (Vol. 18, No. 2, 1989), pp. 163–83; and R.B.J. Walker, 'State Sovereignty and the Articulation of Political Space/Time', *Millennium* (Vol. 20, No. 3, 1991), pp. 445–61.
33. Ruggie, *op. cit.*, in note 31, p. 165.

34. M. Foucault, *The Archaeology of Knowledge* (New York, NY: Pantheon Books, 1972), pp. 190–2.
35. R.B.J. Walker, 'Gender and Critique in the Theory of International Relations', in V. Spike Peterson (ed.), *Gendered States Feminist (Re)Visions of International Relations Theory* (Boulder and London: Lynne Rienner Publishers, 1992).
36. D. Harvey, *The Condition of Postmodernity An Inquiry into the Origins of Cultural Change* (Oxford: Basil Blackwell, 1989).
37. H. Bull, 'European States and African Political Communities', in H. Bull and A. Watson (eds), *The Expansion of International Society* (Oxford: Clarendon Press, 1984); Lauren, *op. cit.*, in note 4; Tinker, *op. cit.*, in note 4; and Vincent, *op. cit.*, in note 7.
38. Vincent, *op. cit.*, in note 7, p. 254.
39. M. Wight, *Systems of States* (Leicester: Leicester University Press, 1977), p. 168.
40. Bull, *op. cit.*, in note 37, p. 107.
41. P. Brantlinger, 'Victorians and Africans: The Genealogy of the Myth of the Dark Continent', in Gates, *op. cit.*, in note 4, pp. 195–222.
42. For example, see R.L. Doty, 'Sovereignty and the Nation: Constructing the Boundaries of National Identity', in T.J. Biersteker and C. Weber (eds), *State Sovereignty as Social Construct* (Cambridge: Cambridge University Press, 1996), pp. 121–47; and K. Manzo, *Racial Nationalism and the Politics of Exclusion* (Boulder, CO: Lynne Riener, 1996); and M. Mitchell, 'Regional Integration and the Formation of Ethnic Identities: The Recasting of Luso-Brazilian Identity', presented at the American Political Science Association Meeting, Washington, DC, 2–5 September 1993.
43. M. Barker, *The New Racism* (London: Junction Books, 1981); Cashmore and Troyna, *op. cit.*, in note 3; and K. Kovel, *White Racism* (New York, NY: Columbia University Press, 1984).
44. F. Halliday, 'International Relations: a New Agenda?', *Millennium* (Vol. 20, No. 1, 1991), pp. 57–72; and P. McGowan, 'State-Agents, International Structures, and Foreign Policy Behavior: Thinking Seriously About Foreign Policy Analysis', *International Affairs Bulletin* (Vol. 13, No. 3, 1990), pp. 39–54.

8 The Cultural Dynamics of Ethnic Conflict[1]
Marc H. Ross

INTRODUCTION

Traditionally, realist analyses of inter-state relations assign a very minor role to culture, arguing that states in conflict are motivated by concerns over concrete economic and strategic interests, and that state-level actors in inter-state conflicts share a common frame of reference. This chapter argues that while there are times when these long-held ideas are adequate to understand conflict, there are also situations where attention to cultural forces contributes a way to understand additional critical dynamics of international conflict. This is particularly true when we consider a matter of great concern in the post-Cold War period – ethnic conflict (Huntington, 1993).[2] Culture affects international cooperation and ethnically rooted disputes in several distinct ways: it provides the context in which collaboration and conflict occur, helping explain why certain issues become significant to one or more states and shaping how conflicts are played out; it defines group differences and how groups compete for scarce resources and recognition; and it points to the deeply held fears and threats to identity which shape how political leaders phrase their demands and garner support from their own populations (Ross, 1997).

Examining the culture of conflict directs our attention to the paths disputes take and the role of institutions, practices and norms in their initiation, escalation and possible settlement. This approach does not ignore the important role that interests play for states. However, it contributes to an understanding of how the pursuit of interests is tempered by psychocultural interpretations – within-group worldviews consisting of desires, assumptions about the motives of others, and deeply held threats to identity which for theoretical purposes I treat as parallel in both states and other actors involved in conflict. To understand this approach, it is necessary to examine how cultural forces produce and reinforce particular interpretations of the world, how these interpretations affect behaviour, and to appreciate their impact on long-term intransigent conflicts such as those rooted in ethnicity. My argument is not that culture differences *per se* cause conflict but rather that the presence of intergroup cultural differences is a vehicle for the expression and organization of conflict and how participants understand it.

In ethnic conflict, groups defined formally or informally in terms of cultural differences which attain political, social and psychological significance pursue what they perceive as conflicting interests and hold incompatible interpretations concerning each other's intentions and motivations. Ethnic conflicts are dynamic phenomena in which what is defined as central to a dispute, and the composition of the parties at odds with each other, often shifts over time. Conflicts can be analysed in terms of the changing strength of forces for accommodation versus those pushing for escalation.[3]

Ethnocentrism, a group identification process that polarizes in-groups versus out-groups, is a key element in almost all ethnic conflict (Ross and Campbell, 1989). Ethnocentrism is variously seen as a cause of ethnic conflict, or as a product of conflicts once they are underway. Yet even if the ethnocentric imagery used to mobilize support is only a symptom of a deeper conflict, it points to ways in which the economic or other individual interests are assumed to include the maintenance of the social group *per se*. Thus, a key element in ethnic group conflict is the idea of group identification which 'rewards' individuals in terms of esteem derived from the group's status *vis-à-vis* other groups. It draws attention to the equation of individual with group interests, and forces us to ask about the conditions under which high costs to individuals are accepted in terms of long-term group gain.

Ethnic interests, which serve as the ostensible rationale for conflict, are easy to justify ideologically and difficult for participants in a conflict to deny. The language of ethnocentric mobilization is the language of kinship; it is imbued with highly charged sacred objects (Horowitz, 1985; van den Berghe, 1981). To advocate the use of strength in defence of such interests is heroic and noble. Those who oppose the defence of the group are easy to characterize as either traitors or cowards. At the same time, there is far weaker ideological support for ideas of peacemaking, compromise or accommodation (except under severe duress).

Elsewhere (Ross, 1993a; 1993b) I have used the concept of 'the culture of conflict' to describe culturally specific norms, practices and institutions which shape conflict in a society. The culture of conflict defines what people consider valuable and worth fighting over, investing particular goods, statuses, positions or actions with meaning; it suggests appropriate ways to wage disputes, identifies suitable targets of conflict; it supports institutions in which disputes are processed;

and it determines how conflicts are likely to end. While economists are fond of translating very diverse values into a common standard of reference, a cultural analysis is more likely to move in the opposite direction, asking why particular objects or positions take on the value they do in a certain setting. An inquiry into actors' choices divorced from the cultural settings in which they are made is incomplete because it cannot account for why and how individual and group interests are established, or why a similar event can produce different reactions in another setting.

Before developing my argument more fully, a few caveats are in order about what I am *not* claiming. First, I am not arguing that there is any simple one-to-one correspondence between culture and conflict. Rather, most of the connections of interest here are more indirect, involving interactions among several key forces, and mediated through political and social structures. Second, I emphasize culture as an emblem, enabling identification of 'us' and 'them' around which conflict is organized. In so doing I want to distinguish between culture as a mechanism for the expression of conflict versus culture as an inherent cause of conflict which is not my argument. Third, I am not arguing that all behaviour can be understood only as the product of culture. Rather, I hope that introducing a cultural perspective can help answer questions which trouble non-cultural analyses such as those grounded in rational choice theory (Jervis, 1976; Keohane, 1983). For example, outside observers have often expressed a lack of comprehension at the intensity of conflicts such as Northern Ireland or Sri Lanka while failing to consider the psycho-cultural forces which have made these conflicts so intransigent. To simply dismiss such conflicts as irrational and the participants as somehow deranged is not useful. Finally, while I argue that ethnic (and other) conflict is a cultural construction, this claim has important qualifications. To focus on how conflict is culturally constructed, does not mean that it is arbitrary or a product of the whims of key actors (Spiro, 1984; 1987). While this is not a central purpose here, to say that conflict is culturally constructed requires showing how it is internalized, maintained and affects behaviour (D'Andrade, 1992). Although constructions are subjective we can study them systematically, emphasizing the dynamics of the production, reinforcement and use of cultural symbols, myths and rituals (Spiro, 1984).

My argument is that appreciating the role of culture and cultural identity in ethnic conflict increases our understanding of the phenomena and our capacity to settle such conflicts in constructive ways. In the following sections, I first argue that conflict is fruitfully viewed as cultural behaviour and discuss the concept of culture as a system of meaning arguing that it plays a central role in defining the dynamics of conflict both within and between societies. Next I contrast realist and neo-realist approaches to conflict with their emphasis on interests and a cultural approach which asks how and why competing parties view a conflict and how their interpretations of the conflict are related to action. Lastly, I examine the role of psycho-cultural interpretations and ethnic identity issues in long-standing intransigent ethnic conflict and its management.

CONFLICT AS CULTURAL BEHAVIOUR

Social scientists examine conflict from a variety of economic, political, social and psychological perspectives. The analysis presented here emphasises psycho-cultural forces in conflict, drawing attention to ways in which social groups share and transmit distinct perspectives. The emphasis on the dynamics of developing and sharing common understandings and ways of life among group members does not deny that in all social groups there are individual differences and subgroup variations but it pays less attention to these dynamics than to the real and perceived within-group commonalities. In this section I develop the notion of the culture of conflict which emphasizes conflict as cultural behaviour and in the next section suggest its relevance for understanding international behaviour.

It is important to emphasize that while the structure of society is an excellent predictor of who might be an enemy, it is a terrible predictor of how conflictual a society is likely to be in the first place. The culture of conflict is a much better predictor of the level of conflict within a society (Ross 1993a). From this it derives its relevance for understanding international behaviour.

Conflict

Conflict occurs when parties disagree about the distribution of material or symbolic resources and act out of an incompatibility of goals or a perceived divergence of interests. Conflict is about concrete interests – differences over specific scarce resources (e.g. land, money, positions) which divide parties in a conflict. At the same time it is also about identities and the interpretations of disputants, including the motives they attribute to themselves and to opponents which are rooted in historical experiences and provide models for action (Ross, 1993a; 1993b; 1995). Interests are important because they are what parties stand to gain and lose in a dispute; interpretations matter because they link individual and group identities and capture the deepest fears and threats groups feel while offering an explanation for the actions (or inactions) of the parties. In ethnic disputes interests and identities are intimately linked as parties perceive attacks on their group's interests as identical to threats to its identity. Examining conflict as a cultural process can tell us a good deal about how such linkage occurs, and suggests ways in which conflict management can separate them.

A good deal of conflict occurs within and between groups with incompatible cultural perspectives or worldviews. In these conflicts, culture plays a central role in defining what is fought about, and how a conflict unfolds. In intergroup conflict, cultural understandings play a role in defining competing interests and incompatible identities, and cultural differences can also prevent effective intergroup communications frustrating efforts to bridge differences (Cohen, 1991).

Culture

Culture is a socially constructed, shared, collective structure which Geertz describes as 'an historically transmitted pattern of meaning embodied in symbols, a system of inherited conceptions expressed in symbolic forms by means of which men communicate, perpetuate, and develop their knowledge about and attitudes towards life' (1973: 89).[4] Culture provides a standard of reference for organizing relations within and between groups and to evaluate the actions of others (Avruch and Black, 1991). Culture is an emergent concept, something which appears on the aggregate, but not individual, level in the sense that a single person cannot have culture; rather culture is those things which many people living in a society share. This definition emphasizes culture as public, shared meanings; behaviours, institutions and social structure are understood not as culture itself but as culturally constituted phenomena (Spiro, 1984).[5]

Culture is usefully thought of as a worldview which explains why and how individuals and groups behave as they do and includes both cognitive and affective beliefs about social reality and assumptions about when, where, and how people in one's culture and those in other cultures are likely to act in particular ways. For purposes of political analysis, to this anthropological conception of culture there needs to be added the idea that the widely shared understandings occur among people who have a common named identity which marks distinctions between the group and outsiders. Culture, in short, marks 'a distinctive way of life' characterized in the subjective we-feelings of cultural group members and outsiders that the way of life is unique. While culture can be understood through the beliefs about the distinctiveness of a life-style and worldview which members of a group hold, it is expressed through specific behaviours (customs and rituals) – both sacred and profane – which mark the daily, yearly and life cycle rhythms of its members and reveal how people view past, present, and future events and understand the choices they face (Kertzer, 1988). These metaphors have both cognitive meaning which describes group experience and high affective salience which emphasizes the unique intragroup bonds – almost like a secret code – which sets one group's experience apart from others.

The Culture of Conflict

The culture of conflict refers to culturally specific norms, practices and institutions which shape conflict in a society and define what people consider valuable and worth fighting over, investing particular goods, statuses, positions or actions with meaning; it suggests appropriate ways to wage disputes, and identifies suitable targets of conflict; it supports institutions in which disputes are processed; and it determines how they are likely to end. Culture is critical to the development and maintenance of in-group and out-group identities. It provides the metaphors and associations which distinguish allies and enemies. Through participation in day-to-day within-group interaction with its primary-process sensory experiences, groups affectively experience salient events around which identities coalesce. Critical differences between groups are not found in the objective dissimilarities between experiences, but in the ways in which even small disparities between groups can mark large emotional gaps.[6]

Culture shapes conflict behaviour when it sanctions particular ways to pursue individual or group interests and disapproves of others. One of the things that anthropologists have learned is the highly stylized form inter-tribal warfare takes in many settings (Davie, 1928; Meggitt, 1976). The same is true of other forms of conflict as well. Most cultures have clear expectations about what behaviour is appropriate when particular grievances arise. There are cultural expectations about what a party should do for itself, who it can turn to for help, and if, and when, it is appropriate to involve the wider community in a dispute. As a result, the same event such as a physical attack on a kinsperson, might result in physical retaliation in one culture, a community meeting to discuss the situation in another, and an appeal to the authorities in a third.

Culture affects conflict behaviour. At the same time, conflict can also be viewed as cultural behaviour since all conflict occurs in a cultural context which shapes its course in critical ways. Knowing something about the cultural context in which a conflict occurs may reveal a great deal about its roots, its likely course and its management, for there are often significant cultural differences in the magnitude, form and responses to what looks to an outsider like similar disputes in different settings.[7] Conflict, of course, can take place outside of a culturally shared frame of reference; when it does, the absence of common assumptions often makes such conflict especially difficult to contain. In such situations one party often uses its own cultural assumptions to try to understand what another has done or is likely to do, with disastrous results. At other times a group decides that an adversary's values and behaviours are completely different from its own and therefore not subject to any of its own within-culture inhibitions on conflict.

Cultural values and practices affect institutional goals and procedures and cultural norms guide behaviour even in the absence of institutions to enforce them. For example, even in as basic a conflict as Axelrod's (1984) prisoners' dilemma game between computer programs, culture is visible in the definition of what constitutes winning and in the payoff matrix (Ross, 1983b: 62). Changes in either or both of these can produce different outcomes.[8]

Culture shapes how people understand their social worlds, how they classify people, and how they evaluate action possibilities, and sanction certain ways of responding over others. Conflict reflects cultural priorities, but also can be used to alter them. Culture is political because control over the definition of actors and actions favours certain people and groups over others. For this reason it is useful to understand that the culture of conflict then both summarizes a society's core values and behavioural practices and reflects the outcomes of prior conflicts which favour some groups and individuals over others.

Examining conflict as cultural behaviour leads us to examine what it is that people get into disagreements about and what they are likely to do about them. In ethnic conflicts there are concrete group differences over the allocation of resources but also incompatible interpretations concerning the meaning of interest differences. I suggest that this cultural perspective on conflict behaviour both clashes with more widely held realist views, and can answer questions which realists have a hard time answering adequately such as the intensity of ethnic conflict.

THE CULTURE OF INTERNATIONAL CONFLICT

The cultural view of conflict behaviour understands international conflict quite differently from realist perspectives, and in talking about the international system the term *the culture of international conflict* refers to the shared norms, practices and institutions which characterize the international system or international regimes at particular periods. Certainly particular international regimes can be described in terms of the assumptions actors make about the motives of both state and non-state actors, what are considered legitimate ways to pursue grievances with them. Often the acceptance of a common frame of reference is at least as important as power relationships among the parties in understanding the outcome of disputes.

Here I outline some major differences between the two and how they understand conflict behaviour in general and ethnic conflict in particular. Realist analyses emphasize the state as the key actor in international politics whereas a cultural analysis sees the role of the state as more variable – sometimes it is the dominant player in a conflict, at other times state actors are far less central. In addition, a cultural perspective suggests important ways in which the cultural construction of the state plays a role in many conflicts. Finally, a cultural analysis, in addition, moves beyond the interests which preoccupy state actors and draws attention to the role of identity issues in conflict.

Realism and Culture

Traditionally realist analyses (and recent rational choice approaches) focus on state-based actions in the pursuit of concrete interests – material resources and strategic advantages. Within the state system, realist theory implicitly (and sometimes explicitly) assumes that states operate out of a commonly shared framework which make the actions of any state more or less comprehensible, if not necessarily acceptable, to all others. It follows that the central motivational force for international behaviour in general, and conflict in particular, is states pursuing their national self-interest (through the maximization of state power) in the context of weak international institutions which develop in a world without centralized authority (Waltz, 1959).

Among the criticisms of this view is that it exaggerates the autonomy (sovereignty for some) of states, ignores significant non-state international actors (such as non-governmental organizations and multinational corporations) and encourages a too rigid distinction between international and domestic politics and offers little appreciation of the role of cultural forces in international politics (Donnelly, 1995). It exaggerates the degree to which the motivations of states and the norms of international actors are distinct from those in the domestic political sphere. Furthermore, even when there is a recognition of cultural differences between states, most international relations scholars assume these have little impact on political leaders and diplomats.

Conflicts between cultural groups are not taken very seriously in international relations[9] except perhaps when they occur in conjunction with claims for self-determination and demands for sovereignty and are often reinterpreted in realist power terms. Often cultural conflicts are seen as noise – domestic issues which impinge on a state's capacity to act effectively in the international arena. By assuming that all states are essentially seeking the same goals, cultural conflicts become threats to a state's ability pursue its 'true' interests. From this perspective, cultural conflicts are distractions at best, and irrational and uncontrollable forces at worst. This lack of attention to cultural and other identity based conflicts makes it easy to dismiss their relevance or the need to understand them.

I argue that even if there are some international behaviours best understood in terms of the dynamics of the interstate system, the evidence also shows that often there are important linkages between domestic and international politics such as a propensity for weak leaders to gain support by fostering a belief in out-group threat (LeVine and Campbell, 1973; Ross, 1993a: 113–28; Stohl, 1980; Wilkenfeld, 1973). In addition to the argument that domestic political considerations affect the international behaviour of state decision-makers, a culturally oriented analysis can make explicit other connections which come into play here. It can point, for example, to widespread continuities in how both domestic and foreign enemies are perceived, or to how experiences in one domain serve as models for behaviour in the other.

Culture and State Definition

A good starting point is the recognition that the definition of each state in the international system is itself a result of particular political, social and cultural processes which affect international behaviour.

The extensive literature on the new states of Africa and Asia in the 1960s stressed the problems associated with the fact that the post-colonial entities brought together diverse cultural groups. It is striking that in virtually none of these discussions is there recognition that most European states followed the same process in earlier centuries. Historian Eugen Weber (1976) argues that even in the case of France, widely seen as a culturally homogeneous state, the development of a common culture *followed* the creation of the centralized state. He argues that as recently as 1860 fewer than half of France's population spoke French as their first language (1976: 67–70). Only by the second half of the nineteenth century was the power of the French state sufficient to establish a system of universal primary education using a common language and curriculum, construct railways and roads, and institute universal military service for young men, all of which served to weaken local culture and loyalties while building a national identity rooted in common cultural experiences (Weber, 1976).

Culture and State Borders

While the composition and boundaries of states is often taken for granted, Lustick argues that the reality is that 'no fact about states is more obvious than the impermanence of their boundaries' (1993: 1). He contends that even state borders which seem more or less stable today have resulted from wars and other processes which are not well understood. Many severe conflicts, he points out, revolve around issues of incorporation or separation as cultural groups compete over the definition of a state and the relationship between different cultural groups within it. While force is a factor in such conflicts, he demonstrates that political, social and cultural processes are also involved in determining the outcomes of such intergroup conflicts (Lustick, 1993).

Boundary conflicts and changes in state borders generally involve competing claims rooted in the language of cultural and national self-determination which take several forms. The claims can support a group separating to form a new state, as Croatia and Slovenia did in withdrawing from the former Yugoslavia. The reverse situation is found when one state seeks to incorporate another, as Lustick argues Britain sought to do in the case of Ireland, and France with Algeria (1993). Another pattern is seen where a group such as the Kurds, who inhabit several states, seeks to form a new entity.[10] Finally, there is the case when a state exists and is primarily populated by a group which seeks to incorporate neighbouring regions where other members of the group live (Germany in the 1930s) or sees itself as representing the interests of the members of the group (e.g. Hungary *vis-à-vis* the Hungarian minorities in Slovakia and Romania).[11]

An international border can be drawn to unite people sharing what they perceive as a common cultural and shared identity and expressed in Wilsonian ideas about self-determination.[12] However, as Lustick and Weber remind us, another sequence is one in which people brought together around a common political boundary subsequently develop a common identity. Effective states have a capacity to mobilize and organize social, economic and military resources, and to create common experiences out of which a common identity and sense of joint purpose emerges after several generations. This is what Karl Deutsch (1957) calls the development of the sense of 'a distinctive way of life', which both unites a domestic population and distinguishes it from outsiders through key symbols, myths and rituals.

Culture and National Identity

Cultural experiences involving the development and participation in shared rituals and the articulation of myths and symbols are central to the creation, strengthening and maintenance of cultural and national identity (Cohen, 1969; Kertzer, 1988). Two distinct parts of the dynamic are the interplay between local and national identities, and those between domestic and international domains. Culture and identity issues can play a central, but not necessarily the same, role in each of these relationships. My own empirical examination of the culture of conflict in a sample of pre-industrial societies suggests what some of these connections can be (Ross, 1993a). One is the clear link between intragroup and intergroup conflict: cross-culturally I found a moderately strong tendency for societies which have more internal conflict to also have more external conflict. At the same time, more careful examination of the results showed two distinct patterns. In most of the cases, which I call *generalizing* societies, the levels of internal and external conflict and violence are positively related, while in a smaller, but not insignificant number of *differentiating* societies, the two forms of conflict are inversely related so that conflict is with either internal or external foes, but not both (Ross, 1993a: chapter 7). What turns out to be especially interesting is that the social and political structures of generalizing and differentiating societies are extremely different. Differentiating societies have a variety of mechanisms which increase cross-cutting ties among various groups within the society which apparently produce high internal solidarity and external hostility. In contrast, in generalizing[13] societies, within-group social ties are more limited and enemies are both internal and external. In addition, although these different social and political structures are good predictors of whether violence is directed inwards, outwards, or both, they are not closely related to the overall level of conflict generated by the members of a society. Rather, the results show that a society's level of conflict and violence is most closely associated with its psycho-cultural dispositions – patterns of early socialization – which are critical to the developments and maintenance of culturally approved styles for dealing with conflict. In societies where early socialization is harsh and physically punishing, where it has little affection or warmth, and where male gender-identity conflict is high, both internal and external conflict and violence are higher (Ross, 1993a: 94–104). These results form the basis of my argument that the social structural features of a society which reflect competing interests are most associated with who fights with whom, while psycho-cultural experiences, the essential building blocks for the development of worldviews and identities, are tied to a society's overall level of conflict.

International conflict can readily be examined from a cultural perspective which identifies both behavioural and normative regularities and says how cultural differences among international actors are associated with variation in behaviour. Such an analysis of international conflict is likely to be particularly useful when we try to understand destructive conflicts such as those rooted in ethnic identity. A psycho-cultural perspective can be useful in understanding the definition of enemies and allies, what they are willing to do to each other and how they interpret one another's actions. Central to such an analysis is the dynamic in which political leaders draw upon deep fears and threats to group identity which emphasize cultural differences in the definition of enemies and achievement of internal political mobilization. To understand the relevance of this argument, I next spell out in greater detail the nature of psycho-cultural interpretations and identity in ethnic conflict.

PSYCHO-CULTURAL INTERPRETATIONS AND IDENTITY IN ETHNIC CONFLICT[14]

Psycho-cultural Interpretations

Psycho-cultural interpretations are internalized, shared orientations rooted in the earliest social relationships which help people in a culture make sense of inherently ambiguous, highly charged events which characterize their lives (Ross, 1995). The term psycho-cultural links the psychological processes central to the construction of these interpretations and a cultural dynamics, emphasizing that these orientations are not just personal, but rather are nurtured and socially reinforced, linking individuals in a collective process, amplifying what is shared and emphasizing differences among groups (Mack, 1983). Psycho-cultural interpretations are central to the dynamics of conflict where the combination of ambiguity about the meaning of others' actions and/or intentions and emotional salience, which characterizes bitter ethnic conflicts, readily produces psychic threat and regression to intense, primitive feelings.

Psycho-cultural interpretation invoked in ambiguous, highly charged situations are linked to dispositions rooted in early experiences and shape how disputants react in a conflict (Ross, 1995). In such situations, provocative but vague comments from adversaries are really taken as literal threats and can easily produce social polarization and further rhetorical and emotional escalation. For example, Cohen (1990) suggests that Israeli interpretations of Nasser's rhetoric in the spring of 1967 were far more precise and literal than he intended and this significantly contributed to the escalation in the region prior to the June war.

While participants in any dispute can often tell someone 'just what the conflict is about' this precision is often illusory. In many situations, different parties do not always agree about what a conflict is about, when it started, or who is involved, for they operate from (but are not aware of) alternative frames of references which shape their actions. Of course, these can be difficult to detect since conflict is less a one-time thing than a fluid, changing phenomenon. Many disputes, whether they are between families in a community or nations in the world, involve parties with a long history, which, of course, includes long lists of accumulated grievances which can be trotted out and appended to newer ones as political conditions shift.

Identity and Escalation

A striking feature of so many conflicts is the emotional investment parties make in what to outsiders often seem like unimportant matters. The fact is, however, that any matter invested with emotional significance is no longer trivial, and intransigent ethnic disputes quickly become characterized by threats to group self-esteem and legitimation (Horowitz, 1985). The dynamic is one in which the parties perceiving themselves as threatened place identity issues at the core of their concerns (Northrup, 1989). Such emotion-laden conflicts can be especially difficult to settle. Sometimes the fact that each side feels the same intense emotions makes it difficult to recognize what is, in fact, shared. For example, although both Protestants and Catholics in Northern Ireland each see themselves as a threatened minority, each has trouble acknowledging the other side's view. One party's emotional concerns make it very difficult to accept another's account, especially when their own action may be the root cause of an adversary's behaviour. Only when steps are taken to address these issues can any progress on the 'substance' of the dispute be made.

The same factors which push actors to make sense of a situation also lead to cognitive and perceptual distortion because the desire for certainty often is greater than the capacity for accuracy. Not only are disputants likely to make systematic errors in the 'facts' underlying interpretations, but the homogeneous nature of most social settings and cultural amplifiers reinforces these self-serving mistakes. What is most crucial, however, about interpretations of a conflict is the compelling, coherent account they offer to the parties in linking discrete events to general understandings. Central to such interpretations is the attribution of motives to parties. Once identified, the existence of such motives seemingly makes it easy to 'predict' another's future actions, and through one's own behaviour to turn such predictions into self-fulfilling prophesies. In this sense, it is appropriate to suggest that rather than thinking about particular objective events which cause conflicts to escalate, we ought to be thinking about the *interpretations* of such events which are associated with escalation and those which are not. This is certainly not a common understanding of how international politics is viewed.

Shared images of the world and plans for action are predicated on a shared conception of the difference between one's own group and others. The interpretive processes involved in intense conflicts emphasize the homogeneity of each party, sometimes using what are small objective differences to mark large social distinctions. Outsiders then can serve as objects for externalization, displacement and projection of intense negative feelings, while dissenting perspectives present inside the group are denied (Fornari, 1975; Volkan, 1988). This dynamic draws attention to the mediating effects of shared and culturally reinforced mental representations of the world.

Shared History and Common Fate

Group members share common developmental experiences and part of the developmental task involves emphasizing those shared experiences as part of the process of incorporating a sense of group identity into one's own personal identity. Anderson (1991) writes of imagined communities, which can link the person and collective identities in powerful ways. This process of within-group identity formation overemphasizes what it is that group members actually share, giving greater emotional weight to the common elements, reinforcing them with an ideology of linked fate, and frequently an overvaluation of the uniformity within groups (Turner, 1988). This dynamic is perhaps best viewed as a psycho-cultural 'regression to the mean' in that what is emphasized both affectively and cognitively are the common elements which individuals share – and related to what Volkan calls the narcissism of minor differences (1988: 103–5). Deviations from the norm are selectively ignored or negatively reinforced as incompatible with group membership.

Psycho-cultural interpretations of ethnic conflict are found in the stories parties locked in struggle recount about past experiences, present difficulties and future aspirations. These accounts are valuable for revealing how participants think about and characterize a conflict. In fact, as we listen to them it is important to consider the extent to which stories from different sides of what is apparently the same conflict differ, without necessarily directly contradicting each other. Each side selects key events which come to have central meaning for their own community. For example, in Northern Ireland, Protestant Unionists find great meaning in the story of William of Orange and the Battle of the Boyne in 1689, while Catholic accounts really say little about King Billy or the battle. In contrast, Catholic Nationalists emphasize the meaning of the 1916 Easter Uprising which for Protestants is far less significant that their sacred pact committing themselves to resist Irish self-rule four years earlier. Even when an event enters into the stories of both sides, such as the hunger strikes of Nationalist prisoners in 1980–1, the metaphors and meanings associated with them can be so different that it is hard to realize one is hearing about the same events in two different ways.

Chosen Traumas

Stories about a long-standing conflict contain the culturally rooted aspirations, challenges and deepest fears of ethnic communities. Volkan

(1988) uses the term 'chosen trauma' to refer to a specific experience which comes to symbolize a group's deepest threats and fears through feelings of helplessness and victimization (1991: 13). Volkan and his collaborators provide many examples of such events including the Turkish slaughter of Armenians, the Nazi holocaust, the experience of slavery and segregation for African-Americans, and the Serbian defeat at Kosovo by the Turks in 1389.[15] If a group feels too humiliated, angry or helpless to mourn the losses suffered in the trauma, Volkan suggests that it then incorporates the emotional meaning of the traumatic event into its identity and passes on the emotional and symbolic meaning from generation to generation.[16] In escalating ethnic conflicts, the key metaphors, such as the chosen trauma serve both as a rallying point and as a way to make sense of events which evoke deep fears and threats to existence (Horowitz, 1985; Kelman, 1978; 1987). Only when the deep-seated threats these stories represent are addressed, he suggests, is a community able to begin to formulate a more peaceful future with its enemies.

Validating Differences

Psycho-cultural interpretations reflect but also strengthen the boundary between in-groups and out-groups. The process of telling – validating[17] if you will – such stories strengthens the link between individual and group identity and emphasizes how threats to the group are also threats to individual group members. In long-term intransigent ethnic conflict, strong threats to identity are an essential part of the conflict dynamic and any efforts to defuse such a situation must take the stories participants recount, and the perceived threats to identity, seriously. The point, after all, is not whether participants' accounts are true or false from some objective point of view but that they are meaningful to the parties involved.

Psycho-cultural interpretations are a central feature of intransigent ethnic conflict. The strong support and reinforcement they receive within an ethnic community make it difficult for dissenting voices to be heard (let alone speak up) in many situations and serves to discredit outsiders (however sympathetic) who do not accept a group's position. In many cases shared interpretations are protected and defended as a sacred shrine might be for they embody a group's existence. Given the fervour with which interpretations are linked to group identity and a group's fate, what are the prospects for settling contemporary ethnic conflicts?

PSYCHO-CULTURAL INTERPRETATIONS AND SETTLING ETHNIC CONFLICTS

The intensity of ethnic conflicts can be reduced when these conflicts are managed constructively (Ross and Rothman, forthcoming). My argument is that this is most likely when each side's deeply felt threats to identity are addressed, since ethnic conflicts are not just about differences on distributive issues. While I have spelled out elements of this process elsewhere (Ross, 1995; Ross and Rothman, forthcoming), here I offer a brief overview suggesting the contribution a cultural approach to ethnic conflict management can make in settling long-standing conflicts such as Northern Ireland, South Africa and the Arab–Israeli conflict, as well as emerging conflicts involving culturally distinct migrant communities in western Europe and regional-based ethnic communities in central Europe and the former USSR. Underlying my argument is that recognizing the role of cultural interpretations and identity issues in ethnic conflicts offers a mechanism for incorporating them into the conflict management process.

Although psycho-cultural interpretations are a powerful feature of intransigent conflicts, they are not all that matter. After all, there are always substantive competing interests at stake as well in group conflict, and cultural differences are only part of what divides groups. One hypothesis is that while there are differences in both interests and identities in ethnic disputes, divergent interpretations must be addressed before there can be progress in bridging interest differences (Ross, 1993b: chapter 8). The argument is that when both fear and anger are great, the parties cannot imagine making an agreement with an enemy or conceptualize what a viable, mutually acceptable agreement could look like. In such situations, interest differences are converted into moral principles and it is especially hard for either side to imagine conceding much of anything to an opponent.

Some Specific Steps

One point to be clear about at the outset is that directly attacking a group's worldview is rarely, if ever, useful and more likely to result in rigid defence than in flexibility and change. Paradoxically, modification is more likely when a group's worldview is not directly challenged but accepted as part of the social and political reality. This means that any meaningful change in culturally rooted worldviews must be consistent with other core elements of a culture. Adoption of new metaphors and understandings is possible when they are linked to other cherished beliefs, not when groups must give up all that they value and place at the center of their identity.

Taking seriously the key metaphors and worldviews of conflicting parties offers a starting point for constructively settling conflicts, but it is only effective as part of a larger process whereby the parties come to agree on a set of mutually acceptable arrangements regarding concrete interests. The emphasis on deep-seated relational issues begins with questions of security, trust and identity as barriers to settlements (Horowitz, 1985; Northrup, 1989). Frequently each party in intense ethnic conflicts sees itself as a highly vulnerable minority but cannot acknowledge that an opponent feels the same thing. In Northern Ireland, for example, Protestants emphasize their minority status in the island as a whole, while Catholics point out their political, social and economic vulnerability in the North. In the Middle East, Jews see themselves as a tiny island in the Arab-dominated region, while Palestinians focus on their powerlessness *vis-à-vis* Israel. In Sri Lanka, Tamils feel vulnerable as a minority on the island, while Sinhalese are fearful of the more than 50 million Tamils nearby in south India.

Culturally focused conflict management efforts seek to address a group's deepest concerns not through denial but by making them a less powerful source of anxiety. Dramatic gestures like Sadat's 1977 visit to Jerusalem and de Klerk's 1990 meeting with Nelson Mandela after his release from prison offered recognition and acceptance between longtime enemies which softened (although hardly removed completely) a hard core of deep distrust. While the actions of key leaders are often noted by all, they are not all that common. An additional path to change is offered by problem-solving workshops and Track II discussions aimed at bringing important, but not high-ranking, government officials and influential persons together to modify each side's interpretation of the conflict by constructing a more nuanced image of the opponent and developing a sense that each side understands and could be responsive to one's own human concerns and deepest needs (Kelman, 1978).

Psycho-cultural approaches to conflict management stress the importance of symbolic and ritual efforts to address feelings of past victimization and loss. Mourning means coming to terms with significant loss and progressively investing past events with lower levels of emotional intensity. As Montville says:

> For the mourning process to occur, however, requires that the victimizers accept responsibility for their acts or those of their predecessor

governments and people, recognize the injustice done, and in some way ask forgiveness of the victims. In many cases, the contrition may have to be mutual. (1990: 538)

ILLUSTRATIONS: SOUTH AFRICA AND NORTH AFRICAN MIGRANTS IN FRANCE

A psycho-cultural perspective towards ethnic conflict does not deny that concrete interests and questions of power are central to long-term disputes. It does, however, say that the inability to address interest differences successfully is often tied to an unwillingness or inability to focus attention on issues of identity. The rapidity of change in South Africa since 1990 and the polarised nature of relations between the French majority and minority North African community in France can be understood in terms of the extent to which psycho-cultural issues have been engaged in the one case but not the other.

South Africa

The case of South Africa is a particularly interesting one from the point of view of psycho-cultural interpretation theory. While the decision of the Afrikaner minority to yield political power to the Black majority in South Africa can be accounted for in terms of *realpolitik* factors such as the changing world political situation at the end of the Cold War, the impact of international sanctions on the South African economy, or the weakening of direct threat in the withdrawal of Cuban forces from Angola, a psycho-cultural analysis would also emphasize various ways in which the Nationalist leaders and their supporters engaged in significant dialogue with the ANC and its backers which altered core elements of their image of each other and the fears each had so that a peaceful transition to majority rule could occur.

Available accounts suggest that more than interest calculations were central to the South African government's decision to release Nelson Mandela from prison in 1990 and to launch the country on the road to majority rule. Sparks (1994) describes a decade of meetings between Mandela and key figures in the government, particularly Minister of Justice, Police, and Prisons Jacobus Coetsee. Not only were there dozens of sessions with Mandela and other ANC figures in South Africa, but Nationalist leaders also met overseas with ANC officials in a variety of settings. An important conclusion which many Nationalists reached was that the Afrikaners' deepest cultural fears and threats to identity would be taken seriously in any negotiated solution with Mandela and other ANC leaders (and their allies). Sparks (1984) documents the increasing respect and ability to listen to the other which developed as leaders on both sides identified common goals and a commitment to achieving them.

One of the more fascinating aspects of the South African transition is how much the negotiations and more informal discussions between the major actors took place without any assistance of outside third parties. One reason this became possible was the existence of groups in South Africa prepared to facilitate the change process and the creation of settings where the major groups were able to talk together. The National Peace Accords (NPA), for example, a framework brokered by church and business leaders, provided a forum where all parties could discuss a wide range of topics and where joint proposals could be developed for pressing immediate problems such as the ongoing violence in the early 1990s (Gastrow, 1995). Although the NPA ultimately was not able either to significantly lessen the violence or move the country towards reconstruction and development, Gastrow suggests its discussions helped develop a paradigm shift towards a new democratic political culture through the work of the national, regional and local peace committees it established (1995: 59–76).

An in-depth psycho-cultural analysis of South Africa would go beyond the strategic judgement of both the Nationalist leaders and the ANC that outright victory was not possible. It would emphasize how through informal contacts and sustained discussions key actors decided that there was indeed someone on the other side worth talking to, how they came to perceive mutual acceptance, a sense of sufficient common concerns, and a joint wish to move past the trauma of apartheid. Only through such an analysis can we explain the rapidity and peaceful character of the political and social transition between 1990 and 1994. While it is often easy to view a particular outcome as consistent with expectations, it is valuable to explain situations where what we expected did not, in fact, take place. In South Africa, only when we ask how key players' psycho-cultural interpretations changed as identity needs were addressed, can we understand why this most intransigent of conflicts was transformed so rapidly.

North Africans in France

In a similar fashion, while underlying psycho-cultural fears and identity issues are at the heart of the conflict-laden relationship between the French and the several million persons, generally Muslim, of North African origin (many of whom are citizens) living in France, here the failure to address these deep concerns explains the rise in ethnic and racial political appeals, and the regular outbreak of divisive conflict which increases the fears and anger on all sides in the 1990s.

Migrants from North Africa and their descendants are now the largest and most visible minority in France, and have been the focus of sometimes intense political and social conflict (Grillo, 1985). Throughout the 1980s and 1990s there have been physical confrontations and local violent incidents, often associated with youth gangs and with the National Front, a neo-fascist political organization, and many occasions where the role of North Africans in France has been questioned from a variety of points of view. Almost exclusively Muslims – but not unified politically, socially or religiously, the North Africans – often called Maghrebians because of their region of origin experience discrimination in a number of domains. In the view of many French, they show little interest in integration.[18] While in the early 1980s François Mitterrand's socialist government first cautiously moved to extend social benefits and citizenship rights, more recently from all sides of the French political spectrum there have been calls to restrict immigration, social programmes, and the availability of citizenship (Balinkska, 1988). For some time hostility between Muslims and non-Muslims has sometimes been high and relations strained in many French cities. Incidents like the one in the summer of 1989 where the mayor of one small city ordered the bulldozing of the local mosque and later claimed it was an accident, are all too common.

Several years ago I studied the bitter conflict which erupted in the Autumn of 1989 (Ross, 1993b: chapters 1–2), when the head of a small secondary school in Creuil 40 miles north of Paris, prohibited three young Muslim girls from wearing in school the *hijab* or headscarf with which traditional Muslim women cover their hair in public from adolescence onward. Here I present an overview of this conflict to suggest how neglect of its underlying psycho-cultural features meant that efforts to manage it were not especially successful.

The issue hit the press when one girl claimed the head had struck her, and her family called in two Islamic fundamentalist organizations to talk to the head. This action then touched off a whirling controversy which quickly involved the nation's leading political figures and raised a series of powerful issues at the core of French political life. What particularly interested me was how the specific dispute rapidly gave way to deeper cultural and political divisions in France. As a result, while the government imposed an outcome to this dispute, it never dealt with the underlying psycho-cultural fears and as a result in the years since other conflicts between the French majority and the North African minority have broken out repeatedly.

As the then Minister of Education, Lionel Jospin (who is presently Prime Minister as well as head of the Socialist Party) was drawn into the conflict over the scarves he declared that the responsibility in this matter rested with school authorities. Their job, he said, was to talk to the families involved to get them to understand the importance of secular public education and to abandon the open expression of religion in school. However, he added, wearing a headscarf is not sufficient grounds for exclusion and if after a long dialogue with the family they refuse to change their minds, the child's education must come first (Beriss, 1990). They must be accepted in the public schools because 'French schools exist to educate, to integrate, not to reject' (Schemla: 1989: 78).

However, this did not calm fears and the rapid transformation of the dispute was marked by the mobilization of both conservative forces who offered well-worn xenophobic, anti-Arab rhetoric, as well as those on the left who offered additional anti-immigrants images. For example, many on the anti-clerical French left supported the head's action as a defence of the school as a secular institution and a symbol of the separation of church and state. The language of many on the left was often as hysterical as on the right and hardly conducive to constructive discussion of the dispute. 'The future will tell if the year of the bicentennial [of the French Revolution] will be seen as the Munich of the public school', declared five leading intellectual figures (Badinter et al., 1989: 58).

For many feminists the central issue in the conflict was the oppression of women in fundamentalist Islam. For others, the critical image associated with the dispute was not of the cherubic faces peering out from under the scarves, but that of Ayatollah Khomeini and the spectre of Islamic fundamentalism and reminded the French that several years earlier there had been a dramatic wave of terrorist bombing in and around the capital, and that French hostages were still being held in the Lebanon. The young girls, some charged, were being manipulated by their fathers in the service of larger political/religious goals.[19] Teachers throughout the country, feeling that their authority and secular principles were under attack, spoke out against the *hijab*, bringing up cases where Muslim students refused to attend gym classes or where they objected to biology, music or even art classes on religious grounds. Teachers said the *hijab* was not only a rejection of secular education, but represented a safety hazard in some situations, and threatened to go on strike if the scarves were not banned.

Soon Jospin realized that there was not much he could do to manage the conflict which was now increasingly revolving around questions of the work habits of North Africans, housing, social services, illegal immigration and integration. The specific issue of the scarves and the more general question of the role of North African immigrants in France divided the ruling Socialists and generated intense emotions so that there was no obvious way to contain the issue and put together a coalition around an acceptable solution. So Jospin kicked the matter upstairs, not to the President or Prime Minister who certainly wanted to deal with it even less than he did, but to the *Conseil d'État*, the nation's top administrative tribunal which offered a narrow decision satisfying neither those who saw the issue as one of religious freedom nor those who wanted to ban the *hijab* from public schools. They said that wearing religious signs was not necessarily incompatible with the idea of a secular public school, but only if the signs were non-provocative, did not put pressure on other students, and were not proselytizing and not objects of propaganda. The Council then told the government to implement its ruling on a case-by-case basis.

When the media stopped covering the issue, it seemed to fade away. Yet, French suspicions about, and anger towards, North Africans clearly increased in intensity, while North Africans felt more vulnerable than ever and uncertain which, if any, of their basic rights the government would protect. Using administrative and judicial procedures to deal with the scarves meant that the deeper, far more divisive, issues raising important challenges to the Socialist policy of supporting limited ethnonational expression from minorities within France remained unaddressed (Safran, 1985), along with deep identity fears.

This dispute, and the deeper conflict can be understood in terms of the real, competing interests at stake. The changing economic situation by 1989 made many French feel insecure about their future, in comparison with the prosperity of the French (and European) economy a generation earlier when there was a great need for labour and the immigration of North Africans (and others) to France was encouraged. At that time, French public and private employers were glad to find inexpensive workers who created few problems (Grillo, 1985). Many North Africans, in many cases, saved a good deal of their modest wages and spoke of returning home, to Morocco, Tunisia or Algeria, when they could afford to do so.

Many, however, stayed in France longer than they had planned, married and had children. Although the children attend French schools and the families have benefited from French social services, the Maghrebians remain socially, political, economically and psychologically segregated in France. Many Maghrebian communities are poor and socially and politically marginal. Many immigrants speak French poorly and participate in the institutions of the wider society only peripherally. They are viewed with widespread suspicion and many of their cultural habits are misunderstood and are objects of derision. When the French economy turned downward in the 1980s the visible North Africans were variously seen as the cause of the problem (they were taking jobs away from the French), and a drain on the economy through their claims on education, health and other social services.

While specific interests were central to the conflict, it is hard to explain its intensity and rapid escalation without considering psycho-cultural interpretations and the deep identity fears and threats they evoked. For many French the critical images were highly emotional and non-negotiable. Permitting scarves in school was returning the country to the Cardinals for some and giving it to the Ayatollah for others. For Muslims, many of whom did not support wearing the scarves, the case provided more evidence of French racism and hypocrisy, rekindling intense feelings of vulnerability and anger.

Why did anyone care what less than a dozen teenagers wore on their heads? Why did the story fill newscasts, papers and the covers of the nation's leading magazines day after day and week after week for several months? Why were the polemics of the debate so extreme, leaving little room for exchange and compromise? Why did the girls' scarves represent such basic threats to identity for so many French and attacks on their identity to the Maghrebians? A psycho-cultural analysis points to the symbolic meanings involved in this highly ambiguous situation, which led the parties to a reliance on fear-laden shared representations of the world. Underlying the different images evoked on many sides in the dispute were perceived threats to a fragile core sense of identity. For the French, since the young girls wearing the head scarves were not themselves a plausible threat, the real responsibility for the actions had to be shifted to their much more potentially aggressive fundamentalist fathers. Only then could a consensus develop around opposition to the scarves even while those against the head scarves disagreed about the specific threat that they posed.

Public opinion, in fact, showed that the issue of minorities in French society was potentially explosive. Not only did large majorities oppose the right to wear the *hijab* in school (which Muslims also opposed by 45–30 per cent), but in addition, surveys showed that French non-Muslims see Muslims in France as past-oriented, violent fanatics who repress women (*Le Monde*, 30 November 1989: 15). There was majority opposition to the idea of a Muslim president or mayor, to Islamic political parties or unions, to the right for foreigners to vote in local elections; 25 per cent even opposed the right of Muslim parents to give their children Islamic first names (which in France must be registered by the civil authorities) at birth (Schneider, 1989: 73).

A psycho-cultural account of the conflict emphasizes the importance of disputants' deeply rooted interpretations of the conflict. It draws attention to how particular events arouse culturally shared fears about threats to self-esteem and identity. It emphasises the importance of how people define their social worlds, the identification of key actors (groups and individuals), their goals, interests and motives. It concerns how individuals process events, and the emotions, perceptions and cognitions they evoke. On the psycho-cultural level, most members of the majority community transformed the question of religious attire into a threat from fundamentalist Islam; for the minority community, many of whom, did not support the wearing of the *hijab*, the hostility and fears of rejection which the incident unleashed were very powerful indeed. The conflict management failure here is the inability of significant individuals and groups in the country to address these polarized images as a way either to bridge the competing interests or lessen the extent to which identities were threatened.

CONCLUSION

Taking cultural differences seriously does not mean that intergroup conflicts are about the differences themselves. Rather, my argument has been that cultural differences are generally not what groups fight about, but rather it is the threats, fears, differences in legitimization or differential access to resources which cultural differences represent which are what is critical. Culture becomes politically relevant in both domestic and international politics when it serves as a threat to a group's legitimacy or a vehicle for what is perceived as privileged access.

Different cultural understandings are not necessarily a problem and indeed we can point to many places in the world in which very different cultural groups have lived together at peace for long periods of time. Differences in meanings become important when they become associated with malevolent intentions of others and when they are linked to motivations which launch groups on escalatory spirals.

Even if the field of international relations was only concerned with interstate relationships, its current neglect of cultural considerations would be problematic. When we recognize both the far larger number of actors, ranging from international organizations, non-governmental organizations, transnational corporations, interest groups and ethnic communities, and their cultural diversity, it is clear that understanding the role of cultural forces in the international arena is important. In addition, cultural dynamics matter because of the fundamental role they play in ethnic conflicts and other matters which bridge domestic and international politics.

Conflicts in which ethnicity is a central focus are expressed in cultural terms, and I have argued that psycho-cultural dynamics are central to how they develop and to defining possibilities for their constructive management. In situations where threats to identity come to the fore, violence and escalation often follow. Culturally organized and reinforced worldviews strengthen group differences and provide metaphors and images to characterize threats to existence which political leaders exploit at particular times. The parties to such conflicts are not simply acting in terms of predetermined primordial identities. Rather it is particularly important to understand how their differences reflect more recent cultural and political processes and reflect incompatible worldviews.

Constructive conflict management often requires taking these alternative perspectives seriously and asking why it is that each side finds it so hard to comprehend the most central concerns that the other feels. Often, I suggest (following Kelman, 1982), a party finds itself in a situation where recognizing the other side's most basic concerns and acknowledging their right to exist, raises questions concerning its own right to exist. In this, as in other situations, a conflict readily escalates when it is only understood in zero-sum terms in which one side wins and the other loses. A cultural approach to conflict and conflict management, on the other hand, hopes that efforts which address an opponent's most basic identity concerns can lead to a situation in which the parties redefine the substantive issues which divide them into more integrative problems which allow, and even require, joint action for their settlement.

NOTES

1. I wish to thank Donald T. Campbell and Katherine Conner for the thoughtful comments and suggestions on an earlier draft of this chapter.
2. Almost all the ethnic conflicts of interest here can be described as both domestic and international conflicts and the two terms imply an overly rigid boundary not reflective of how participants treat them. Conflicts such as Sri Lanka or Northern Ireland, which at one level first appear as domestic conflicts involving two or more parties within a single state, also involve additional states as one or both sides appeals for outside support for its claims or material assistance in its campaign.
3. Sometimes differences in interests and identities can push a conflict in one direction or another. Often, however, there are some interests and interpretations which work in one direction and some which work in the other. In addition, most ethnic communities themselves are sufficiently heterogeneous that there are factions within any group for whom the forces for accommodation are relatively high and those for whom escalation are more important.
4. D'Andrade (1984: 88) points out the radical shift from the view of culture as behaviour which could be understood within a stimulus–response framework and culture as systems of meaning is found in a number of fields. For a more complete discussion of culture as meanings and symbols see the excellent discussions in Schweder and LeVine (1984).
5. While culture involves shared 'structures of meaning', to understand how meanings can be shared Strauss (1992) and D'Andrade (1992) argue we need to consider the cultural assumptions (what they call internalized schema) people employ to derive meaning from events, and the psychocultural dynamics involved in rendering events meaningful. While schemas may be widely shared in a culture, LeVine (1984) makes the important point that common understandings of the symbols and representations they communicate means there is not necessarily a problem with within-cultural variation in thought, feeling and behaviour (1984: 68). In addition, Strauss cautions that while there may be some variation in schemas across individuals in the same culture, even those with very similar schemas may not internalize exactly the same things, and that the ambiguity of metaphor produces variation in responses (Strauss, 1992: 10–11).
6. Volkan (1988), drawing on Freud, uses the phrase 'the narcissism of minor differences' to describe the situation where what seem to be small objective differences between groups or individuals take on large emotional, and political significance.
7. This does not deny the effect of individual differences within any cultural community. Surely there will be people who are more or less assertive, ambitious, or pugnacious in any setting, and often this makes a difference in understanding response to the actions of others. Knowing something about the cultural context in which they are located will tell us something about how such traits will be valued and how they can affect behaviour.

The Cultural Dynamics of Ethnic Conflict 183

8. Axelrod's rules favour players seeking absolute rather than relative gains over opponents over time. Winners never beat an opponent in any given round, but do best over all rounds played. These 'cultural' rules are quite different from those which are accepted in many cultures in such domains as athletic contests.
9. The same can be said about cultural differences among key state level actors. Consider, for example, how little analysis of the escalation prior to the Gulf War is explained in terms of cultural terms, as opposed to the power motivations of key participants. For an excellent overview of the question of the role of problems of international miscommunication due to cultural differences in understanding the meaning of key messages and the motives underlying them see Cohen (1990; 1991).
10. In the nineteenth and early twentieth centuries, Croats and Serbs united under the banner of pan-Slavism and sought the creation of Yugoslavia – a southern Slav state – in the context of the break-up of the Austro-Hungarian and Ottoman empires.
11. Gurr (1993) analyses 233 ethnic conflicts in the world from 1945 to 1990. He categorizes politicized communal groups as national ethnonationalists, indigenous peoples, ethno-classes, militant sects, and advantaged and disadvantaged communal contenders and analyses the extent to which each type of group is likely to pursue political autonomy, political rights other than autonomy, economic rights, and social and cultural rights.
12. Of course, people brought together under the banner of nationality and self-determination can also later emphasize internal differentiation as in the case of Croats and Serbs in Yugoslavia.
13. Ross (1993a: 113–28) provides more detail and examples of differentiating societies such as the Huron of North America and Buganda Kingdom of Africa and generalizers such as the Mbuti of the former Zaire and the Tiv of Nigeria.
14. The argument in this section is based on Ross (1995).
15. See the special issue of *Mind and Human Interaction* (1992) devoted to the question of ethnic and nationalistic traumas.
16. The flip side is the *chosen glory* in which a group perceives triumph over the enemy; this is seen clearly in the Northern Irish Protestant celebration of the Battle of the Boyne in 1689 every 12 July (Cecil, 1993).
17. What is validated is the meaning of a story to participants on each side. This does not necessarily mean the acceptance of such accounts as accurate. The notion of empathy is useful here. It suggests an acceptance of the account as meaningful to the recounter without necessarily meaning agreement from the listener.
18. France has historically been willing to accept immigrants. During the period between the wars, for example, they were the largest immigrant nation in Western Europe. Most came from Spain, Italy and Poland, all Catholic nations, and had little difficulty in acculturating, and consequently were not problematic for the French majority.
19. Beriss (1990) suggests that for some French there were also strong images of the Algerian war invoked as well as the role some Muslim women played as carriers of bombs to be used against the French.

REFERENCES AND BIBLIOGRAPHY

Anderson, B. (1991) *Imagined Communities: Reflections on the Origin and Spread of Nationalism*, revised edition. London and New York: Verso Books.
Avruch, K. and P.W. Black (1991) 'The Cultural Question and Conflict Resolution', *Peace and Change*, 16: 22–45.
Axelrod, R. (1984) *The Evolution of Cooperation*. New York: Basic Books.
Badinter, Elisabeth et al. (1989) 'Profs, ne capitulons pas', *Le Nouvel Observateur* (2–8 November) 1304: 58–9.
Balinkska, Maria (1988) 'SOS-Racisme', *Patterns of Prejudice*. 22: 46–8.
Beriss, David (1990) 'Scarves, Schools, and Segregation: The *Foulard* Affair', *French Politics and Society*. 8: 1–13.
Cecil, R. (1993) 'The Marching Season in Northern Ireland: an Expression of Politico-religious Identity', in S. Macdonald (ed.) *Inside European Identities: Ethnography in Western Europe* (pp. 146–66). Ann Arbor: Berg Publishers.
Cohen, A. (1969) *Custom and Politics in Urban Africa*. Berkeley and Los Angeles: University of California Press.
Cohen, R. (1989) *Culture and Conflict in Israeli–Egyptian Relations*. Bloomington: Indiana University Press.
—— (1991) *Negotiating across Cultures: Communication Obstacles in International Diplomacy*. Washington, DC: USIP Press.
D'Andrade, R.G. (1984) 'Cultural Meaning Systems', in R.A. Schweder and R.A. LeVine (eds) *Culture Theory: Essays on Mind, Self, and Emotion* (pp. 88–119). Cambridge: Cambridge University Press.
—— (1992) 'Schemas and Motivation', in R. G. D'Andrade (eds) *Human Motives and Cultural Models* (pp. 23–44). Cambridge: Cambridge University Press.
Davie, M.R. (1928) *The Evolution of War: A Study of its Role in Early Societies*. New Haven: Yale University Press.
Deutsch, K. et al. (1957) *Political Community and the North Atlantic Area*. Princeton, NJ: Princeton University Press.
Donnelly, Jack (1995) 'Realism and the Academic Study of International Relations', in James Farr, John S. Dryzek and Stephen T. Leonard (eds) *Political Science in History: Research Programs and Political Traditions* (pp. 175–97). Cambridge: Cambridge University Press.
Fornari, F. (1975) *The Psychoanalysis of War*. Bloomington: Indiana University Press.
Gastrow, Peter (1995) *Bargaining for Peace: South Africa and the National Peace Accord*. Washington, DC: United States Institute for Peace Press.
Geertz, C. (1973) 'Religion as a Cultural System', in Clifford Geertz, *The Interpretation of Cultures* (pp. 87–125). New York: Basic Books, Harper Torchbooks.
Grillo, R.D. (1985) *Ideologies and Institutions in Urban France: The Representation of Immigrants*. Cambridge: Cambridge University Press.
Gurr, T.R. (1993) *Minorities at Risk: A Global View of Ethnopolitical Conflicts*. Washington, D.C.: United States Institute for Peace Press.
Horowitz, D. (1985) *Ethnic Groups in Conflict*. Berkeley and Los Angeles: University of California Press.
Huntington, S. (1993) 'The Clash of Civilizations', *Foreign Affairs*, 22–49.

Jervis, R. (1976) *Perception and Misperception in International Politics*. Princeton, NJ: Princeton University Press.

Kelman, H. (1978) 'Israelis and Palestinians: Psychological Prerequisites for Mutual Acceptance', *International Security* 3: 162–86.

—— (1982) 'Creating the Conditions for Israeli–Palestinian negotiations', *Journal of Conflict Resolution* 26: 39–75.

—— (1987) 'The Political Psychology of the Israeli–Palestinian Conflict: How Can We Overcome the Barriers to a Negotiated Solution?', *Political Psychology*. 8: 347–63.

Keohane, R.O. (1983) 'Theory of World Politics: Structural Realism and Beyond', in Ada Finifter (ed.) *Political Science: The State of the Discipline* (pp. 503–40). Washington D.C.: American Political Science Association.

Kertzer, D.I. (1988) *Ritual, Politics, and Power*. New Haven and London: Yale University Press.

LeVine, R.A. (1984) 'Properties of Culture: An Ethnographic View', in R.A. Schweder and R.A. LeVine (eds) *Culture Theory: Essays on Mind, Self, and Emotion* (pp. 67–87). Cambridge: Cambridge University Press.

LeVine, R.A. and D.T. Campbell (1973) *Ethnocentrism: Theories of Conflict, Ethnic Attitudes and Group Behaviour*. New York: John Wiley.

Lustick, I.S. (1993) *Unsettled States, Disputed Lands: Britain and Ireland, France and Algeria, Israel and the West Bank-Gaza*. Ithaca: Cornell University Press.

Mack, J. (1983) 'Nationalism and the Self', *Psychohistory Review*, 2, 47–69.

Meggitt, M. (1976) *Blood is Their Argument: Warfare among the Mae Enga of New Guinea*. Palo Alto: Mayfield.

Mind and Human Interaction (1992) 'Probing Ethnic and Nationalistic Traumas', Vol. 3, No. 3.

Montville, J.V. (1990) 'The Psychological Roots of Ethnic and Sectarian Terrorism', in V.D. Volkan, D.A. Julius and J.V. Montville (eds) *The Psychodynamics of International Relationships. Volume I: Unofficial Diplomacy at Work* (pp. 163–80). Lexington, MA: Lexington Books.

Northrup, T.A. (1989) 'The Dynamic of Identity in Personal and Social Conflict', in L. Kriesberg, T.A. Northrup and S.J. Thorson (eds) *Intractable Conflicts and Their Transformation* (pp. 55–82). Syracuse: Syracuse University Press.

Ross, M.H. (1993a) *The Culture of Conflict: Interests, Interpretations and Disputing in Comparative Perspective*. New Haven: Yale University Press.

—— (1993b) *The Management of Conflict: Interests, Interpretations and Disputing in Comparative Perspective*. New Haven: Yale University Press

—— (1995) 'Psycho-cultural Interpretation Theory and Peacemaking in Ethnic Conflicts', *Political Psychology*. 16: 523–44.

—— (1997) 'The Relevance of Culture for the Study of Political Psychology and Ethnic Conflict', *Political Psychology*. 18: 299–336.

Ross, M.H. and D.T. Campbell (1989) 'The Role of Ethnocentrism in Intergroup Conflict and Peacemaking: A Collaborative Integration of Theories'. Unpublished research proposal.

Ross, M.H. and J.R. Rothman (forthcoming) 'The Conflict Management Implications of Major Theories of Ethnic Conflict'. Special paper. Kandy, Sri Lanka: Institute for Comparative Ethnic Studies.

Safran, William (1985) 'The Mitterrand Regime and its Ethnocultural Accomodation', *Comparative Politics*. 18: 41–63.
Schemla, Elisabeth (1989) 'Jospin: Accueillez les Foulards!', *Le Nouvel Observateur*. 1303: 78–9.
Schneider, Robert (1989) 'Immigrés: L'Enquête qui Dérange', *Nouvel Observateur*. 1307: 72–3.
Schweder, R.A. and R.A. LeVine (eds) (1984) *Culture Theory: Essays on Mind, Self, and Emotion*. Cambridge: Cambridge University Press.
Sparks, Allister (1984) 'The Secret Revolution'. *New Yorker*, 11 April: 57–78.
Spiro, M.E. (1984) 'Some Reflections on Cultural Determinism and Relativism with Special Reference to Emotion and Reason', in R.A. Schweder and R.A. LeVine (eds). *Culture Theory: Essays on Mind, Self, and Emotion* (pp. 323–46). Cambridge: Cambridge University Press.
—— (1987) 'Culture and Human Nature', in *Culture and Human Nature: Theoretical Papers of Melford E. Spiro* (pp. 3–31). Chicago: University of Chicago Press.
Stohl, M. (1980) 'The Nexus of Civil and International Conflict', in T.R. Gurr (ed.) *Handbook of Political Conflict* (pp. 297–330). New York: Free Press.
Strauss, C. (1992) 'Models and Motives', in R.G.D'Andrade (eds) *Human Motives and Cultural Models* (pp. 1–20). Cambridge: Cambridge University Press.
Turner, J.C. (1988) *Rediscovering the Social Group: a Self-categorization Theory*. Oxford: Basil Blackwell.
van den Berghe, P.L. (1981) *The Ethnic Phenomenon*. New York: Elsevier.
Volkan, V.D. (1988) *The Need to Have Enemies and Allies: From Clinical Practice to International Relationships*. New York: Jason Aronson.
—— (1991) 'On "Chosen trauma" ', *Mind and Human Interaction* 3: 13.
Waltz, K.N. (1959) *Man, the State and War*. New York: Columbia University Press.
Weber, E. (1976) *Peasants into Frenchmen: The Modernization of Rural France, 1870–1914*. Stanford: Stanford University Press.
Wilkenfeld, J. (1973) 'Domestic and Foreign Conflict', in J. Wilkenfeld (ed.) *Conflict Behaviour and Linkage Politics* (pp. 107–23). New York: David McKay.

9 Cultural Aspects of Peacekeeping: Notes on the Substance of Symbols
Robert A. Rubinstein

In 1957, following the truce which ended the Suez War, the United Nations deployed its first peacekeeping force to monitor the separation of Egyptian and Israeli troops in Gaza and in the Sinai. On the first evening that the United Nations Emergency Force (UNEF) was deployed in Gaza, UNEF troops sprayed with machinegun fire a minaret from which a *muezzin* was calling the faithful to prayer. The UNEF soldiers, not understanding Arabic or Islam, had mistaken this as a call for civil disobedience.[1] Ten years later UNEF withdrew from Gaza and the Sinai at the behest of the Egyptian President Nasser. This withdrawal was a key factor leading to the June 1967 Arab-Israeli War and was widely cited as evidence of the failure of the United Nations' foray into the field of peacekeeping. Further, it set off a continuing debate about what Nasser's statements and actions *really* meant, underscoring the importance of cultural questions to the establishment and success of peacekeeping.[2]

Since this inauspicious event the United Nations has organized dozens of peacekeeping missions, in all hemispheres of the globe. In 1988 the significant contribution of these efforts to the maintenance of peace and international security was recognized when the UN peacekeeping forces were collectively awarded the Nobel Peace prize. Since that award there have been many changes in the world, including the dissolution of the Soviet Union and the increasing gravity of interethnic conflicts.

Peacekeeping missions have traditionally been deployed to separate fighting groups that are motivated to cease their military conflict, to maintain a buffer zone between these groups and to monitor the subsequent ceasefire, however imperfect this may have been. Since the late 1980s, peacekeeping missions have been contemplated, and some actually deployed, which create new roles for peacekeeping, like the monitoring of local elections, the delivery of humanitarian aid and the mediation of civil conflicts at more local levels.[3] The renewed promise that multilateral peacekeeping operations appears to hold is widely attributed to the end of the Cold War and the opportunity that this affords for the construction of a 'new world order'. It is said that the end of the Cold War will bring about an era of cooperation in the United Nations Security Council which will make for a 'virtually unanimous international constituency for promoting the concept of international authority through consensus and joint action, conciliation, diplomatic pressure, and where necessary, peacekeeping operations to monitor and tranquilise the area of conflict'.[4] Indeed, peacekeeping is being widely cited as perhaps the major instrument of diplomacy available to the United Nations for insuring peace and international security.[5]

There is no doubt that the change in relations between the 'big powers' has had a salutary effect on international relations in general. Yet, it seems to me that discussions of the promise of peacekeeping are being carried out in an idiom that perpetuates a limited view of intergroup relations that unfortunately dominated international relations during the Cold War. Elsewhere I have argued that foreign policy establishments – especially those of the 'big powers' – had institutionalized a shortsighted view of the kinds of information necessary for wise decision-making.[6] Mary LeCron Foster and I showed how this institutionalized view led to outcomes that were often contrary to those intended by the policies that had brought them about. I further argued that the policies themselves were unrealistic because they did not integrate an understanding of the social and cultural dynamics of the groups in conflict.[7] One point of this work was to suggest that anthropological analysis could provide a much needed corrective because anthropologists learn about a group's system of implicit meanings by listening to and observing the ways group members express themselves. In doing this we seek to understand a group's symbolic environment and learn how symbols are manipulated. We see how some symbols evoke powerful affective and cognitive responses from group members.[8]

A hallmark of the views of the international security communities that we examined was a tendency to arrive at models and methods that were intended to be applied interchangeably to different problem situations.[9] Moreover, when local knowledge seemed necessary to qualify the formal models, it too often came in an ethnocentric, self-absorbed form. One striking example of this is a RAND study of constraints on American policy in relation to conflicts in the Third World which are largely instances of ethnic conflict. The report treats the policy constraints from a military perspective and, although it is 130 pages long, cites not a single local concern, focusing instead on supposed Soviet or Chinese interests.[10] This idiom of ethnocentric, formal analyses focused on military concerns is being extended to discussions of the new roles that United Nations peacekeeping forces might assume now that the Cold War is over. Put simply, many analysts in the international affairs community are moving to extend its methods and models to the all too common ethnic and other local-level conflicts that now hold our attention, despite the failure of those approaches to treat adequately the social dynamics of conflicts during the Cold War. This movement is seen in at least two areas. First, in discussions which seek to define new rules for United Nations peacekeeping in a 'new world order', the concept of *collective security* is increasingly being glossed as the need for the United Nations to field a militarily effective force for imposing order. Second, models of strategic negotiation that in the past have produced fundamentally flawed agreements are being extended to problems of ethnic conflicts and preventive diplomacy.[11]

It is wrong to try to understand the recent flourishing in the prospects of multilateral peacekeeping in the old idiom of international affairs. Because discussions in international affairs often focus on dramatic, high-profile issues of broad policy scope, it may seem difficult to see why attention ought to be paid to the rather mundane (and apparently trivial) anthropological concern with culture and symbolism.[12] I argue that, in contrast, the conditions necessary for the establishment and success of peacekeeping are to be found in large measure in the smaller, ordinary activities of daily life.

The position developed in this chapter is part of an analysis which seeks a revitalized role for culture in international affairs by updating the way culture is treated in analyses. Currently, in most instances where culture is considered in international affairs discussions, it is taken to be relatively stable patterns of behaviour, actions and customs. I discussed in detail elsewhere the reasons for the use of this view of culture in the international affairs literature: the 'culture as behaviour' view characterized anthropological and sociological thought during the post-Second World War period up until about 1960 and fitted particularly well with the then emerging paradigm of political realism.[13] In the past 30 years, however, anthropological analyses have shifted emphasis and recognized the fundamental role of meaning construction, symbolism and rituals in human social life. The result is a view of 'culture as meaning' system. R.G. d'Andrade, for instance, sees:

culture as consisting of learned systems of meaning, communicated by means of natural language and other symbol systems, having representational, directive, and affective functions, and capable of creating cultural entities and particular senses of reality. Through these systems of meaning, groups of people adapt to their environment and structure interpersonal activities.[14]

There have been many attempts to codify formal definitions of culture during the past 50 years.[15] These efforts have not been particularly fruitful, in part because, as LeVine points out, 'clarification [of culture] is only possible through ethnography'.[16] The culture as meaning view, then, requires that analysis proceeds by examining social life as a communicative construction and enactment of meaning, and gives prominence to methods which explore the dynamics of the symbolic system.[17]

In addition to describing some of the symbolic material of peacekeeping, I describe some activities, especially rituals, that help shape social cognition in relation to peacekeeping and international affairs. Ritual behaviours are: (1) conventionalized, i.e. their performance adheres to some specific set of rules which cannot be easily breached; (2) repetitive, both in their performance and their occurrence; (3) essentially social, i.e. they evoke communal experience; (4) emotionally involving, because they shape participants' affective images of themselves and of others; and (5) convey meaning on several levels simultaneously.[18] Of particular interest with regards to peacekeeping are rites of reversal. These are ritualized activities that induce ideological shifts so that the impossible or unthought of becomes possible and acceptable. I argue here that the proper understanding of the emergence and potential for the continuation of peacekeeping as a respected instrument of diplomacy depends on recognizing the crucial role of symbolic forms of representation and behaviour in shaping political perceptions about and within peacekeeping missions. I will show in a preliminary way how the legitimacy of peacekeeping in general, and of its ability to play a nonpartisan role in mediating conflicts in particular, results from the symbolic transformation of the political contexts within which peacekeeping is carried out. In large measure, peacekeeping has attained, and may retain, its legitimacy by restructuring the context of political action through developing and manipulating symbolic representations of international consensus and joint action and by elaborating and repeating ritual behaviour which reinforces these representations. There are many levels at which the use of symbols and ritualized behaviour effects ideological shifts in relation to peacekeeping. Among these, for example, can be the 'temporary ceding' of national sovereignty over a nation's military when mission command and control functions are held by officers from another country, the sharing of information and daily duties with troops from countries that are potential adversaries, and the renunciation of military force by military units. My comments in this chapter are intended to set out in a preliminary way how a meaningful link might be made between such seemingly mundane activities and the more sweeping policy concerns involved in constructing international order.

SYMBOL AND RITUAL IN PEACEKEEPING

The most obvious sense in which symbols have invested legitimacy in peacekeeping is that the blue beret or blue helmet is now widely recognized as denoting UN peacekeeping troops. This was not always so. Rather the creation of this most durable symbol of peacekeeping was constructed out of the hurried need to distinguish UN troops from those of the other armed forces they were separating during the 1956 Suez crisis, when surplus allied combat helmet liners were painted blue.[19] Following on the *ad hoc* origin of this and other peacekeeping symbolism, the legitimacy accorded to peacekeeping today has grown through nearly 40 years of relatively ordinary symbolic representation and ritual repetition.

The substance of symbolic action in day-to-day transformations of political perceptions is often overlooked because it is not especially glamorous. Likewise, for peacekeeping, it is easy to overlook the importance of symbols and rituals for legitimating peacekeeping because its symbols and rituals are individually unremarkable.[20] Yet, it is not from the isolated symbols and rituals that the legitimacy of peacekeeping is constructed. Rather, the power of peacekeeping symbolism derives from the deployment of symbols and rituals in a variety of arenas, and from the symbolic restructuring this often entails.

In order to illustrate this, I briefly describe some of the symbols and rituals which have channelled perceptions of peacekeeping during the decade prior to 1992. The material presented is drawn from data collected during an ongoing research project on cultural aspects of peacekeeping, begun in 1987. The field sites for this project have been diverse: from formal diplomatic settings in New York, Vienna, Cairo, Jerusalem and elsewhere to isolated outposts in the Sinai dessert. I have had formal and informal interviews with scores of diplomats and hundreds of military personnel who serve or served with United Nations or other peacekeeping missions.

I do not intend here to give an exhaustive account of the operation of ritual and symbol in peacekeeping; my purpose is exploratory and suggestive. Here I propose that in discussing the effect of peacekeeping on political relations (and of political relations on peacekeeping), it is hard to separate its material success from its symbolic success. To some degree, the descriptions of peacekeeping ritual and symbolism presented here are selective and a composite of many missions. Because of its unique role in UN peacekeeping, I have concentrated my study on the United Nations Truce Supervision Organization (UNTSO) and on its several observer groups, which therefore figure disproportionately in my descriptions.[21] Observer groups and peacekeeping forces differ in their missions and in their formal organization, and these differences are important.[22] Nevertheless, to a great degree, both rely on an overlapping set of rituals and symbolism for their legitimacy and coherence.

The ritual symbolism of peacekeeping is evident in the conventionalized actions through which peacekeeping missions are created, such as: those of the Security Council consultations and resolutions authorizing missions; the tasks assigned to peacekeeping troops, the uniforms, insignia and accoutrements associated with peacekeeping in general and with particular missions; and the social activities organized under the auspices of peacekeeping missions.[23]

Peacekeeping involves the use of military personnel to establish and maintain order. The diplomatic rationale often expressed is that by bringing together troops from many nations to work under one command, the deployment of a peacekeeping mission directs international attention on a crisis area. The deployment of a peacekeeping mission is thus said to be a visible demonstration of international consensus and joint action. In fact, establishing a peacekeeping mission may mean many different things to different people, because each may have a different political understanding of the situation.[24] Peacekeeping operations take place in the context of the daily lives of multiple communities: diplomatic, military and local. Each of these communities embodies culturally constituted ways of behaving and understanding the objectives and practices of the operation. Sometimes the intersection of these cultural spheres is problematic. In order to appreciate fully how peacekeeping has become a legitimate instrument of diplomacy, it is important to understand the problems entailed by the overlapping of the multiple cultural spheres concerned and the ritual and symbolic mechanisms that to a great extent resolve them.

For instance, the meaning of serving in a Middle East mission of UNTSO for a military officer may reflect a commitment to a vision of global order based on universal principles of social justice. Equally, however, that service may represent, among other things: (1) an opportunity for financial gain; (2) a chance to see the Holy Land; (3) a strategy in planning for career advancement; (4) an opportunity to improve one's skills as a foreign area officer; (5) a chance to see how one would react under fire; or (6) an unfortunate posting. One of the most immediate problems facing the institution of peacekeeping then is the need to integrate individuals with diverse backgrounds, understandings and agendas into a quasi-corporate entity: 'the mission'. In such situations, the use of symbols which can carry multiple meanings is an extremely useful tool for coordinating perceptions.[25] Since symbols represent and unify disparate meanings they can be used to embody and bring together diverse ideas. Through symbolic representation, 'these various ideas are not just simultaneously elicited but also interact with one another so that they become associated together in the individual's mind'.[26]

United Nations Military Observers (UNMOs) in UNTSO wear the blue beret and display the UN flag. These symbols serve to integrate the local activity of the mission with higher levels of political organization. More locally, however, UNMOs share a number of symbols which serve to establish an individual's identification with the group. For instance, each wears on his uniform a badge unique to the mission. These badges are designed specifically for the mission and often are locally produced. These badges help to integrate members from many different national services into the mission. All denote the international nature of the operation by including reference to the United Nations through its symbols or in words. Sometimes, the integrative task is explicit and the badge includes symbols of national identity as well. Wearing these symbols of the mission helps UNMOs to be recognized as a member of 'a group' and integrates them into it. For instance, in 1990, the People's Republic of China began to contribute troops to UNTSO. Nine officers joined the observer groups. At one, Observer Detachment Damascus (ODD), the Chinese presence led to the redesign of the mission badge. Previously the ODD badge showed the UN symbol as well as elements of the French, Soviet and American flags. To this was added the Chinese flag.

These and other symbols help integrate individuals into peacekeeping missions. Such symbols help to establish continuity in the mission despite changes in the political environment or shifts in the purpose of the organization. After the 1973 war, UNTSO deployed a group of observers to monitor the military situation in the Sinai. This Sinai Observer Group (SOG) worked with the second United Nations Emergency Force (UNEFII). Following the Camp David Accords UNEFII had to withdraw. The Egyptian government asked UNTSO to maintain its presence in Egypt, and the Sinai Observer Group was reorganized as Observer Group Egypt (OGE). The operational tasks assigned to the OGE differed substantially from those of the SOG, yet the continuing presence of an observer group in the mission area projects an image of continuity of concern and purpose locally and internationally.

Another symbolic means of establishing continuity for the mission as operational realities change is in the names used to describe revised duties. Although OGE no longer has significant official observing and reporting functions, its members still go 'on patrol,' and they do so from 'OPs', as did the SOG, but now patrols have no operational elements beyond their execution and they originate from outposts rather than observation posts. Patrolling and manning OPs are two activities that are shared with all other UNTSO observer groups as well, though in other groups patrolling includes the operational responsibilities of inspecting troop concentrations, monitoring ceasefire agreements and reporting on these. Patrols and OPs thus link the local activities of UNMOs and OGE with those of other groups, providing for a kind of internal continuity.

The symbols and ceremonies used in peacekeeping are not original to it. Rather as peacekeeping has developed, well-known symbols from other spheres of social life – especially from military organizations and some from family and community life – have been appropriated and invested with new meanings. This borrowing improves rather than diminishes the efficacy of these symbols because when encountering them people draw on their stock of past experiences and associations with such symbols.[27]

Symbols are most effective when they are experienced in ritual context. Just as peacekeeping has appropriated symbols from other domains of social life, it has appropriated rituals. Together with symbols which signal group membership and organizational continuity, life in an Observer Group is marked by activities that are ritually delineated. It is not an exaggeration to say that much of the activity of an observer group follows a ritual cycle which marks off various life-events, like comings and goings and changes in status. It is a fact of life in an Observer Group that people are constantly arriving and departing. This is partly related to movement between the station headquarters and week-long OP duty. These kinds of arrivals and departures are marked by regular events within the station including, before leaving, a general briefing and planning of logistics for the week and, upon returning, debriefing and perhaps a free drink at the station bar. It is interesting that OP duties conform neatly to the steps of rites of passage: separation, transition, incorporation. These rituals have powerful effects on those experiencing them, adjusting their cognitive and affective perceptions and integrating them into a corporate group.[28]

In part the constant movement also results from that fact that the tour of duty for officers serving as UNMOs with UNTSO is relatively short, varying in length of posting at a particular Observer Group from six months to three years. Although total length of UN service varies from country to country, in the Middle East UNMOs are usually required to spend half of their tour posted in an Arab country and half posted in Israel. Because of this, every week new UNMOs arrive and current members leave from a given observer group. The military custom of *hail and farewell* has been appropriated in the ritual cycle of the observer groups in a fashion directed at incorporating UNMOs into the larger group at the station (not just into their country detachment).

The military custom acknowledging arriving and departing individuals in a public ritual has not, however, simply been transferred unchanged to the peacekeeping context. Rather, it has been reinterpreted and fitted into the ritual cycle of the group. At OGE, for instance, the hail and farewell is part of a weekly rite of intensification which serves to reinforce identification with the group. Each Friday evening the observer group assembles for a 'happy hour', which is sponsored by one of the national contingents.[29] These have a regular structure throughout the month and each 'happy hour' has a regular internal structure. The hail and farewell takes place in the context of this repetitive group activity. Not only are arriving and departing members identified, but the activity is used to structure and reinforce perceptions of the nature of OGE and of UNTSO. For instance, in addition to providing information about arriving members, the happy hour is also an occasion where it is stressed that the UNMO is entering the 'OGE family' or the 'OGE community'. During farewells there is nearly always explicit reference to the ways in which the departing UNMO contributed to dissolving the boundaries of nationality and of service branch between himself and others in the group. Metaphors of family and community are woven throughout these occasions and serve to focus perceptions of the group. Since local diplomatic and military personnel are frequent guests at these activities, their perceptions of OGE are also shaped in part by this shared experience.

The themes supported by the ritual cycle of the local group also link the activity at the station to the larger UNTSO organization. In the magazine *UNTSO News*, for instance, which is distributed to UNMOs and to a limited number of local diplomats and military officers, there are repeated references to the metaphorical peacekeeping family. The message redundantly delivered is that UNTSO is a stable organization, with historical continuity, that has bridged gaps in national understandings in order to provide neutral, nonpartisan observers of the political situation in the Middle East and elsewhere.

Traditional military ritual and symbolism is appropriated and given new meanings in the context of peacekeeping. This allows for those who serve in them and for those who are aware of them for the elaboration of a myth of stability, continuity, joint action and neutrality. In addition to the structuring of perceptions that result from activities within peacekeeping missions, additional legitimacy has resulted from the cognitive restructuring entailed by peacekeeping missions collectively as rites of reversal. The use of unarmed military personnel for peacekeeping missions has not simply been logistically useful. Rather, because it involves a certain amount of ritualized activity to authorize and field a peacekeeping mission, physical separation from their national armed forces and ceding of command sovereignty to the force commander, the use of military personnel buttresses a system of cultural reversals. These reversals symbolically allay fears of domination and promote the restructuring of political perceptions to legitimate actions that would otherwise be unacceptable.[30] Through the use of symbols and rituals the instrument of UN peacekeeping develops and maintains an authority and legitimacy that it would otherwise lack. This makes it possible to substitute into the position of 'neutral observer' a changing set of individuals each of whom may personally hold a partisan view.

PEACEKEEPING AND THE SUBSTANCE OF SYMBOLS

In calculating the effect of peacekeeping on political relations it is hard to distinguish its 'real' success from its symbolic success. While some peacekeeping missions have been very successful in mediating conflicts, many of the peacekeeping missions deployed by the United

Nations have been less successful in concrete outcome. In those partial successes, which include some of the most prominent missions, the problems which the peacekeeping mission were to address have remained unresolved or even worsened.

Three examples of the partial success of United Nations peacekeeping will suffice here.[31] The United Nations Peacekeeping Force in Cyprus (UNFICYP) was established in March 1964 to prevent Greek and Turkish Cypriot inter-communal fighting. In the nearly 30 years since that time the Force has maintained a presence on the island, but order has not always prevailed. Indeed, during this period, relations between the communities periodically have deteriorated and fighting requiring stronger UNFICYP action has broken out. In 1974 ceasefire lines were redrawn, and the Force now patrols a 180-kilometre long buffer zone between the sides. Although attempts to mediate the conflict continue, with occasional promise of success, it seems unlikely that a solution to the root problem will be worked out in the near term. What UNFICYP does is provide an administrative structure and a measure of calm amidst the general belligerence.

The United Nations Interim Force in Lebanon (UNIFIL) is a second example. Established in 1978 following Israeli incursions into southern Lebanon, its mission is to confirm the withdrawal of Israeli forces from the area, to establish peace there and to assist the Lebanese government in regaining effective control of the area. Rather than withdrawing, in 1982 Israeli troops moved beyond the UNIFIL mission area. Now, Israeli troops move through the mission area at will and the political situation in southern Lebanon is inherently unstable. While the Force has not succeeded in achieving its mission, its 5800 troops now try to contain violence as best they can and to provide humanitarian assistance in the area. Over the years of its existence UNIFIL troops have been drawn into the local social, economic and political life. According to one observer, 'UNIFIL has come to function as a pseudo-government for the south whose chances of being replaced by the appropriate authorities in the foreseeable future seems remote.'[32]

The United Nations Military Observer Group in India and Pakistan (UNMOGIP) was set up in January 1949. Its operational charge included observing and reporting the India–Pakistan ceasefire line and investigating violations of that ceasefire. As recently as Autumn 1989, Sir Brian Urquhart described UNMOGIP as 'a backwater of peacekeeping'.[33] Within the following year renewed fighting in the area forced a reassessment of the nature of that mission.

Since the success of peacekeeping missions has been partial at best, the perception of the success of peacekeeping depends largely on the symbolic restructuring of the field of political action that has been achieved through the use of symbols and rituals. To the extent that this has been achieved it has been accomplished through the elaboration of symbols and activities that assert the consensual, nonpartisan nature of missions. In contrast to this ideal, individuals serving in missions have strong personal political feelings. These views are sometimes affected by service in a mission area and also affect service there as well. UNMOs in OGE, for instance, report a wide range of reactions to the activities they witness while serving with the observer group and in other UNTSO Middle East stations. It is widely acknowledged by UNMOs that their views of the local political situation have changed during their UN service. For instance, UNMOs serving with UNTSO in the Middle East report that their experiences restructured their understanding of Arab–Israeli affairs. Most frequently reported was a shift away from a pro-Israeli stand, held prior to UNTSO and UNIFIL service, to a more neutral or pro-Arab position. These shifts are based on a variety of specific experiences, including observation of the relative strengths of Arab and Israeli militaries, disparagement of UN missions by Israeli border guards and military officials, and interactions with local populations. In addition, it is clear that these altered views are carried home and influence public opinion there, especially for Western observers, like those from Canada, Ireland and the Scandinavian countries.[34]

The fact that UN peacekeeping as an institution is perceived as independent of those who make it up and that it is viewed as implementing joint consensus and nonpartisan action allows the institution to be accepted as a fair witness. This perception derives at least as much from the symbolism and ritualization of peacekeeping as it does from the mixed record of the success of various missions. The legitimacy of peacekeeping depends upon a radical restructuring of political perceptions in such a way that the unthinkable is rendered plausible. Moreover, because this reframing is emotionally charged it must be done in a way that insulates it from ordinary critiques. A mechanism for this process – ritual reversal – is found in nearly all human societies.[35] Ritual reversals provide culturally legitimate social space in which actions are sanctioned that would at other times not be allowed.[36] In the case of UN peacekeeping, the rituals in the individual missions and in the Security Council create the ritualized social space where activities, like the surrender of control over elements of a nation's armed forces, are possible.

CIVIL CONFLICT: CHALLENGES FOR PEACEKEEPING

Among the more intransigent conflict situations for peacekeeping are civil conflicts, especially ethnic conflict below the national level. Such civil conflicts are the most common source of warfare today. These often lead to situations in which civilian populations are at great risk due to the effects of conflict on food supplies or access to clean water, and are in need of humanitarian aid. For example, in the south of Sudan war has meant the near cessation of drilling of boreholes for fresh water, exceptionally high infant mortality and prevalent malnutrition among children 12 and younger. In Zimbabwe, from 1978 to 1980, the military destroyed crops, livestock and food supplies as a means of dealing with civil conflict there. This resulted in widespread malnutrition and increased infant and childhood mortality. In Guatemala, civil conflict and military responses to it have distorted the economy causing food costs to soar which resulted in extreme nutritional consequences for the local population.[37] It is in the context of dealing with such civil conflicts that new roles for peacekeeping are being explored.

It is well recognized that such new roles will not be a simple extension of the traditional concept of multilateral peacekeeping. In part this is because traditionally peacekeeping has depended upon obtaining the consent of the parties to the conflict. With this foundation, the myths, symbols and rituals of peacekeeping could be brought to bear on the restructuring of political perceptions. In the situation of civil conflict, obtaining such agreement is often not possible. Furthermore, it is sometimes difficult to determine who speaks for the local belligerents. Additionally, the political environment is made more complex by the intersection of cultural groups. It is thus especially important in contemplating new missions to take account of the important role that ritual symbolism plays in legitimating peacekeeping missions. It is only under the auspices of a peacekeeping organization which has an established reputation as neutral and nonpartisan that such interventions can hope to succeed. This representation depends upon symbolically developing the desired view of political order in which the mission is to operate.

The symbolic restructuring of the field of political action is especially important because neutrality in any given conflict situation is context specific. Neutrality is a social construct. An act that may appear to outsiders to be nonpartisan may be thought highly biased by others. While this may include the traditional peacekeeping activities of observing and reporting, in nontraditional peacekeeping contexts it may apply to the delivery of humanitarian aid.[38] For instance in the Sudan withholding of food and access to humanitarian aid has been used as a weapon in the war between the Muslim north and the non-Muslim south.[39]

It is only in a situation where the particular peacekeeping mission can be symbolically assimilated to an institution with a history of perceived nonpartisan activity that intervention can hope to work. The recent unfortunate intervention in Liberia of the West African Peace-keeping Force (ECOWAS) provides grim evidence of this. ECOWAS was fielded by a consortium of neighbouring countries, the governments of which had a stake in the pacification of Liberia.[40] Conceived as a humanitarian relief effort to a country where people were 'becoming increasingly desperate as food supplies ran out, with no end of fighting in sight',[41] the development of the force paid insufficient attention to the symbolic relations among its troop contributors and the Liberian belligerents. Despite its multilateral nature and even before its first deployment, the West African Peacekeeping Force was perceived as partisan by all of the Liberian belligerents. In part because there was no institutionalized structure for joint neutral action that could be symbolically legitimated, the force was soon embroiled in the local conflict and fought as desperately as the combatants they were meant to disarm. The current UN intervention in Somalia appears to be repeating this experience, in no small measure because of efforts to 'put teeth' into the mission, efforts that are allowing the symbolic legitimacy of the mission to dissolve. This dissolution is evidenced by, among other things, the decreasing willingness of participating nations to submit their troops to joint UN command and control and in the growing belief among some Somalis that the mission is a neo-colonial effort to Christianize their country.

CONCLUSION

Much current political commentary anticipates the onset of a new world order because of the end of the Cold War. As part of this new order, many envisage an increased role for multilateral peacekeeping in the maintenance of international peace and security. In this chapter I have suggested that realizing such a role will depend upon developing an adequate understanding of the role of symbol and ritual in the structuring of political perceptions.

Civil and ethnic conflicts are now the most frequent and important threat to international security.[42] These conflicts have not proved amenable to solution by a 'power politics' which focuses on military power to the exclusion of symbolic and normative considerations.[43] Some analysts have expressed a growing dissatisfaction with the political realist view and there are escalating calls for alternatives to it.[44] Anthropological analyses show that in many instances understanding ethnic and civil conflicts depends upon taking account of the dynamics of cultural meaning systems.[45]

Understanding the prospects for peacekeeping is then a special case of a broader choice that now confronts us. This 'new era' presents us with the opportunity to develop a more complex, complete and adequate view of political relations than that which has prevailed in the past. We can, on the one hand, continue to pursue the understanding of political relations through the technical-rationalist analysis of self-interests embodied in the philosophy and method of political realism. Or, on the other hand, we can develop fuller accounts of the role of culture – and the place of symbols and rituals – in contemporary international affairs. By pursuing this second direction, we can, I hope, develop more satisfactory and humane ways of confronting as well as resolving situations of conflict, both among nations and at more local levels.

NOTES

1. B. Urquhart, *A Life in Peace and War* (New York: Harper and Row, 1987), p. 136.
2. R. Cohen, *Culture and Conflict in Egyptian–Israeli Relations: A Dialogue of the Deaf* (Bloomington, IN: Indiana University Press, 1990), pp. 98–110; I.J. Rikhye, *The Sinai Blunder: Withdrawal of the United Nations Emergency Force Leading to the Six Day War June, 1967* (New Delhi: Oxford and IBH Publishing Company, 1978), p. 240.
3. I.J. Rikhye and K. Skjelsbaek (eds), *The United Nations and Peacekeeping: Results, Limitations and Prospects: Issues in Peacekeeping and Peacemaking* (London: Macmillan, 1990), p. 199; T.G. Weiss (ed.), *Humanitarian Emergencies and Military Help in Africa: Issues in Peacekeeping and Peacemaking* (London: Macmillan, 1990), p. 136; and I.J. Rikhye, *Strengthening UN Peacekeeping: New Challenges and Proposals* (Washington, DC: United States Institute of Peace, 1992), p. 48.
4. B. Urquhart, *Decolonization and World Peace* (Austin, TX: University of Texas Press, 1989), p. 105.

5. C.W. Maynes, 'Containing Ethnic Conflict', *Foreign Affairs* (Vol. 90, No. 3, 1993), pp. 3–21.
6. R.A. Rubinstein and S. Tax, 'Power, Powerlessness, and the Failure of "Political Realism" ', in J. Brøsted, et al. (eds), *Native Power: The Quest for Autonomy and Nationhood of Indigenous People* (Bergen: Universitetsforlaget AS, 1985), pp. 301–8; R.A. Rubinstein, 'International Conflict, Decision-Making, and Anthropology', *Anthropology Today* (Vol. 2, No. 1, 1986), p. 14; and R.A. Rubinstein, 'The Collapse of Strategy: Understanding Ideological Bias in Policy Decisions', in M.L. Foster and R.A. Rubinstein (eds), *Peace and War: Cross-Cultural Perspectives* (New Brunswick, NJ: Transaction Books, 1986), pp. 343–51.
7. R.A. Rubinstein, 'Cultural Analysis and International Security', *Alternatives* (Vol. 13, No. 4, 1988), pp. 529–42; R.A. Rubinstein, 'Ritual Process and Images of the Other in Arms Control Negotiations', *Human Peace* (Vol. 6, No. 2, 1988), pp. 3–7; R.A. Rubinstein, 'Culture, International Affairs and Peacekeeping: Confusing Process and Pattern', *Cultural Dynamics* (Vol. 2, No. 1, 1989), pp. 41–61; R.A. Rubinstein, 'Methodological Challenges in the Ethnographic Study of Multilateral Peacekeeping' Paper presented at the 1989 Annual Meeting of the American Anthropological Association, Washington, DC, 15–19 November; and R.A. Rubinstein, 'Culture and Negotiation', in E.W. Fernea and M.E. Hocking (eds), *The Struggle for Peace: Israelis and Palestinians* (Austin, TX: University of Texas Press, 1992), pp. 116–29.
8. R.A. Rubinstein and M.L. Foster, 'Revitalizing International Security Analysis: Contributions from Culture and Symbolism', in R.A. Rubinstein and M.L. Foster (eds), *The Social Dynamics of Peace and Conflict: Culture in International Security* (Boulder, CO: Westview Press, 1988), pp. 1–14.
9. P.K. Davis and J.A. Winnefeld, *The RAND Strategy Assessment Centre: An Overview and Interim Conclusion about the Utility and Development of Options* (Santa Monica, CA: RAND Corporation, 1983), p. vii.
10. S. Hosmer, *Constraints on U.S. Strategy in Third World Conflict* (Santa Monica, CA: Rand Corporation, 1985), p. 130.
11. C.W. Maynes, *op. cit.*, in note 5, pp. 3–21; and R.A. Rubinstein, 'Culture and Negotiation', *op. cit.* in note 7, pp. 116–29.
12. R.A. Rubinstein and M.L. Foster, *op. cit.* in note 8, pp. 3–5.
13. Political realism is an approach which privileges certain kinds of information in the analysis of political relations. Especially it: (1) treats the state as the unit of analysis; (2) construes useful knowledge as objective fact; (3) treats the state as a rational actor the behaviour of which conforms to the objective realities; and (4) restricts calculations of power and interest to material resources. See Rubinstein, 'Cultural Analysis', *op. cit.*, in note 7, pp. 530–2; and Y.H. Ferguson and R.W. Mansbach, *The Elusive Quest: Theory in International Politics* (Columbia, SC: University of South Carolina Press, 1988), p. 300.
14. R.G. d'Andrade, 'Cultural Meaning Systems', in R. Shweder and R. LeVine (eds), *Culture Theory: Essays on Mind, Self, and Emotion* (Cambridge: Cambridge University Press, 1984), pp. 88–119. Similarly,

in his *Interpretation of Cultures* (New York: Basic Books, 1973), p. 89, Clifford Geertz defines culture as 'an historically transmitted pattern of meanings embodied in symbols, a system of inherited conceptions expressed in symbolic form by means of which men communicate, perpetuate, and develop their knowledge about and attitudes towards life'.

15. See, for instance, G. Weiss, 'A Scientific Concept of Culture', *American Anthropologist* (Vol. 75, No. 5, 1973), pp. 1376–413.
16. R.A. LeVine, 'Properties of Culture', in R. Shweder and R. LeVine (eds), *loc. cit.*, in note 14, p. 67.
17. For surveys of the importance of symbolism to cultural analysis, see M.L. Foster and S. Brandes (eds), *Symbol as Sense: New Approaches to the Analysis of Meaning* (New York: Academic Press, 1980), p. 416; J.L. Dolgin, D.S. Kemnitzer and D.M. Schneider (eds) *Symbolic Anthropology: A Reader in the Study of Symbols and Meanings* (New York, NY: Columbia University Press, 1977), p. 523; and R. Shweder and R.A. LeVine (eds.) *loc. cit.*, in note 14, p. 359.
18. For discussions of the nature of ritual symbolism see, E. d'Aquili et al., *The Spectrum of Ritual* (New York: Columbia University Press, 1979); C.D. Laughlin et al., 'The Ritual Transformation of Experience', *Studies in Symbolic Interaction* (Vol. 7, No. A, 1986), pp. 107–36; and D.I. Kertzer, *Ritual, Politics, and Power* (New Haven, CN: Yale University Press, 1988), p. 235.
19. B. Urquhart, *op. cit.*, in note 1, p. 134.
20. This is equally true whether considering the construction of legitimacy for local populations, diplomats, the international community generally or peacekeeping troops themselves. For discussions of the importance of ritual in international diplomacy and political life, see R.A. Rubinstein, 'Ritual Process', *op. cit.*, in note 7; and D. Kertzer, *op. cit.*, in note 18.
21. I am grateful to the International Peace Academy (IPA) for permitting me to conduct research through their training seminars and meetings which bring together senior diplomats and military officers involved in multilateral peacekeeping. From January 1989 until June 1992 I conducted an intensive study of the United Nations Truce Supervision Organization (UNTSO), especially Observer Group Egypt (OGE), which involved participant observation, a questionnaire survey and formal and informal interviews of Military Observers, United Nations personnel and regional diplomats. I am grateful for the support and encouragement given to this project by General Indar Jit Rihkye, former President of the IPA, Lieutenant General Martin Vadset, formerly Chief of Staff of the UNTSO, Lieutenant Colonel Alen D. Clarke, formerly Chief OGE, and Lieutenant Commander James Robinson, formerly Senior Liaison Officer United Nations Liaison Office in Cairo. The methodological challenges of the ethnographic study of peacekeeping are described in R.A. Rubinstein, 'Methodological Challenges', *op. cit.*, in note 7.
22. See I.J. Rikhye, *The Theory and Practice of Peacekeeping* (New York: St. Martin's Press, 1984), p. 255.

23. R.A. Rubinstein, 'Culture, International Affairs and Peacekeeping', *op. cit.*, in note 7.
24. Ibid., pp. 52–4.
25. E. d'Aquili et al., *op. cit.*, in note 18, p. 29.
26. D. Kertzer, *op. cit.*, in note 18, p. 11. See also V. Turner, 'Ritual Aspects of Conflict Control in African Micropolitics', in M. Swartz, V. Turner and A. Tuden (eds), *Political Anthropology* (Chicago, IL: Aldine, 1966), pp. 239–46; V. Turner, *The Forest of Symbols* (Ithaca, NY: Cornell University Press, 1967); and V. Turner, *The Ritual Process* (Chicago, IL: Aldine, 1969).
27. D. Kertzer, *op. cit.*, in note 18, p. 45.
28. E. d'Aquili, et al., *op. cit.*, in note 18, pp. 250–1.
29. A fuller description of the happy hour cycle and of the internal organization of OGE is presented in R.A. Rubinstein, 'Methodological Challenges in the Ethnographic Study of Peacekeeping', *op. cit.*, in note 7.
30. M.L. Foster, 'Reversal Theory and the Institutionalisation of War', in J. Kerr, S. Murgatroyd and M. Apter (eds), *Advances in Reversal Theory* (Amsterdam: Swets and Zeitlinger, 1993), pp. 67–74; and D.I. Kertzer, *op. cit.*, in note 18, p. 132.
31. See I.J. Rikhye, *op. cit.*, in note 22, for details of some of the various UN missions.
32. M. Heiberg, 'Peacekeepers and Local Populations: Some Comments on UNIFIL', in I.J. Rikhye and K. Skjelsbaek (eds), *The United Nations and Peacekeeping: Results, Limitations and Prospects* (London: Macmillan, 1990), p. 151. See also E.A. Erskine, *Mission with UNIFIL: An African Soldier's Reflections* (New York: St. Martin's Press, 1989).
33. Personal communication, Cairo, October 1989.
34. See also M. Heiberg, *op. cit.*, in note 32. The relation of these shifts in political perception to their service in UNTSO and afterward is itself an interesting case study of the role of symbols in shaping political perceptions.
35. M.L. Foster, 'The Growth of Symbolism in Culture', in M.L. Foster and S. Brandes (eds), *Symbol as Sense: New Approaches to the Analysis of Meaning* (New York: Academic Press, 1980), pp. 367–97. For discussion of ritualized role reversal in human societies, see also E. Leach, *Rethinking Anthropology* (London: Oxford University Press, 1961), pp. 132–6.
36. See M. Bloch, 'Ritual Symbolism and the Nonrepresentation of Society', in M.L. Foster and S. Brandes (eds), *loc. cit.*, in note 35, pp. 93–5.
37. R.A. Rubinstein and S.D. Lane, 'International Health and Development', in T.M. Johnson and C.F. Sargent (eds), *Medical Anthropology: a Handbook of Theory and Method* (New York: Greenwood Press, 1990), p. 380.
38. See R. Cohen, *op. cit.*, in note 2.
39. R.A. Rubinstein and S.D. Lane, *op. cit.*, in note 37.
40. ECOWAS was not a United Nations Force. Scant attention appears to have been paid to forming the ECOWAS troops into a corporate group independent of national governments and their interests. Indeed, accounts of the development of ECOWAS often highlighted the nation-

alities of different troops. ECOWAS's failure undercuts analyses which contend that the success of the Multinational Force and Observers in the Sinai is directly due to its independence from the United Nations bureaucracy.
41. *The Times*, 4 August 1990, p. 22.
42. E.E. Rice, *Wars of the Third Kind: Conflict in Underdeveloped Societies* (Berkeley, CA: University of California Press, 1988), p. 186.
43. R.A. Rubinstein and S. Tax, *op. cit.*, in note 6; and R.A. Rubinstein, 'Cultural Analysis', *op. cit.*, in note 7.
44. See for example, D.P. Moynihan, *Pandaemonium: Ethnicity in International Politics* (Oxford: Oxford University Press, 1993), p. 22; and Z. Brzezinski, *Out of Control: Global Turmoil on the Eve of the 21st Century* (New York: Charles Scribner, 1993), p. 240.
45. See the papers in R.A. Rubinstein and M.L. Foster (eds.), *loc. cit.*, in note 8.

10 Towards an International Theory of State–Non-state Actors: A Grid–Group Cultural Approach
Veronica Ward

The neo-realist construction of IPE [with its] particular reaffirmation of the importance of the state is doubly worrying, for not only are non-state actors pushed into the background in this construction of the international domain, but there is also no place left for investigations of the contribution of 'private actors' in shaping the social structures which lie behind state apparatuses.... Within this straitjacket, one could not go beyond simple categorizations of state apparatuses.... Hence possibilities which were once open for constructing an international political economy capable of linking the changing behavior of states to their evolving social structures fell to others, most especially the historical sociologists.[1]

During the 1980s, non-state, private actors, such as multinational corporations and international banks, disappeared from studies in International Political Economy (IPE), while most attention was focused on the state. The re-emergence of the state as an autonomous, influential actor worthy of theoretical attention was in response to a period of scholarship when, to quote Stephen Krasner, 'students of international relations ... multi-nationalized, transnationalized, bureaucratized, and transgovernmentalized the state until it [had] virtually ceased to exist as an analytic construct.'[2] By the mid-1980s the pendulum had swung back in favour of a state-centric approach; today this perspective is again under assault as scholars attempt to gain a greater understanding of the domestic/international nexus. This study challenges the primacy of the state as an analytical construct. The theory advanced here reintroduces the 'revolutionary' potential identified by Richard Leaver in the opening quotation in the early work of IPE, including non-state actors and 'the possibility of inquiring into the triadic relationship between the form of the state, the structure of the society over which it exercised its theoretical sovereignty, and the patterns of international behaviour that were generated in the interaction of these state–society complexes.'[3]

Unfortunately, efforts to explore the state–society complex – more specifically, to evaluate the relationship between authority and market, between state and non-state actors in the international arena – have foundered on the lack of an adequate framework linking domestic social factors that shape state capabilities and behaviour as well as specific outcomes seen at the global level. What is called for is a theoretical framework that will enable the researcher to classify state–society linkages in such a way as to explain the extent to which any particular state can exercise authority effectively and manipulate and constrain nonstate actors operating beyond its territorial borders. The grid–group cultural theory developed here provides such an explanatory tool.

The remainder of this chapter first discusses the present state of research on the state–society relationship. Thereafter, a presentation of the grid-group approach follows. Any analysis of the potential effectiveness of state policies satisfactorily address the related phenomena of power and authority. In the next section, Nicholas Onuf's work on rules and rule, and the schema developed by Richard Flathman, which nicely complements and reinforces Douglas's approach, is combined with grid–group cultural theory.[4] A brief discussion of the authority–market relationship is followed by a conclusion, which provides an example of the application of this framework. I should note that this example is based on a much larger study in which two cases have been selected to explore the relationship between the domestic and international realm. The two cases focus on Japan and the United States. The substantive issue area chosen is international financial/monetary policy, where the principal non-state actors are commercial banks. In the interests of space, only a few comments will be made about these cases in the conclusion.

THE STATE AND SOCIETY

Debate among scholars over the role of the state is closely tied to the question of the source(s) of control and power. Typically, the question is asked: are these sources located in the state, society, or international system? In the 1960s and 1970s, the period described by Krasner, scholars 'started to peer within the "black box" or "billiard ball" of the state, explicitly or implicitly questioning its autonomy and stressing the degree to which policy outcomes are shaped by domestic political actors and processes.' In addition, the position of the state as an autonomous force was challenged by the perception of an increase in international interdependence.[5] Thus the state was assaulted from 'below' (society) and from 'above' (the international system); its disappearance as an independent player seemed imminent. Work by Katzenstein, Krasner, Nordlinger, Ikenberry and Skocpol, along with the often-cited edited volume by Evans, Rueschemeyer and Skocpol, served to 'bring the state back in'.[6] Causal primacy is assigned to the state by these researchers in explanations of policy formulation and implementation. To argue in favour of the autonomy of the state, however, requires a distinction be made between state and society, a difficult task. In one of the first and most important studies, Katzenstein's *Between Power and Plenty*, just such a distinction was made by contributors to the volume. Katzenstein, engaged in comparative analysis of foreign economic policy, concludes that variations in the relative autonomy of the state *vis-à-vis* society, expressed in terms of 'strong state/weak state', lie in differences in the range of policy instruments available, and the character of the relationship between business and the state.[7] A decade later a similar divergence is posited in Ikenberry, Lake and Mastanduno's *The State and American Foreign Economic Policy*. Focused on the United States alone, Ikenberry et al. do not reject the 'weak' designation assigned to the American state by Katzenstein; although they do find that the 'state matters more' than previously acknowledged.[8]

The distinction between state and society captured in the strong/weak continuum has found a place in the international relations and comparative politics literature as other scholars adopt this framework to evaluate state autonomy. Unfortunately, the definition of state varies with each application; so too do the indicators of state strength and weakness. Some researchers have made efforts to locate and measure domestic organizational capabilities through analysis of state extractive powers such as taxation.[9] One researcher includes the depth and breath of penetration of the state into society, and its permeability, as indicators of state vulnerability.[10] In a recent volume, several authors introduced institutional and normative factors to distinguish states in terms of their relative capabilities and effectiveness. Along these lines, James Rosenau writes that 'to distinguish between *strong* and *weak* states is to differentiate not between those that have large and small armies, but rather between those whose norms, habits, and practices facilitate deeply rooted coherence and those whose tendencies favoring the whole system's integrity and sovereignty are superficial';[11] the latter are weak, while the former are strong. Stephen Krasner, in the same volume, presents an institutionalist perspective that 'regards enduring institutional structures as the building blocks of social and political life.'

> The preferences, capabilities, and basic self-identities of individuals are conditioned by these institutional structures. Historical developments are path dependent; once certain choices are made, they constrain future possibilities. The range of options available to policy makers at any given point in time is a function of institutional capabilities that were put in place at some earlier period, possibly in response to very different environmental pressures.[12]

Although these works have advanced efforts to link the domestic arena to the global (particularly with the inclusion of normative and institutional factors), only a list of suggestive possibilities and variables is left and no more. With the institutionalist perspective, for example, the position of the state is unclear. If we grant that the state is a set of historically conditioned institutional arrangements, then can any generalizable statements be made about state autonomy? Michael Loriaux notes, after reviewing four books that provide detailed studies of the political economy of several countries: 'We look in vain . . . for traces of a strong, autonomous state, which uses its interventionist powers to implement policies designed to preserve its own interests.'[13] Interestingly, the countries investigated include Austria, Switzerland, Britain, France and Japan.

More troubling than the presence of competing indicators of state strength is the fact that the boundaries between state and society remain unclear and shifting; often society remains an undefined, underdefined or residual category. The latest challenge to the state-centred approach comes as analysts delve ever deeper into the domestic realm in an effort to understand and explain the policies advanced and diplomatic positions taken by state officials. We see this with discussions of 'two-level games' and the development of the negotiation-analytic approach.[14] Differentiation between state and society, an essential element in statist arguments, appears increasingly tenuous and questionable.

It is my contention that if we are to explain policy choices and outcomes we must integrate state and society in our analytical frameworks as they are integrated in the real world. 'Political institutions cannot be studied in isolation from the political cultures in which they function,' writes Loriaux, 'while political cultures cannot be studied in isolation from the political institutions which give them expression.'[15] The state is a social entity, a 'sociocultural phenomenon', to use J.P. Nettl's phrase, which should neither be ignored or defined away, nor treated as a disembodied entity sitting above society.[16] The state, coterminous with a specified piece of territory, is a set of complex institutions populated by individuals who identify themselves as both state agents and members of an identifiable society. Institutions are integrated patterns of social practices. Governing then refers to the practices of specific persons, state authorities. The specific set of institutionalized practices defined and identified as the state serve to *enable* and *constrain* action.

State practices vary in time and space, though in each instance reflect the society of which they are a part. As Bruce Andrews correctly notes: 'The purposes of states are not autonomous phenomena. [T]hey rely on a network of domestic conventions, boundaries, and meanings that provide a framework for both the goals and considerations of the actors.' Hence, a state's policies are 'guided and constrained by an array of domestic expectations which are considered legitimate, and by social conventions which both define and delimit those broader social purposes.'[17] A society is a group, an organized aggregate, with its own culture(s). The principles of social organization that shape a society also vary; although I will argue in my presentation of grid–group theory that the range of variation is limited which permits classification.

'An amorphous complex of agencies with ill-defined boundaries, performing a great variety of not very distinctive functions', the state is indeed 'elusive'.[18] Not surprisingly, identification of the extent of the authority and power of the state apparatus *vis-à-vis* specific non-state private actors is difficult to establish *a priori*, or even 'after the fact', particularly for comparative purposes. Yet, if we are to gain some purchase on this core relationship for both comparative politics and international relations studies, we must proceed to develop an analytical model. It is the purpose of this chapter to provide such a model. If successful, this research should clarify the state/society relationship through its analysis of the interaction between authority and market, between the state apparatus and commercial banks. By doing so, the domestic/international nexus is explored as possible limitations on state authority beyond its territory borders are identified.

FRAMEWORK OF ANALYSIS: GRID–GROUP CULTURAL THEORY

The intent behind the development and application of the grid–group framework is to provide a tool that will enable us to understand and explain a pattern of policy outcomes. To do this requires not only explaining the consequences that followed the implementation of a specific policy, but also 'how that state and its choices were possible in the first place'. In doing so, as Alexander Wendt notes, the '"rules of the game" of social action' are revealed.[19] The relationship between human agents and social structures comprise the game. The 'agent-structure problem' identified by Wendt in such an endeavour is to find a satisfactory conceptualization of 'these entities and their relationships'. Operating on the assumptions that 'human beings and their organizations are purposeful actors whose actions help reproduce or transform' their society; and that society is comprised of 'social relationships which structure interactions between these purposeful actors', sociocultural theory, reprising Wendt, sets out to solve this problem,[20] and thereby to clarify the state–society nexus.

Grid–Group Cultural Theory

Grid–group theory owes its origins to the work of cultural anthropologist Mary Douglas. Over several decades Douglas refined a framework to bring order and coherence to a welter of information and insights on diverse cultures.[21] Interested in producing a 'sociological understanding of culture', she devised a typology based on extensive fieldwork. The purpose of this scheme is to permit social scientists to engage in cross-cultural analysis in order to increase their understanding of social and cultural relations and how they direct individual choices and behaviour. Applications of this approach have been undertaken by Douglas and others to explicate a wide range of social behaviour.[22] A recent effort to refine and extend this theory is Michael Thompson, Richard Ellis and Aaron Wildavsky's *Cultural Theory*. Building on Douglas's pioneering work, they present a theory of 'sociocultural viability that explains how ways of life maintain (and fail to maintain) themselves'.[23] In advancing this theory, the authors also argue that they are bridging an 'unjustified' dichotomy between theories that purport to explain how individuals interpret and apply meaning to social reality, and those theories that explain social structures and patterns of behaviour.[24] They are engaged in an effort, perhaps unknowingly, to solve the agent–structure problem noted above.

After detailing the grid–group model and discussing epistemological and methodological issues, an extensive analysis of rules, and their role in the articulation of ways of life and the exercise of authority and power is undertaken.

The Grid–Group Typology: Dimensions of Social Control

> Among all living beings, humans are the only ones who actively make their own environment, the only ones whose environment is a cultural construct. Culture is no passive object of investigation; it is not a solid deep-storage system, nor a fixed set of logical pigeonholes for retrieving embedded memories. With some pliability and some toughness of its own, there are yet limits to the negotiability of culture. *To discover these limits is the problem I discern.*[25]

> [A]lthough nations and neighborhoods, tribes and races, have their distinctive sets of values, beliefs, and habits, their basic convictions about life are reducible to only a few cultural biases.[26]

Without denying the existence of features unique to each society, all social contexts or cultures can be distinguished from each other in terms of their 'permitting and constraining effects upon the individual's choices'.[27] For individuals located in a social context with its own 'pattern of rewards and punishments', the task will be to find principles to guide their behaviour in acceptable ways, as well as enable them both to judge others and justify themselves to others. Douglas, in identifying this method as a 'social-accounting approach to culture', writes that 'it selects out of the total cultural field those beliefs and values [defined as a cosmology] which are derivable as justifications for action.'[28] The specific character of beliefs and social actions found in any particular setting are a consequence of a variation in two structural dimensions – group and grid.

Group and grid, described as 'a paradigm for the analysis of social organization', are two polythetic variables which incorporate 'fundamental cultural constraints';[29] they are variables that represent the 'ordered relations' that are society. Group, to quote Thompson et al., 'refers to the extent to which an individual is incorporated into bounded units'. 'The greater the incorporation, the more individual choice is subject to group determination.'[30] Identifying the strength of group identity in any particular social context is the researcher's task. To what extent is the individual's life shaped, constrained, absorbed or supported by the group? Does the individual explain, justify and judge his or her own and others' behaviour in terms of its relevance and importance for the group, for the collectivity? Group strength refers to the degree of solidarity present, the extent to which there is identity with others. 'High group strength . . . requires a tight identification of members with one another as a corporate entity.' For this reason, membership is not easy to gain; barriers to entry, to borrow an economic phrase, may be quite high. 'Individuals are expected to act on behalf of the collective whole, and the corporate body is expected to act in the normative interests of its members.'[31] Such collectivities have their own purposes and goals. Douglas, writing with Isherwood, argues that 'the stronger the group the greater its capacity to accumulate assets in its own name and the less the power of its constituent members to accumulate assets for themselves.'[32] Douglas and Isherwood point to the Catholic Church and the modern corporation as examples; communes and monastic orders also epitomize strong groups. Exclusion carries a high cost for an individual whose sense of security is identified with such a group.

Low or weak group boundaries are present 'when people negotiate their way through life on their own behalf'; absent is solidarity, with its accompanying sense of responsibility towards others. Individuals choose 'with whom they will associate'. Reflecting 'a competitive, entrepreneurial way of life . . . the individual is not strongly constrained by duty to other persons.'[33] Instead, value is placed on self-reliance and self-expression. Thus, the extent of solidarity, as a group property, provides the basis for a comparative analysis of collectivities.

Grid refers to the extent to which rules structure the relations between and among individuals, the rules 'that relate one person to others on an ego-centered basis'.[34] Imagine a situation in which there is no clear delineation of social roles, no formal classifications, no hierarchy. Being low grid, the character of relations between members would be established by each individual. For the investigator the relevant question is, what is the scope for personal choice; how prescribed are relations? In evaluating the grid dimension of a social context,

Mary Douglas identifies as key elements the degree of autonomy, control and competition. As one moves 'up grid', the individual will be subject to more rules and role definition; position and status will not be open to negotiation. At the high end, role will be assigned; individual control and autonomy will be markedly reduced, if not eliminated in the extreme case. In a high grid setting, symbolic action is, as David Ostrander notes, 'extremely routinized in terms of how, where, when, and why it may take place'; whereas low grid action is 'more spontaneous, flexible, and personalized'.[35] A caste system would be both high grid and high group. At the same time, the establishment of group boundaries will assume greater importance as relations become more structured and constrained. Alternatively, maintenance of strong group boundaries, while permitting individual negotiation of relations (low grid), may prove difficult. This is, in fact, commonly the case with respect to egalitarian groups or collectivities whose members have rejected, in principle, any forms of authority or hierarchy in social relations.

What is particularly important in differentiating high from low grid is not just the actual number of rules or the extent to which social life is ordered, but the character of the rules. Douglas reports that even 'as individuals are supposed to transact more and more freely, the rules governing transactions may ... multiply'.[36] Similarly, there may be a body of rules in place which protect an individual from interference from other persons or the state; such rules enlarge the arena of personal choice, and thus enable rather than restrict or restrain social conduct. An extensive analysis of the different types of rules, and their presence in different types of societies will be undertaken at a later point.

The two dimensions that focus attention on social processes of inclusion and social processes of classifications are depicted below. Moving horizontally from 0 toward B, individual conduct becomes more group-focused. Movement from 0 towards A indicates an increasing classification and formalization of social relations. To measure a downward shift towards 0 tells 'how freely a person disposes of his time, of his own goods, chooses his collaborators, chooses his clothes and food'.[37]

The theoretical relationship assumed between the constructs grid and group is not causal; the presence or absence of strong group boundaries is *not* assumed to cause the presence or absence of restrictive codes of conduct. Rather, the relationship is associational, one does not presuppose the existence of the other; variation in the two dimen-

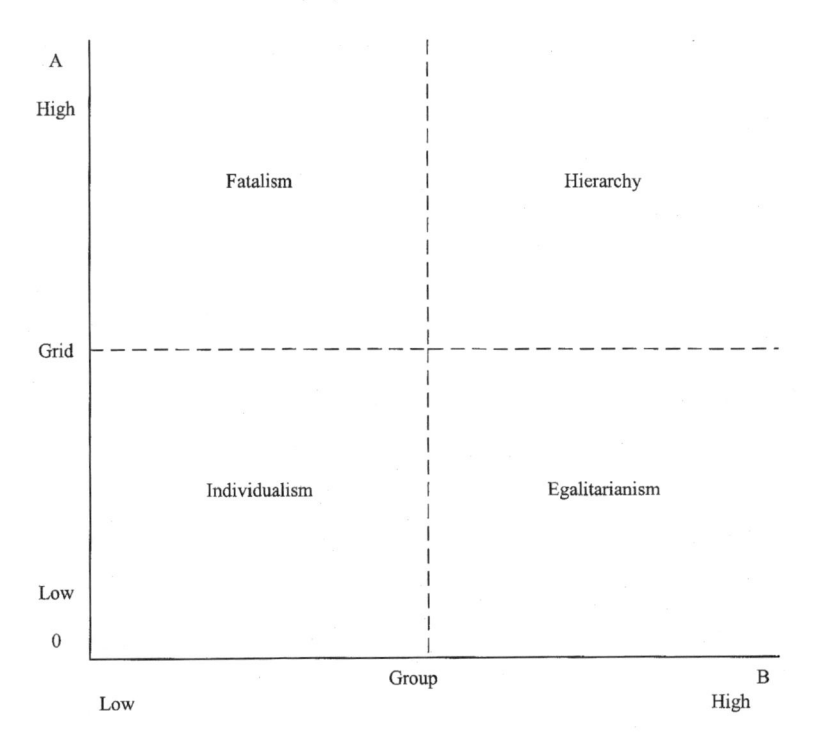

```
A                    |
High                 |
                     |
          Fatalism   |      Hierarchy
                     |
                     |
                     |
                     |
Grid  ---------------+----------------
                     |
                     |
       Individualism |     Egalitarianism
                     |
                     |
Low                  |
 0                   |
                  Group                B
     Low                               High
```

Source: Adapted from Mary Douglas, 'Cultural Bias', in Mary Douglas, *In the Active Voice* (London: Routledge and Kegan Paul, 1982).

sions results in the construction of a typology.[38] The four ways of life or 'social environments' constructed by Douglas from grid and group are individualism (low grid, low group), fatalism (high grid, low group), hierarchy (high grid, high group) and egalitarianism (low grid, high group). Each of these categories should be viewed, according to Douglas, not as an ideal type but as an 'extreme representation' of a specific configuration of social relations. As an exercise in social mapping, the grid–group model locates 'the sociological position of a society (or a social unit within society) in order to predict the "cosmological" presuppositions of that social unit or society'.[39] Along with each way of life is a moral order or cosmology that reinforces and invigorates the social context. The process between the two elements is interactive; neither values nor social relations are assigned causal primacy. 'Relations and biases are reciprocal, interacting, and mutually reinforcing. Adherence to a certain pattern of social relationships generates a distinctive way of looking at the world; adherence to a certain world view legitimizes a corresponding type of social relations.'[40] This approach owes a debt to Emile Durkheim. According to Thompson et al., Durkheim argued that

> Social relations generate ways of perceiving the world that contribute to the maintenance of those relations . . . [He] held that the roles and norms that constitute social situations are both inside the individuals who have internalized them and outside those individuals in that, once established, these norms exercise an independent influence on their creators.[41]

Unlike the work of Durkheim, however, this approach does not fall victim to mechanistic determinism and reification where society is assigned a life of its own external to the individuals who comprise it. Neither can it be classified as 'voluntaristic idealism' where, to quote Roy Bhaskar, 'social objects are seen as the results of (or as constituted by) intentional or meaningful human behavior.'[42] Instead, the cultural model developed here follows the ontology advanced by Bhaskar:

> Society must be regarded as an ensemble of structures, practices and conventions which individuals reproduce or transform, but which would not exist unless they did so. Society does not exist independently of human activity (the error of reification). But it is not the product of it (the error of voluntarism).[43]

Individuals and society are ontologically distinct, for people act on the basis of reasons, intentions and plans, while society provides the 'ever-present *condition* (material cause) and the continually reproduced *outcome* of human agency';[44] neither should be reduced to the other. Thus, social activity, 'may . . . be described either in terms of the agent's reason for engaging in it or in terms of its social function or role'.[45] Mark Granovetter makes a similar point in his discussion of the 'embeddedness' of economic action in society:

> Actors do not behave or decide as atoms outside a social context [as portrayed by economists], nor do they adhere slavishly to a script written for them by a particular intersection of social categories that they happen to occupy [as portrayed by some sociologists]. Their attempts at purposive action are instead embedded in concrete, ongoing systems of social relations.[46]

The social context, considered the material basis of action, is open to change, to transformation through the activities of persons; society is not set in stone. 'Because social structures are themselves social products,' notes Bhaskar, 'they are themselves possible objects of transformation and so may be only relatively enduring.'[47] Thus, the state itself is subject to transformation. Similarly, to return to the terminology of cultural theory, no way of life is immune to change; it may gain or lose adherents. Social change occurs, together with movement along one or both dimensions. Even while recreating their cultures, individuals encounter events (Bhaskar refers to 'historically significant events'[48]) which may raise doubts about the appropriateness of long-standing patterns of conduct and the correctness of the existing moral order. The appearance and persistence of problems or social dilemmas may lead to a reflection on and reconsideration of commonly accepted practices, roles and values. Individual justifications and explanations for actions taken or contemplated may no longer seem convincing. Summarizing their discussion of change, Thompson et al. note:

> Ways of life . . . have an impressive array of ways of reinforcing commitment by directing attention away from discomforting facts. But surprises – the cumulative mismatches between expectation and result – . . . can and do dislodge individuals from a way of life. If they are to ensure the continued allegiance of individuals, ways of life must deliver at least some of what they promise.[49]

Maintenance of a way of life, of society itself, depends upon the continuation of activities and support of values that are consistent with and appropriate for its reproduction.[50]

When individuals will abandon one way of life and move towards another is difficult to predict. What can be accomplished, though, is applying this framework to compare and contrast different social settings across time and space. This structured typology can 'trace certain patterns of behavior through the whole system of social interactions, perceptions, values and justifications'.[51] Categorizing social contexts will more clearly expose the underpinnings of specific cultures and thereby illuminate the state–society relationship. Explaining, within a way of life, a pattern conduct is also possible. Specifically, 'cultural bias rules out certain courses of action as incongruent with a way of life'; however, 'they do not necessarily rule in a specific alternative'.[52] Grid–group theory argues that individuals' preferences are derived from their ways of life. Individuals 'deduce their preferences from their way of life' on the basis of what they believe supports its continuation. 'An egalitarian, for instance, need only ask whether a policy or practice will increase or diminish differences among people.' Alternatively, 'preferences emerge as unintended consequences of attempting to organize social life in a particular way. In choosing how to relate to others, people unwittingly commit themselves to a number of other choices.'[53] This perspective supports Bhaskar's point that social structures do not exist independently of people's conceptions 'of what they are doing in their activity'. What he terms a 'theory of these activities' is the cosmology associated with each way of life; a cosmology which is itself subject to change.[54]

Before proceeding to a fuller description of the four ways of life constructed through a combination of grid and group, three additional issues must be addressed. The first relates to the nature of the polythetic concepts of grid and group and the appropriate unit of analysis, the second refers to the presence and interaction between ways of life in any particular society, and the third is a discussion of the functional element in this approach.

The word polythetic comes from *poly* (many), and *thetos* (arrangement). Grid and group are polythetic properties of society. 'Polythetic classification is the formation of classes according to a number of characteristics, such that no single characteristic has to be present in every member of any class.' This classification, used in the biological sciences, captures family resemblances. It differs from monothetic classes where a specific property is identified as necessary and sufficient for inclusion in the class. With polythetic classes, designation is assigned, write Gross and Rayner,

> according to a set of properties subject to the following general conditions: 1) Each individual possesses a large but unspecified proportion of the chosen properties; 2) Each property is more commonly found among individuals in the class than among individuals outside the class but in the same domain. It is not required that any property in the set must occur in every individual in the class.[55]

Family resemblance is provided through identification of *basic predicates*, which are 'formal features' of the cultural model. Predicates identify the boundaries of the polythetic categories; they enable the researcher to assign membership. Similar to a type-concept, grid and group are combined to create the four-fold table described earlier.[56] The entries in the cells (egalitarianism, individualism, fatalism and hierarchy) are prototypes. Assignment of specific social units, in this case societies, is achieved through the predicates of the polythetic categories.

As Gross and Rayner note, the choice of basic predicates depends, as does the choice of the basic social unit, upon the situation under investigation. For researchers such as Mary Douglas, interested in individual face-to-face encounters, the basic predicates and units of analysis differ from the predicates and unit appropriate for an analysis of the authority–market, state–society relationship that guides this project. In measuring group we are identifying the strength and closeness of the social network of specific societies.

It is not feasible to devise interval scales that permit precise measurements. Instead, well-informed judgements are reached on the basis of a careful analysis of the societies under investigation. We cannot question or interview each relevant member of society; however, we can establish a defensible position of the relative location of a society with respect to the predicates of grid and group.[57]

Group Predicates

The extent of solidarity present in a society may be indicated by the presence of *deferential involvement* in terms of allocation of resources, a sense of investment in and commitment to the well-being of society as a whole. To what extent is there deference to group as opposed to individual concerns? *Commonality of experience* is another indicator of strong social ties. Commonality of experience is realized through a 'particular subset of special activities perceived as identifying a group'.[58] For example, there may be group rituals that function as signs of inclusion; there may be the perception of a common social background; or there may be a distinctive creation or ritual myth, a shared story that set members off from nonmembers.[59] *Impermeability of boundary* is a third indicator. How difficult is it to become a member or citizen of a society with all the attendant rights and duties? Evidence of boundary markers is present when sanctions are applied, either coercive or noncoercive, for the breaking of taboos that express a concern for the purity of the group. The sanctions themselves relate to participation and acceptance as a member of the society; exclusion, expulsion and abuse are common forms of punishment. There is the use of the 'we–they' metaphor. Is there a perception of danger to the society associated with taboos?[60] In addition, the extent to which members perceive that their *life-support* is gained from the larger group is a predicate of group strength.[61] Finally, and implicit in the other predicates, is the extent to which *controls* on behaviour are exercised in the name of the larger society.

Grid Predicates

With grid, focus is on differentiation in a social network. How restricted is conduct? The extent of *standardization*, the extent to which activities are formalized and prescribed is a predicate of grid.[62] *Asymmetry*, a predicate associated with role, refers to a lack of symmetry in role exchanges. High asymmetry is present in a master/slave, lord/serf relationship where there is little or no role exchange between persons. The more asymmetrical the society, the more hierarchical.[63] In any society the question is 'do categories of role-based social hierarchy affect the choices available to members of a society?'[64] The greater institutionalized authority, the less control persons have. *Entitlement* refers to role access; what is the balance between ascribed and achieved roles? Are roles limited to certain categories of persons or open to all?[65] *Accountability*, which refers to the extent to which sanctions may be applied based upon role performance, reflects hierarchical relationships. Accountability, as Atkins notes, will produce 'sensitivity to categorical distinctions'. If a society is high grid, then there should be 'social mechanisms that reinforce role specialization'; while if the setting is low grid, then 'social mechanisms should reinforce individual freedom'.[66] Finally, there is *autonomy*; how much independence in decision making is granted to persons in a specific social setting? Are members free to choose what to do with their time, with their possessions? Are individuals able to choose with whom they will associate, what they will wear, what they will eat? Autonomy implies freedom from control by others.[67] Autonomy raises the question of not only the density of rules governing social life, but also their character. The character of rules may be well captured in a society's legal system. In fact, the place of law in a society is a valuable indicator of the degree of circumscription placed on conduct. Evidence of the presence or absence of these predicates, and their extensiveness, are used to identify the relative strength of grid and group, which in turn is used to categorize societies.

With respect to the interaction between ways of life, Thompson et al. hypothesize that all ways of life are present in varying degrees in all societies. Thus, Thompson et al. write: 'the differences between regimes ... are to be found in the differing configurations of this perpetual dynamic imbalance between the ... ways of life.' In any society, one or two ways of life dominate, but all will be present. All must be present, the authors argue, for each needs rivals 'either to make up for its deficiencies, or to exploit, or to define itself against.' Thus, individualists need hierarchy to enforce contract laws, egalitarians need individualists and hierarchists to rail against, and all to differing degrees need fatalists to exploit or recruit.[68] At the same time, alliances between different ways of life will form and re-form.

Every bias (or combination of biases) encounters situations it did not predict, cannot explain, and is ill equipped to cope with. What is anomalous from one perspective, however, is predictable and solvable from another. As one bias (or alliance of biases) becomes discredited, other previously excluded biases are bolstered.[69]

Functionalism, as a form of explanation, has come under repeated, often well-deserved, attack. The most important and damaging criticism has been the charge of illegitimate teleology. For example, the functionalist arguments of Talcott Parsons have been found wanting for this reason. Pitched at the level of the society, certain functions are then identified as essential for maintenance and stability. This approach seems to require the existence of what Thompson et al. term a '"group mind", i.e., endowing institutions with human qualities of intention and purpose'. At the same time, social conflict dropped out. Instead, society was pictured as coherent, orderly and stable. Social change occurred as the society gradually adapted itself to a changing environment. Cultural theory does not fall victim to either of these failings. No group mind is implied, and conflict as a social phenomenon is not neglected; rather, it is implicit in competing ways of life.[70] Institutions do not have purposes or intentions; as noted above, only persons do. Individuals can and often do sustain social arrangements supportive of certain values and norms; to deny this is to deny the incidenceof purposive behaviour. This is what is meant by a functional explanation; one 'in which the *consequences* of some behaviour or social arrangement are essential elements of the *causes* of that behaviour'.[71] To ask for the cause of something is to ask '"what makes it happen", what "generates", or more weakly, "enables" or "leads to" it'.[72] In this case, the 'it' is the effectiveness of the designated policy. We wish to know how, by what processes or mechanisms, the outcome occurred as it did. In proceeding in such a fashion, we avoid 'the fallacy of affirming the consequence', a common occurrence in social science research.[73]

Individuals operating through institutions reinforce and sustain a given behavioural pattern. To use an example provided by Stinchcombe, if a group organizes itself as a business, we can infer that it wants profits and will probably change its activities if necessary to get them.[74] In this case, 'wanting' provides the mechanism that leads to the pattern of conduct. Wanting, as Stinchcombe notes, is not the only mechanism that may lead to the selection of a certain type of behaviour; although all too often it is treated as such. Evolution, competition, satisfaction, reward from others and planning, along with wanting, may produce action and activities that will support a desired outcome.[75] The consequences generated by a way of life, whether intended or not, 'are not random but instead serve to bolster the way of life that spawned them.'[76] None of this is meant to suggest immunity from change for, as discussed earlier, all societies are subject to change. The tensions always present in society may lead to dissatisfaction with the existing 'way of proceeding'.

Four Ways of Life

Each of the ways of life described below sets out a specific social context with its accompanying cosmology. Following John McKinney, this typology represents a constructive type: 'a purposive, planned selection, abstraction, combination, and (sometimes) accentuation of a set of criteria with empirical referents that serves as a basis for comparison of empirical cases.'[77] All constructed types, as McKinney notes, are heuristic devices generated for comparative, predictive, and I would add, explanatory purposes.[78] Thus, the four types presented here function to isolate conduct that is deemed theoretically significant. In doing so, these ways of life serve 'as a means by which concrete occurrences can be compared and comprehended within a system of general categories . . . underlying the types'; in this case, grid and group.[79] These ways of life should not be viewed as ideal types in the Weberian sense for they are not abstractions devised as 'conscious deviations from concrete experience'. Instead, the typology developed by Douglas lies much closer to the 'extracted' pole of the ideal–extracted continuum described by McKinney. 'The extracted type is based upon the notions of average, common, and concrete.'[80] Abstraction is obviously involved in the selection of predicates of grid and group; however, the model itself is grounded in the study of numerous societies from which has come the four ways of life typology. As Sayer notes, 'the understanding of concrete events or objects involves a double movement: concrete–abstract, abstract–concrete.'[81]

As approximations or prototypes, perfect fit between a hypothesized way of life and a specific social setting is not to be expected. Deviations, as McKinney notes, are always present, as they are in the physical sciences with the use of the constructed types of perfect

A Theory of State–Non-state Actors 223

vacuum and perfect surface. 'A type implies a predictive [and explanatory] schema.' To paraphrase McKinney, there is an expectation of conduct associated with constructed type.[82] The researcher then compares the extent to which the pattern of behaviour occurs. For purposes of the research undertaken here, what is most relevant is the identification of the presence or absence of predicates of grid and group that satisfy the requirements of the types.

Individualism

Recall that individualism as a way of life ranks low on both grid and group; thus, few prescriptions define or classify the individual's role in society. Status is not ascribed as it is in a hierarchical setting but is earned through the demonstration of skills and the acquisition of resources. For example, the Igbo of southeast Nigeria purchase their position in society; 'they believe that the world is a marketplace where status symbols can be bought.'[83] The role ambiguity associated with the individualist way of life assures maximum scope for personal choice. Where classifications are established, they are the product of bargaining and thus open to future negotiation and adjustment. The agent is sovereign and autonomous, with no identity with or acceptance of solidarity with others except to further one's own interests. The 'social experience of the individual is not constrained by any external boundary.'[84] Life is a series of exchanges between equal individuals.

Not surprisingly self-regulation through bidding and bargaining is the favoured method of social interaction. Agreement is achieved through negotiation, culminating in contractual arrangements, thereby minimizing the need or desirability of external authority. The fewer society-wide rules, the further down grid, the more relationships and rules are subject to negotiation. In this setting, mediators and brokers play a major role. In the individualist way of life, leadership is accepted only reluctantly and only when deemed necessary to deal with a crisis or specific task.

The larger environment from this cosmology is dominated by impersonal forces beyond any one agent's control. Through competition, success in such an environment becomes possible. Individualists may strengthen or advance their interests or position through network building and through formation of alliances. Rules are established to manage competition, but they actually facilitate individual transactions. This process can be seen in the behaviour of the 'big-man' of New Guinea. By definition, the big-man is one who has developed a network of exchange relations; the larger and more extensive the network, the more influence and power. At the bottom of this social arrangement are the 'rubbish men', described as soft, humble and weak. They are unable to make 'persuasive talk that "sticks"', and they lack 'grease' (wealth).[85] The rubbish men exemplify the reverse of negative freedom, or autonomy, implicit in the individualist way of life. They are under the control of those who have succeeded in the competitive game. These individuals may be pushed up grid to the point where they become fatalists.

The former Zaire provided a real-world example of a society where a big-man, in this case Joseph-Desiré Mobutu, established networks of support based on pay-offs. Bill Berkeley reports: 'Control of the printing and distribution of money is a vital tool of Mobutu's; it is not only the means by which he enriches himself but also his means for supporting his friends and co-opting his enemies.'[86] The widespread existence of 'passivity' among the population, described as 'a version of the "battered-woman syndrome"', was not surprising in a society that slid rapidly into a state of anarchy; fatalists abounded.[87]

The stipulated environment of the individualist way of life is an uncertain one because role restrictions and group identity are absent. This in turn tends to produce a relatively short-term perspective that emphasizes quick gains and resource exploitation. The long term is left to take care of itself. A natural equilibrium is believed to exist so that if and when a disturbance occurs, a built-in tendency returns the system to a stable point. Thus, the best, most appropriate, management is *laissez-faire*, with no more called for.

Human nature, perceived to be stable and self-seeking regardless of time and place, is unchanging and unchangeable. Therefore, institutions must be adjusted accordingly to take account of the self-interested agent.

Fatalism

Fatalism consists of strong prescriptions imposed by others and weak group ties. Fatalists believe that life is a lottery. Any good that comes their way is simply a matter of luck, with their needs and resources seemingly controlled by others. (A well-known study of fatalism is Edward Banfield's *The Moral Basis of a Backward Society*.)[88] 'Controlled from without', their 'sphere of individual autonomy', like the hierarchists, is restricted. Unlike the hierarchists, however, they are 'excluded from membership in the group responsible for making the decisions that rule their life'.[89] Survival comes by coping with what life throws at them. Fatalists would like to improve their lot, but they see no direct relationship between their efforts and rewards, and winning or losing is a matter of chance. Fatalists often find themselves on the periphery of those networks built by successful individualists.

Human nature is viewed as unpredictable, thereby generating feelings of distrust. Not surprisingly, the fatalistic cosmology generates feelings of apathy, disengagement and social inactivity. Their very inactivity would reinforce their positions, which would in turn reconfirm the correctness of their perspective. Fatalists become the target of members of the active ways of life. A society where a high proportion of its citizens are judged to be fatalists would not pose a direct challenge to state officials because they would not initiate actions. Alternatively, though, officials might find it difficult to induce change in patterns of social behaviour.

Egalitarianism

The guiding norm for the egalitarian way of life is equality of condition; thus, all actions are directed towards diminishing differences between individuals through sharing out. (In the individualist cosmology, the concern is with equality of opportunity.) For this reason, the exercise of authority is condemned. Granting authority to someone creates and sustains inequality by empowering one person at the expense of others. So-called radical egalitarian groups, such as the antinuclear Clamshell Alliance, the Student Non-Violent Coordinating Committee (SNCC) of the 1960s, and numerous feminist organizations, reject any authority structures; formal leadership is explicitly eschewed.[90] When decisions must be made, members seek agreement through consensus, with each individual assigned an equal voice. This decision rule, along with emphasis on open and unlimited participation, usually leads to extensive discussion. For an egalitarian, methods are as important as the desired goal. This can create tensions that may lead to the collapse of the group, as occurred with SNCC, or fissioning or splitting, a common phenomenon with radical environmental groups.

Because individuals are not to be coerced, prescriptions on behaviour are few. With no fixed roles or positions, there should be no stratification, regimentation or segregation: in cultural terms, low grid. As with individualism, personal relationships are ambiguous, yet egalitarians identify with others similarly committed to this way of life.[91] Adherents tend to divide the world into 'them' and 'us', with 'them' assigned blame for the existing state of oppression, inequality and environmental degradation. Boundaries are then defined negatively in terms of enemies. Solidarity in the face of such evil and repression is essential. Compromise under such circumstances is to be avoided and in cases of total commitment not countenanced. For a small radical group such as SNCC, compromise led to a sense of betrayal and failure that undermined the organization.[92]

Contrary to individualists, egalitarians believe that human beings are inherently good but have been corrupted by evil institutions such as markets, which place a premium on self-seeking, competitive, aggressive behaviour. This suggests that human nature, which is seen as malleable, can be changed through the advent of a noncoercive, egalitarian society.

According to the egalitarian perspective, resources are not limitless; they are fixed and cannot, contrary to the individualist's claim, be expanded. Therefore, needs must be brought under control in order to fit within available supply. Conspicuous consumption must be eliminated. The simple life, while meeting the basic needs of all, is the preferred life style. Not surprisingly, the physical world is believed to be quite fragile; any jolt may trigger collapse. Egalitarians could not believe otherwise and still justify their commitment to sharing out for if they believed, like the individualists, that nature is cornucopian, 'there would be so much of everything valuable that there would be no point in sharing out'.[93] The viability of this way of life requires strict accountability from nature, which is seen as a zero-sum or even negative sum game. For the egalitarian, the long term, which the individualist allows to fend for itself, is fairly close and threatening. Threats of the future are an important part of the political attack mounted against the existing system and its supporters.[94] In addition, egalitarians argue that failure to act in time may have disastrous social consequences. Social systems unable to cope will be delegitimized and rejected by the mass of their now apathetic (read fatalistic) populations. They call for movement away from existing hierarchies and large institutions to smaller, decentralized methods of governance where individuals have direct control over their lives.

Hierarchy

With its sacrifice of parts to whole, deference to superiors, and belief in the value of order, this behavioural pattern, which is generated by strong group boundaries and restrictive prescriptions, dominates hierarchical relations (high group, high grid).[95] In this social context, the individual is subject to the control of other members of the group and the demands of socially imposed rules of conduct. Unlike egalitarianism, which also has group boundaries but few methods for constraining members' behaviour, hierarchy 'has an armoury of different solutions to internal conflicts [including] upgrading, shifting sideways, downgrading, resegregating, redefining'.[96] Acting on their own, individuals have little manipulative ability; however, acting collectively enables members to increase their share of available resources but not at the cost of displacing the group above them. Position and rank must be maintained. In this highly regulated environment, the problem is 'one of keeping everything in its place'.

Their view of nature – as a mirror to society – reinforces the correctness of a hierarchical order, for as nature is governed by regularities, so too is the social order. Going against social arrangements is acting 'against nature'. Nature itself may be either tolerant or perverse in impact. To manage such uncertainty, to determine what nature will tolerate, requires experts. The central role assigned to experts reflects the respect for authority based on the belief that decisions should be made by the right people in the right place. Hence, '[t]he exercise of authority . . . is justified on the grounds that different roles for different people enable people to live together more harmoniously than alternative arrangements.'[97] Unlike the egalitarians, then, blame is not and cannot be directed at the system but instead is hidden, diffused among many, or pinned on 'deviants'. 'Blame-shedding' is a valued and important skill in hierarchies. When hard times do occur, 'hierarchies go on the defensive. They demand sacrifices, institute rationing, and stress that their scrupulous fairness and their highly ordered system of distribution will protect those who otherwise would find themselves most at risk.'[98]

But what of human nature? The hierarchists' way of life sees humans as evil but redeemable through good institutions. Of course, this outlook supports a complex of institutional rules and restraints. 'Hierarchy teaches its adherents to reject the egalitarians' sunny view of human nature because it would undermine the need for the painstaking regulation of human activities.'[99]

One commentator on this model writes that the types 'seem to be describing personality profiles'. This is not surprising as it is individuals that comprise society, and it is through their activities that society is sustained and transformed. Assuming there is a relationship between personality traits and social behaviour, one would expect substantial overlap between a dominant way of life and the conduct and expressed values of individuals. It is the daily encounter and interaction with individuals in other societies that many visitors find unsettling, confusing, and uncomfortable. A similar point is made by Lasswell and Kaplan, who note 'that traits of culture may be *personality types*'.[100] Douglas addresses this issue when she writes: 'This argument closes no doors upon psychological theories of personality. It presupposes that some mixture of self-selection and of adaptation accounts for a fit between personality measurements and grid-group social position.'[101] Individuals, as Douglas observes, choose 'to deal with their social problems in one way or another'. Cultural theory sets forth the range of 'possibilities' available to them.[102]

Extending Cultural Theory

The value of cultural theory, and its accompanying typology, in explicating the authority–market, state–society relationship, lies in its power to explain the extent to which any state's agents are able to establish and/or enforce rules that govern the market activities of private actors. Their ability to do so will be a function of which way(s) of life dominate. Thompson et al. argue that power relations are present in each way of life, yet how power is exercised varies according to the culture. Douglas, for example, writes that in social settings located at the strong end of grid, insulations, through

> an explicit set of institutionalized classifications [that] keeps [individuals] apart and regulates their interactions . . . are the result of effective power. They are also a means of making it effective all the way down from its source to the boundaries of control. Classifications are enforced in an effort to stabilize power, to filter information, ration it, limit access.[103]

Hence, government officials' ability to manipulate or constrain behaviour in specific social contexts will depend on limitations stipulated by the dominant way(s) of life and the extent to which their actions violate or reinforce these way(s) of life. Thus, the rules constitutive of any particular society should reflect the cultural bias of the predominate way(s) of life. The type of rules and the function(s) they are intended to fulfil should be consistent with the cosmology embedded in a given way of life.

Rules that constitute and regulate social practices are central to this approach, yet Thompson et al. do not provide a satisfactory account of the nature of rules. Neither do they analyse their role in the exercise of authority by state officials. Although Douglas is careful to note, as mentioned earlier, that the character of rules varies among ways of life, there has been a tendency in the presentation of cultural theory to focus only on variation in the density of rules. A better understanding of the characteristics of rules and how they are tied to the authoritative practices of state officials must be established, however, to develop an adequate explanation of authority–market relations. To assist in this effort, Nicholas Onuf's work on rules and Richard Flathman's on political authority should prove helpful. A more detailed analysis of the market as an arena of social action will follow.

Rules

Onuf presents two general properties that, he argues, should characterize all political societies – the presence of rules and rule. 'The condition of rule' for Onuf 'is the persistence of asymmetric social relations' created through the 'unavoidability of rules'.[104] He identifies three functional categories of rules: instructive, directive and commitment. Instructive rules, grounded in assertive speech-acts, state a belief that the speaker wishes to or intends the hearer to accept. Hence, principles are considered a special kind of instruction-rule.[105] Directive-rules, reflective of directive speech-acts 'ask, command, demand, permit [and] caution'. Commitment rules, through commissive speech-acts that 'reveal the speaker's intention of being committed to a stated course of action', involve promising and offering, and thereby entail duties and rights.[106]

The purpose of both directives and commissives is to get the subject 'to do something'. Where they differ is in the location of obligation; with directives, it is the hearer's behaviour that is to be regulated. Commitments may entail an obligation to oneself, another, or both.[107] 'Casual revocation' is unlikely to occur when rules are institutionalized and value – whether good or bad – is assigned to them.[108]

Onuf concludes that 'Rules in all three categories . . . are doubtless present in all cultures, though in different mixes.' As expected with a liberal, or to use Douglas's term individualist, culture commitment-rules are presumed to dominate because, as Onuf notes, 'these rules constitute the structure of rights and duties defining our cherished individuality.'[109] Thus, the privileged should be 'merchants and property owners'. Privilege holders in an instruction dominated society would be 'elders, priests and those upon whom honorifics are bestowed'.[110]

The instrumentally skilled would gain privileged status in a directive society.

The similarity with Douglas's description of the essential features of the ways of life is striking. Echoing Douglas, Onuf believes that individuals actively create and recreate their own social reality.[111] Neither the individual nor the social world is assigned priority; rather it is an interactive process. Thus, Onuf agrees with Anthony Giddens that

> The basic domain of study of the social sciences... is neither the experience of the individual actor, nor the existence of any form of social totality, but social practices ordered across space and time. Human social activities... are recursive. That is to say, they are not brought into being by social actors but continually recreated by them via the very means whereby they express themselves *as* actors. In and through their activities agents reproduce the conditions that make these activities possible.[112]

All social practices are constituted and regulated by rules, hence the primacy of rules; however, this does not mean that agents are automata blindly following rules. Although this may occur in some situations, in most instances individuals choose whether to follow a rule based on the consequences of their choice. Given the importance of rule-accepting and rule-guided behaviour, people must not only learn rules but learn what is involved in using different types of rules. This 'consciousness', Onuf argues, 'is the internal dimension of support for rules, which, in each category, also have a characteristic external dimension of support'.[113]

Instructive-rules, including principles, do not involve punishment or formal authority but produce conformity of behaviour by reference to shared values. Examples may be cited or appeals made. Failure to conform may lead to ostracism, denigration and mockery. If punishment is used, we have directive-rules that involve imposition, raise the possibility of resistance and require external support from a system of sanctions.[114] In fact, 'to act authoritatively [is to] issue directive-rules.'[115] With commitment-rules, a given structure of rights and duties provides external support; however, because commitment-rules are the most difficult to practice, they are commonly converted to instructions or directives.[116] Where embedded in a legal order, rule enforcement becomes the responsibility of state officials.

For rules to be considered legal and thus to provide the foundation for exercise of state authority, certain conditions must be met. Onuf argues that 'legality is a function of the degree to which (1) rules are

A Theory of State–Non-state Actors 231

formally stated, (2) their external dimension of support is institutionalized, and (3) the personnel responsible for formalizing and institutionally supporting rules are specifically and formally assigned these tasks.'[117] Most relevant for this project is the institutionalization of rules. Onuf notes that with instructive-rules, particularly principles, exhortation by chosen agents (for example, priests in a religious setting) leads to the establishment of 'injunctions and imprecations'. Threats towards violators accompany directive-rules, with the promise of punishment in the hands of role occupants granted the authority to do so. Opinions and interpretations provide support for commitment-rules. The issuance of judgments is presumably in the hands of 'impartial third parties'. Institutionalization is achieved through 'procedural guidelines and ... precedents'.[118] Therefore, a culture dominated by commitment-rules should see the widespread use of judicial bodies.

As all four ways of life are found to varying degrees in all societies, so too are all categories of rules along with their bases of support 'combined in different proportions in historically distinct cultures'.[119] How, then, do the rule categories fit with the ways of life – individualism, fatalism, egalitarianism and hierarchy?

Egalitarians present a problem given their rejection and distrust of formal authority. Institutionalized rule, correctly seen to create inequality between ruler and ruled, is to be avoided due to its low grid way of life. The difficulties with maintaining such social arrangements were noted above. Other than splintering – a common phenomenon – the other alternative identified by Thompson et al. is governance by a charismatic leader who rules while seeming not to do so. This type of rule, labelled hegemony by Onuf, operates through instruction-rules:

> Hegemony refers to the promulgation of manipulation of principles and instructions by which superordinate actors monopolize meaning which is then passively absorbed by subordinate actors. These activities constitute a stable arrangement of rule because the ruled are rendered incapable of comprehending their subordinate role. They cannot formulate alternative programs of action because they are inculcated with the self-serving ideology of the rulers who monopolize the production and dissemination of statements through which meaning is constituted.[120]

In general, however, egalitarianism as a way of life has proven quite fragile. The likelihood of this way of life dominating any society is quite small. Rule, as Onuf notes, is both inevitable and exploitative based as it is upon rules which always privilege 'some people over others.'[121] (This suggests that the egalitarian quest may be futile.) However, an alliance with either hierarchists to assist in the redistribution of wealth or with individualists to prevent excessive restrictions on individual behaviour is quite possible.

Directive-rules, which play a prominent role in all ways of life with the exception of the egalitarian, predominate with hierarchy and fatalism, both high grid. Neither are instruction-rules uncommon in a hierarchy-dominated society. A caste system is a case where superordinate/subordinate relations are buttressed by principles that exhort individuals to behave in the expected or appropriate manner. Violations would carry both legal and social consequences for the offender. Japan is one noncaste society where both directive-rules and instructive-rules seem to dominate.

Commitment-rules predominate the individualist way of life, with heteronomy the associated paradigm of rule. 'Heteronomous relations characterize situations of exchange among apparent equals', apparent because the rights and duties articulated in commitment-rules are not symmetrical in their effects, and property owners are privileged. Neither are individuals autonomous given the contingent nature of social situations, and their 'inability to control outcomes'.[122] Formal autonomy and equality are guaranteed through a legal order based on commitment-rules, but rule is present:

> [The] asymmetrical consequences of commissively defined relations, combined with the illusion of independence for all parties to these relations, produce the conditions of rule in which rulers, simply cannot be identified by discovering the authors of rules. The ruled join the rulers as authors and audience; rules rule their joint proceedings.[123]

Like Douglas and Thompson et al., Onuf contends that the rules constitutive of different cultures (or ways of life) reflect a set of values and beliefs (cosmology in Douglas's terms) that privilege certain groups and/or individuals who will, of course, act to protect and thus recreate those ways of life as long as they continue to provide 'at least some of what they promise'. The actions of state officials will then be circumscribed by a legal and normative order comprised of rule-types reflective of the dominant way(s) of life. This does *not* mean that state agents have no flexibility or manoeuvrability; they certainly do. State officials may, and often do, initiate or advance new policy directions. But their success in winning the necessary support and acceptance will depend on the extent to which they can either sell or package a proposal as consistent with the dominant values embedded in the dominant way(s) of life or as a necessary change in light of a changed environment. For example, change in the global arena may raise doubts about the continual efficacy of long-standing state policies, thereby producing calls for major adjustments. The emergency of global financial markets is a case in point. Then state policy-makers will have to demonstrate that the old ways can no longer deliver the desired 'goods' in the desired way, a difficult, although not impossible task. Success would be possible during those very periods noted by Thompson et al., the appearance of 'cumulative mismatches between expectations and result'. In most instances, however, the boundaries established by the dominant way(s) of life will set limits. Anything does not go.

Authority and Power

The effective exercise of authority by state agents, writes Richard Flathman, depends on the extent of its consistency with the 'values and beliefs that have *authoritative* standing among the preponderance of those persons who subscribe to the authority of the rules', effective meaning the ability to bring about the desired outcome.[124] Perceived deviations from accepted values and beliefs would raise the spectre of avoidance and disobedience.

Careful to distinguish between brute force, the exercise of power, and the exercise of authority, Flathman identifies authority as 'a *reason for* thinking or acting in a certain way'.[125] As with rules, individuals choose whether to accept obligation(s) entailed by an authority relationship. What is important, writes Flathman, is not so much

> that there are beliefs that lead to the acceptance of certain types of rules which presuppose [persons] *in* authority, [but] the *reasons* why beliefs are accepted or not and the ways they are tied to a variety of other beliefs that make up the authoritative in societies and associations.[126]

The 'reasons' for the beliefs and how they 'make up the authoritative' are provided by both grid–group theory and Onuf's analysis of rules and rule. Similarly, Flathman's contention that the 'practice of authority cannot be fully understood apart from its connections with substantive values and beliefs' finds support in Douglas's and Onuf's work. To gain an understanding of authority requires its location within a specific social setting. For this reason, Flathman warns against efforts to devise a 'nonrelativized notion of authority'.[127] Hence, the exercise of authority by any particular state's officials will entail for any agent that recognizes that authority a specific set of obligations. As Flathman notes, if we are to identify 'the conditions under which authority is effective or ineffective [we must understand] what authority is and is not.'[128] This leads us to

> a study of the values and beliefs shared among [society's] members; of their content at various times; of how they form and change; of the relations among various beliefs and between them and the institutions and patterns of action that are . . . reflections of those beliefs.[129]

Grid–group cultural theory provides the information necessary for understanding the practice of authority and of the specific contours of the authority relationship between state officials and a member (individual or group) of that society. A more extended discussion and example of this point with respect to the authority–market relationship is provided below.

While granting the importance of explicating the authority relationship, there remains the question of state power. The exercise of power is not the same as the exercise of authority. The acceptance of authority entails acceptance of an obligation, a fact not true of power relationships. In addition, authority unlike power provides legitimacy to policies and/or actions. Where power and authority seem to merge is when the threat of 'a punishment is attached to the rule or command [itself a directive-rule] to do X [then] the exercise of authority and the exercise of something that is at least very much like power become conceptually linked.'[130] As Flathman correctly notes, the exercise of power then appears to enter a relationship when an agent refuses to recognize a state official's authority and is confronted with possible punishment. Care is needed here, however, as Flathman argues:

> It is a part of A's authority that he is entitled to assign punishments for failure to discharge the obligations that are attendant upon B's recognition of A's authority. But the question whether A can make those sanctions credible, whether B will believe, and will act on the belief, that the punishments will be effectively imposed in any particular case, has to do with power.[131]

Therefore, authority is still operative if an agent who has been judged guilty of violating a rule accepts the punishment. Rejection of the punishment means rejection of authority, and here the question of state power becomes relevant. This does not mean, however, that a culture's values and beliefs become irrelevant because power, different from raw force or violence, is a relationship between two or more agents or groups 'acting intentionally'.[132] Thus, the agent decides whether to change behaviour in light of prevailing values. 'Power', Flathman writes, 'is impossible in the absence of values and beliefs shared between those who wield power and those subjected to it.'[133] Following Robert Dahl, Flathman identifies the exercise of power with 'the extent that A successfully gets B to do something that he (B) would not otherwise do'.[134]

> [The A–B power relationship] is partly constituted by a more or less elaborate web of norms, beliefs, and accepted patterns of action that are at least partly shared among the A's and the B's. If the strands of this web were to unravel entirely, the exercise of power would become altogether impossible. If the pattern of the web becomes so confused or so internally contradictory as to be difficult to comprehend and to act within, the exercise of power will become difficult and problematic.[135]

Domestically, pre-revolutionary France and Russia provide examples of a breakdown in the power relationship. Internationally, the invasion of Kuwait by Iraq capped Saddam Hussein's failure to exercise power over Kuwaiti officials: hence the resort to raw force. As with authority, the effectiveness of any particular exercise of power can be evaluated only within a given social context.[136]

AUTHORITY AND MARKET

Bringing these intellectual strands together, to understand the authority–market relationship means to understand the cultural factors that underpin the practice and exercise of authority, that establish the contours and limits of rule, itself reflective of a given set of rules compatible with the dominant way(s) of life. The success of a particular state's agents in restraining or guiding the conduct of its private market actors will depend in large measure on what is permitted and what is forbidden. To reiterate Thompson et al., 'cultural bias rules out certain courses of action'. Limits are set on what a state's policy-makers can do, and a perception that a state's agents have stepped outside those established boundaries may create a compliance problem. Direct or indirect challenges to state authority, whether in the form of evasions or appeals to an alternative authoritative source (such as a judicial body or 'higher principles'), will occur when a state's officials are seen to have violated the accepted ways of proceeding, of 'carrying on'.

Although in the cases which comprise the larger study, state officials focus on activities in international financial markets, the relative success of efforts to effectuate a change in conduct, or a change in the consequences of a pattern of behaviour in this arena, is dependent upon the pre-existing relationship with market actors. For example, state agents' relationship with private market participants in the domestic arena delineates the bounds for permissible or possible action against private actors operating overseas. Therefore, it is particularly important to explicate the nature of interaction between what are commonly considered two separate spheres of social action: the state apparatus and the marketplace. A fundamental assumption which underlies the analysis is that the degree of autonomy granted to the marketplace, to market exchange, is reflective of the dominant way(s) of life. Thus, we should expect that for a society dominated by the individualist way of life, greater freedom of action will be granted market participants than in a hierarchical society. Having said that, however, there remains the question of the market itself – what is it?

Somewhat surprisingly, given the enormous attention focused on the market by both economists and non-economists alike, little effort has been expended on establishing a common definition. The term is repeatedly used, but rarely defined. The description adopted for this study is taken from the work of Cantor, Henry and Rayner, one of whom is an economist, the other a sociologist, and the third an anthropologist.[137] Beginning with the assumption that markets 'regulate or engage in economic exchange', the authors, after a review of the social science literature, identify five characteristics that comprise market processes. First, the process must stipulate property rights that 'define control over goods and services'. Property rights systems may vary from private to common, but they are all predicated on the assumption that 'theft is not legitimate in a market process [as it] implies the absence of a shared definition of the rights that establish control over goods and services.' Second, there is a presumed desire to exchange grounded in differences in 'tastes, endowments, or both'. Third, transaction costs (identified as identification costs, negotiation costs and enforcement costs), 'do not exceed the perceived gains from completing the exchange'. Fourth, there exists a choice 'over trading partners, trading periods, or both'. Where there is no choice, there can be no market. And fifth, there is trust that the 'transaction [will be] completed in an atmosphere of noncoercion'; violence is assumed to be absent.[138]

Having described the market process, however, Cantor et al. are quick to point out that certain key questions remain. For example, we do not know the 'extent of competition' or 'allocation outcomes'. These characteristics, although providing a definition for identifying markets, do not tell us about the extent of government intervention. To do so requires the specification of 'institutions that govern or constrain the market process'. What must be understood, Cantor et al. correctly note, is the 'structure of rules that govern demand, supply, and transaction options for a particular set of transactions'. Termed an exchange structure, Cantor et al. argue that 'all market processes are governed by exchange structures'.[139] Cantor et al. go on to develop a typology of exchange structures.

What is relevant for the purposes of this study, is the importance of social context to understand market processes. The rules that specify the exchange structure reflect the larger society; following grid–group theory, they reflect the dominant way(s) of life. Thus, to understand the authority–market relationship we must delve much deeper into the rules, normative and descriptive, that shape and inform the activities and conduct of the relevant social actors – state agents and private agents. The beliefs and values that comprise the cosmology associated with each way of life provide the necessary starting point; although it alone cannot provide specific answers to some of the questions raised by Cantor et al., for instance, identifying allocation outcomes. Cosmologies can, however, identify the contours of acceptable behaviour. They can tell us a great deal about the values and beliefs that channel behaviour in both spheres and that structure relations between them. The very clarity of the social and legal lines drawn between private and public realms, between state and nonstate actors in any social environment can be explicated through an identification of the dominant way(s) of life. Thus, to argue that the public sector and private sector can or cannot be distinguished one from the other is itself an empirical question which can only be answered through an investigation of the social setting; so too is this the case with the authority–market relationship.[140]

CONCLUSION

Through the application of the grid–group cultural theory we can identify the dominant way(s) of life, and their accompanying cosmologies, present in any society. The specific configuration of the authority–market relationship will then be exposed. The articulation of this relationship will then permit an explanation of the relative success of state officials in their efforts to achieve specific policy outcomes. At the same time, we should be able to make some estimates about future success on the part of state agents to direct the activities of key economic actors, particularly relevant in an era of presumed deregulation or liberalization of market activities.

To provide some 'flavour' of the application of this model a brief description of the cases that comprise the larger study is in order. With respect to the United States, grid–group cultural theory would indicate that US officials operating in a society dominated by the individualistic way of life would be hard-pressed to restrain the activities of private actors. This would explain why, when confronted with external market activities considered damaging to the achievement of domestic economic goals, the Nixon administration, in 1971, chose to change the rules of the exchange rate system rather than impose direct restrictions on banks. The former option may well have been the most feasible and least politically costly on domestic policy. The intent was to neutralize the effects of commercial banks' and bankers' operations in international financial markets, with their attendant capital flows. The policy chosen failed to achieve the objectives desired. Alternatively, Japanese policy-makers, embedded in a hierarchically dominated way of life with a heavy 'dose' of instructive-rules, found their task easier than the American government when they imposed a set of restrictive controls on their commercial banks in the mid-1970s, the purpose of which was to reverse the deterioration of their balance of payments position. The source of the variation, I argue in the larger study, lies in the nature of the state/society relationship explicated by the grid–group framework. This theory offers a valuable tool to explain the relative ability of states, to quote Kenneth Waltz, to 'remake the rules by which other actors operate'.[141]

NOTES

1. Richard Leaver, 'Restructuring in the Global Economy: From Pax Americana to Pax Nipponica?', *Alternatives* 14 (1989), p. 440.
2. Stephen D. Krasner, 'State Power and the Structure of International Trade', *World Politics* 28 (1976), p. 317.
3. Leaver, 'Restructuring in the Global Economy', p. 438.
4. Nicolas Greenwood Onuf, *World of Our Making: Rules and Rule in Social Theory and International Relations* (Columbia, SC: University of South

Carolina Press, 1989); Richard E. Flathman, *The Practice of Political Authority: Authority and the Authoritative* (Chicago: University of Chicago Press, 1980).
5. Yale H. Ferguson and Richard W. Mansbach, *The State, Conceptual Chaos, and the Future of International Relations Theory* (Boulder, CO: Lynne Rienner, 1989), p. 14.
6. Stephen D. Krasner, *Defending the National Interest* (Princeton, NJ: Princeton University Press, 1978); Peter Katzenstein, *Between Power and Plenty* (Madison: University of Wisconsin Press, 1976); Eric Nordlinger, *On the Autonomy of the Democratic State* (Cambridge, MA: Harvard University Press, 1981); Theda Skocpol, *States and Social Revolution* (New York: Cambridge University Press, 1979); and Peter Evans, Dietrich Rueschemeyer, and Theda Skocpol (eds), *Bringing the State Back in* (Cambridge: Cambridge University Press, 1985).
7. Katzenstein, *Between Power and Plenty*, pp. 20–1.
8. G. John Ikenberry and David A. Lake, 'Introduction: Approaches to Explaining American Foreign Economic Policy', Special Issue *International Organization* 42 (1988), p. 12.
9. Jacek Kugler and William Domke, 'Comparing the Strength of Nations', *Comparative Political Studies* 19 (1986), pp. 39–69; Alan C. Lamborn, 'Power and the Politics of Extraction', *International Studies Quarterly* 27 (1983), pp. 125–46; A.F.K. Organski and Jacek Kugler, 'Davids and Goliaths: Predicting the Outcomes of International Wars', *Comparative Political Studies* 11 (1978), pp. 141–80.
10. Evenly B. Davidheiser, 'Strong States, Weak States: the Role of the State in Revolution', *Comparative Politics* 24 (1992), pp. 463–75.
11. James N. Rosenau, 'The State in an Era of Cascading Politics: Wavering Concept, Widening Competence, Withering Colossus, or Weathering Change?', in James A. Caporaso (ed.) *The Elusive State: International and Comparative Perspectives* (Newbury Park, CA: Sage, 1989), p. 19.
12. Stephen D. Krasner, 'Sovereignty: an Institutional Perspective', in Caporaso (ed.) *The Elusive State*, p. 70.
13. Michael Loriaux, 'Comparative Political Economy as Comparative History', *Comparative Politics* 21 (1989), p. 373.
14. See Robert Putnam, 'Diplomacy and Domestic Politics: the Logic of Two-Level Games', *International Organization* 42 (1988), pp. 427–60. A recent application is Leonard J. Schoppa's 'Two-level Games and Bargaining Outcomes: Why *Gaiatsu* Succeeds in Japan in Some Cases but not Others', *International Organization* 47 (1993), pp. 353–86. Early work in the negotiation-analytic approach was begun by Howard Raiffa in *The Art and Science of Negotiation* (Cambridge, MA: Harvard University Press, 1984). Further elaboration has followed in the work of James Sebenius in *Negotiating the Law of the Sea: Lessons in the Art and Science of Reaching Agreement* (Cambridge, MA: Harvard University Press, 1984), and 'Challenging Conventional Explanations of International Cooperation: Negotiation Analysis and the Case of Epistemic Communities', *International Organization* 46 (1992), pp. 323–65.

15. Loriaux, 'Comparative Political Economy', p. 355.
16. J.P. Nettl, 'The State as a Conceptual Variable', *World Politics* 20 (1968), p. 566.
17. Bruce Andrews, 'Social Rules and the State as a Social Actor', *World Politics* 27 (1975), p. 523.
18. Philippe Schmitter, 'Neo Corporatism and the State', in Wyn Grant (ed.) *The Political Economy of Corporatism* (New York: St. Martin's Press, 1985), p. 33.
19. Alexander E. Wendt, 'The Agent–Structure Problem in International Relations Theory', *International Organization* 41 (1987), p. 363.
20. Wendt, 'The Agent–Structure Problem', pp. 338, 337–8.
21. Mary Douglas, *Purity and Danger: an Analysis of Concepts of Pollution and Taboo* (London: Routledge & Kegan Paul, 1966); *Natural Symbols: Explorations in Cosmology* (New York: Pantheon Books, 1970); *Implicit Meanings: Essays in Anthropology* (London: Routledge & Kegan Paul, 1975); 'Cultural Bias', in Mary Douglas, *In the Active Voice* (London: Routledge & Kegan Paul, 1982); *How Institutions Think* (Syracuse: Syracuse University Press, 1986).
22. See, for example, the studies in Mary Douglas (ed.), *Essays in the Sociology of Perception* (London: Routledge & Kegan Paul, 1982); Mary Douglas and Baron Isherwood, *The World of Goods: Towards an Anthropology of Consumption* (New York: Basic Books, 1979); Mary Douglas and Aaron Wildavsky, *Risk and Culture: an Essay on the Selection of Technical and Environmental Dangers* (Berkeley: University of California Press, 1982); Richard Ellis and Aaron Wildavsky, *Dilemmas of Presidential Leadership: From Washington through Lincoln* (New Brunswick: Transaction Publishers, 1989); and Robert A. Atkins, Jr, *Egalitarian Community: Ethnography and Exegesis* (Tuscaloosa: University of Alabama Press, 1991).
23. Way of life refers to 'a viable combination of social relations ... defined as patterns of interpersonal relations ... and cultural bias [as] shared values and beliefs.' Michael Thompson, Richard Ellis and Aaron Wildavsky, *Cultural Theory* (Boulder: Westview Press, 1990), p. 1.
24. Thompson et al., *Cultural Theory*, pp. xiii–xiv.
25. Douglas, 'Cultural Bias', pp. 189–90.
26. Thompson et al., *Cultural Theory*, p. 5.
27. Douglas, 'Cultural Bias', p. 190.
28. Douglas, 'Cultural Bias', p. 190. Thompson et al. refer to shared values and beliefs as cultural bias. The two terms, cosmology and cultural bias, can be treated as synonymous.
29. Jonathan L. Gross and Steve Rayner, *Measuring Culture: a Paradigm for the Analysis of Social Organization* (New York: Columbia University Press, 1985), p. 5.
30. Thompson et al., *Cultural Theory*, p. 5.
31. Gross and Rayner, *Measuring Culture*, p. 5. Laswell and Kaplan make a similar point in their discussion of groups. For them, solidarity means an 'integration of diversified perspectives (thinking and feeling together)'. It is not just a number of individuals making the same demand,

A Theory of State–Non-state Actors 241

but a demand that is being made on behalf of oneself and others. H.D. Lasswell and A. Kaplan, *Power and Society* (New Haven, CT: Yale University Press, 1950), pp. 30–1.
32. Douglas and Isherwood, *The World of Goods*, p. 36.
33. Gross and Rayner, *Measuring Culture*, p. 6.
34. Douglas, *Natural Symbols*, p. viii. Thompson et al. argue that Douglas's two dimensions of 'sociality' capture 'the fundamental mathematical distinction in patterns of relationships: groups and networks'. The former pattern has already been noted. With respect to the latter, Thompson et al. write that 'if relationships are organized into networks, the pattern you trace out will be unique to the individual you have chosen.' This does not mean, however, that there are no patterns with networks. Groups of networks are commonly identified as markets. Thompson et al, *Cultural Theory*, pp. 11–12.
35. David Ostrander, 'One- and Two-Dimensional Models of the Distribution of Beliefs', in Mary Douglas (ed.), *Essays in the Sociology of Perception*, p. 26.
36. Douglas, 'Cultural Bias', p. 192.
37. Douglas, 'Cultural Bias', p. 202.
38. The same point is made by Atkins, *Egalitarian Community*, p. 65. Relations between grid and group are not *necessary*, or internal, meaning one can exist without the other. Master/slave is an example of a necessary relationship. See Andrew Sayer, *Method in Social Science: a Realist Approach* (London: Hutchinson Publishing, 1984), pp. 82, 84.
39. Atkins, *Egalitarian Community*, p. 64.
40. Thompson et al., *Cultural Theory*, p. 1.
41. Thompson et al., *Cultural Theory*, p. 130.
42. Roy Bhaskar, *The Possibility of Naturalism: a Philosophical Critique of the Contemporary Human Sciences* (Atlantic Highlands, NJ: Humanities Press, 1979), pp. 39–40.
43. Bhaskar, *The Possibility of Naturalism*, pp. 45–6.
44. Bhaskar, *The Possibility of Naturalism*, pp. 42–3.
45. Bhaskar, *The Possibility of Naturalism*, p. 45.
46. Granovetter correctly points out the undersocialized conception of human action developed by economists, and the oversocialized conception applied by some sociologists. Mark Granovetter, 'Economic Action and Social Structure: the Problem of Embeddedness', *American Journal of Sociology* 91 (November 1985), pp. 483, 487.
47. Bhaskar, *The Possibility of Naturalism*, p. 48.
48. Bhaskar, *The Possibility of Naturalism*, p. 47.
49. Thompson et al., *Cultural Theory*, p. 80.
50. Bhaskar makes a similar point in his discussion of the role of socialization in the reproduction and transformation of society. Bhaskar, *The Possibility of Naturalism*, pp. 45–6.
51. Douglas, 'Cultural Bias', p. 247.
52. Thompson et al., *Cultural Theory*, p. 272.
53. Thompson et al., *Cultural Theory*, p. 57.
54. Bhaskar, *The Possibility of Naturalism*, p. 48.

55. Gross and Rayner, *Measuring Culture*, p. 58. This classification scheme was first developed by philosophers Gilbert Ryle and Ludwig Wittgenstein.
56. For a discussion of the type-concepts and the creation of typologies, see Arthur L. Stinchcombe, *Constructing Social Theories* (Chicago: University of Chicago Press, 1968), pp. 43–6.
57. The predicates chosen for this study are based upon the earlier work of Gross and Rayner, *Measuring Culture*, and Atkins, *Egalitarian Community*. Adjustments have been made to account for the difference in subject matter.
58. Atkins, *Egalitarian Community*, p. 88.
59. Atkins, *Egalitarian Community*, p. 88.
60. Atkins, *Egalitarian Community*, pp. 87–91.
61. Gross and Rayner, *Measuring Culture*, p. 70.
62. Gross and Rayner, *Measuring Culture*, p. 70.
63. Atkins, *Egalitarian Community*, pp. 95–6; Gross and Rayner, *Measuring Culture*, p. 80.
64. Atkins, *Egalitarian Community*, p. 96.
65. Gross and Rayner, *Measuring Culture*, p. 81.
66. Atkins, *Egalitarian Community*, p. 101.
67. Douglas, 'Cultural Bias', pp. 202–3.
68. Thompson et al., *Cultural Theory*, p. 4.
69. Thompson et al., *Cultural Theory*, p. 93.
70. Thompson et al., *Cultural Theory*, pp. 105–7. See also Mary Douglas's discussion of functional explanations in *How Institutions Think*, pp. 31–43.
71. Stinchcombe, *Constructing Social Theories*, p. 80.
72. Sayer, *Method in Social Science*, p. 95.
73. For a discussion of the dangers associated with affirming the consequence, see Sayer, *Method in Social Science*, pp. 191–200.
74. Stinchcombe, *Constructing Social Theories*, p. 85.
75. Stinchcombe, *Constructing Social Theories*, p. 88.
76. Thompson et al., *Cultural Theory*, p. 208.
77. John C. McKinney, *Constructive Typology and Social Theory* (New York: Meredith Publishing, 1966), p. 18.
78. McKinney, *Constructive Typology*, p. 6.
79. McKinney, *Constructive Typology*, p. 7.
80. McKinney, *Constructive Typology*, p. 24. McKinney, while devising a typology of types, notes that all too often researchers mistakenly identify all types with Weber's ideal-types.
81. Sayer, *Method in Social Science*, p. 81.
82. McKinney, *Constructive Typology*, pp. 13, 62.
83. Victor C. Uchendu, *The Igbo of Southeast Nigeria* (New York: Holt, Rinehart and Winston, 1965), p. 16.
84. Douglas, 'Cultural Bias', p. 207.
85. Andrew Strathern, *The Rope of Moka: Big-Men and Ceremonial Exchange in Mount Hagen, New Guinea* (Cambridge: Cambridge University Press, 1971), pp. 187–8.
86. Bill Berkeley, 'An African Horror Story', *The Atlantic* 272 (August 1993), p. 23.

87. Bill Berkeley, 'An African Horror Story', p. 28.
88. Edward C. Banfield, *The Moral Basis of a Backward Society* (Glencoe, IL: Free Press, 1958).
89. Thompson et al., *Cultural Theory*, p. 7.
90. See Gary L. Downey, 'Ideology and the Clamshell Identity: Organizational Dilemmas in the Anti-Nuclear Power Movement', *Social Problems* 33 (1986), pp. 101–17; Emily Stoper, 'The Student Non-Violent Coordination Committee: Rise and Fall of a Redemptive Organization', in Jo Freeman (ed.) *Social Movements of the Sixties and Seventies* (New York: McKay, 1983); Andrea J. Baker, 'The Problem of Authority in Radical Movement Groups: a Case Study of Lesbian-Feminist Organizations', *The Journal of Applied Behavioral Science* 18 (1982), pp. 323–41.
91. These values are quite compatible with Jürgen Habermas's 'ideal speech situation', wherein every individual has the same chance to initiate and to perpetuate a truth-claim; to call statements into question; to express attitudes, feelings, and emotions. Each individual has the same chance to permit and forbid so that the norms that bind only one party are excluded. External authority is bracketed. The only source of authority is the speaker himself or herself. If these conditions were fulfilled, and if the only decisions reached were those in which complete consensus were achieved, then we could say that the outcome was fair, was equitable, and would be philosophically justified. (See Jürgen Habermas, *Legitimation Crisis* [Boston: Beacon Press, 1975].)
92. Stoper, 'Student Non-Violent Coordination Committee', p. 326.
93. Thompson et al., *Cultural Theory*, p. 262.
94. See Douglas and Wildavsky, *Risk and Culture*.
95. Thompson et al., *Cultural Theory*, p. 262.
96. Douglas, 'Cultural Bias', p. 206.
97. Thompson et al., *Cultural Theory*, p. 6.
98. Thompson et al., *Cultural Theory*, p. 46.
99. Thompson et al., *Cultural Theory*, p. 35.
100. Lasswell and Kaplan, *Power and Society*, p. 47.
101. Douglas, 'Cultural Bias', p. 200. The charge of deviance in personal behaviour levelled by some members of society against others may be traced to the fact that certain individuals behave in ways judged inconsistent or violations of the dominant way of life.
102. Douglas, 'Cultural Bias', p. 200.
103. Douglas, 'Cultural Bias', p. 192.
104. Onuf, *World of Our Making*, p. 22.
105. Onuf, *World of Our Making*, p. 85.
106. Onuf, *World of Our Making*, p. 87.
107. Onuf, *World of Our Making*, p. 88.
108. Onuf, *World of Our Making*, p. 85.
109. Onuf, *World of Our Making*, p. 121.
110. Onuf, *World of Our Making*, p. 123.
111. Onuf, *World of Our Making*, p. 114. Unlike the cultural model used here, with its grounding in grid and group, however, Onuf grants rules, or grid, primary consideration. For Onuf, groups are products

of sets of rules and thus can be subsumed under grid. Personal communication with Onuf, 27 August 1992.
112. Quoted by Onuf, *World of Our Making*, p. 58.
113. Onuf, *World of Our Making*, p. 97.
114. Onuf, *World of Our Making*, p. 120.
115. Onuf, *World of Our Making*, p. 118.
116. The difficulty is, how does one learn what is involved in making commitments unless one engages in the practice itself? Writes Onuf, 'Why would one risk rule practice in the absence of rule consciousness?' Onuf, *World of Our Making*, pp. 118, 120. This highlights the problem with Robert Axelrod's 'niceness' rule. Why would someone use this rule on the first play of a game unless he or she had had 'practice' with it? The niceness rule already requires what is to be investigated, the effectiveness of norms. Robert Axelrod, *The Evolution of Cooperation* (New York: Basic Books, 1984).
117. Onuf, *World of Our Making*, p. 136.
118. Onuf, *World of Our Making*, p. 139.
119. Onuf, *World of Our Making*, pp. 97, 121.
120. Onuf, *World of Our Making*, pp. 209–10.
121. Onuf, *World of Our Making*, p. 122.
122. Onuf, *World of Our Making*, p. 197.
123. Onuf, *World of Our Making*, p. 217.
124. Flathman, *The Practice of Political Authority*, p. 6.
125. Flathman, *Political Authority*, p. 80.
126. Flathman, *Political Authority*, p. 85.
127. Flathman, *Political Authority*, p. 76.
128. Flathman, *Political Authority*, p. 159.
129. Flathman, *Political Authority*, p. 26.
130. Flathman, *Political Authority*, p. 157.
131. Flathman, *Political Authority*, p. 158.
132. Flathman, *Political Authority*, p. 129.
133. Flathman, *Political Authority*, p. 6. Lasswell and Kaplan make a similar point when they argue that limits to power may be set by technical factors and by the social order. Mores, meaning cultural traits, may set boundaries and thereby limit the scope of power. Lasswell and Kaplan, *Power and Society*, pp. 95–6.
134. Flathman, *Political Authority*, p. 130.
135. Flathman, *Political Authority*, p. 161.
136. This position echoes the arguments made by David Baldwin on the nature of power. 'Power Analysis and World Politics: New Trends Versus Old Tendencies', *World Politics* 31 (1979), pp. 161–94.
137. Robin Cantor, Stuart Henry and Steve Rayner, *Making Markets: An Interdisciplinary Perspective on Economic Exchange* (Westport, CT: Greenwood Press, 1992)
138. Cantor et al., *Making Markets*, pp. 21, 23.
139. Cantor et al., *Making Markets*, pp. 23, 24.
140. A somewhat similar point is made by Mitchell, 'The Limits of the State'.
141. Kenneth Waltz, *Theory of International Politics* (Reading, MA: Addison-Wesley, 1979), p. 94.

Index

accountability, 220
accumulation, social structures, 72
action, teleological, 100
aesthetics, 101, 102
affirmative action, 144
agency, human, 96
ahistoricism, 15
Almond, Gabriel, 2
Amarna letters, 119
Analects, 92, 103
anarchy, 95–6, 108
anti-rationalism, 100
apology, 124
Aquinas, Thomas, 108
Arab-Israeli War 1967, 187
arbitration, 117, 128
Aristotle, 100
Aron, Raymond, 105
articulation, high-/low-context, 121
ASEAN, 122
asymmetry, in role exchange, 220
Australia, 121; *see also* Keating, Paul
authority, acceptance/rejection of, 234
authority–market relationship, 235–7
autonomy, 31, 164, 220
awareness, detached, 102

banks, international, 206
behaviour, controls on, 219; cultural, 159–63; maximizing, 37; rule-guided 230
Beitz, Charles, 71
Bentham, Jeremy, 102
Bhaskar, Roy, 216, 217, 218
binarism, 5
black power movement, 136, 143
blame-shedding, 227
blood feuds, 126
borer, 127
boundaries, 11, 20–1, 146–51, 165–6; and access to wealth 75; conflicts 165; core/periphery, 146; as

economic units 71; feudal, 20; group, 213; impermeability, 219; linear, 20; markers, 219; sovereign, 71; and territoriality, 146
Bourdieu, Pierre, 3, 4
Bozeman, Adda, 106
British Mandate in Palestine, 128
Bull, Hedley, 62, 69, 76, 104

Camp David strategy, 130
capital accumulation, 70
capitalism, 61
Carr, E.H., 91
Carter, Jimmy, 130
caste, 28, 214, 232
Center on International Race Relations, 137
central banks, 18
China, 134
Chinese philosophy, 90–109
Chirac, Jacques, 134
Christendom, 69
Chuang Tzu, 99–100, 101, 102
citizenship, 150
civic culture, 2
civil conflict, 199–200
civilizations, clash of, 24
Clamshell Alliance, 225
classification, polythetic, 218
Clausewitz, Claus von, 96
coercion, 76
Coetsee, Jacobus, 174
coexistence, non-violent, 108
Cohen, Raymond, 39
Cold War, 22, 188
collectivism, 121
colonization, 77
commitment-rules, 230, 232
common sense, local, 39; shared, 117
commonality of experience, 219
communication, 37; intergroup, 160

communication theory, 138
competition, 61–80; economic, 72; global, 73; military 74; strategic, 75–6
Concert of Europe, 21, 77
conciliation, 127, 128
conflict, 91, 159–60; behaviour, 162; cultural, 62; escalation, 168–9; intergroup, 160; interstate, 96–7; resolution, 116–31
Confucianism, 92–6, 103–6
Confucius, 97, 102, 103, 106
consociationalism, 31
constructivism, 12, 13, 15, 65
control, social, 219
conventions, 117
cosmic order, 105
courtesy, 123
Cox, Robert, 95
critical theory, 90, 91, 95, 102
culture, 160–1; adaptation, 6; awareness, 55; civic, 2; coherency, 4; of competition, 62 and ch. 4 passim; of conflict, 62, 157, 161–3; definition, 2, 64, 190; difference, 35; diplomatic, 38; domination, 91; high/low-context, 121; homogeneity, 91; of international conflict, 163–7; invisible, 36; as meaning, 116–18; national, 2; v. nature, 65; tribal, 40
customs, 117, 161
Cyprus, 197

Dante, A., 108
de Klerk, F.W., 173
decision-making, consensual, 122; intuitive, 100; maximizing, 37
decolonization, 150
defence, group, 157
deferential involvement, 219
dependence, mutual, 72
Derrida, Jacques, 109, 144
Deutsch, Karl, 108, 136, 138, 139, 166
diplomacy, 38–9; and power politics, 106
directive-rules, 230, 232

discourse, 109; rational, 100; war and peace, 96
discrimination, 28
dispute management, Arab-Israeli, 128
disputes, intercultural, 119
dissonance, cultural, 122
division of labour, global, 61
dominance, 118
Douglas, Mary, 211, 212, 214
Du Bois, W.E.B., 141
dualism, 94, 101
Durkheim Emile, 216

economic growth, 70
economic order, international, 72
egalitarianism, 3, 215, 225–6
egoism, 102
elites, 28, 30
Enlightenment, 101
entitlement, 220
environment, symbolic, 188
epistemology, 107
equality, 69–70
ethics, 97
ethnic cleansing, 37
ethnic conflict/strife, 28, 156–81, 199; and identity, 167–71; intransigent, 171
ethnic interest, 157
ethnicity, 27–8, 142
ethnocentrism, 41, 90–3, 157; and language, 119
Eurocentricity, 15
European Union, 22, 31, 150
exclusion, 145, 213, 219
expectations, cultural, 161
expulsion, 219

face-saving, 123
fatalism, 3, 215, 224–5
fate, common, 170
Fiji, 134
Fischer, Markus, 95
Flathman, Richard, 233–5
force, 77
force majeure, 39, 40
Foucault, Michel, 97–8, 99, 144, 147
'fragemegration', 22, 31

Index

France, 175–80
free association, 46
freedom, individual, 105
Fukuyama, Francis, 23, 28
functionalism, 91, 221

Gaza, 187
Geertz, Clifford, 117, 160
Gellner, Ernest, 28
gender, 28
general theory of action, 2
Giddens, Anthony, 108
Gilpin, Robert, 100
Giscard d'Estaing, Valéry, 34
globalization, 62
Great Powers, 76
grid predicates, 220–2
grid–group theory, 3, 4, 207, 211–38
grid–group typology, 212
Gross, Leo, 69
Grotius, Hugo, 16, 97
group boundaries, 213
group defence, 157
group identity, 157, 170
Group of 7, 77
group predicates, 219
Guatemala, 199
Gulf War, 39, 40

Habermas, Jürgen, 102
habitus, 4
Han Fei Tzu, 97
Hayek, Friedrich, 63, 65, 66, 72
hegemony, 231
Henry, Patrick, 26
hierarchies, 3, 66, 124; in Chinese culture, 104–5; competitive, 73–4; political communities, 74
hierarchy, 215, 226
hijib, dispute on France, 176–80
Hobbes, Thomas, 91, 97, 103, 104
Hofstede, Geert, 3, 121
holism, 98
Holsti, K.J., 90, 96
honour, 124
Hui Shih, 100
humility, 123
Huntington, Samuel, 24, 62

Hussein, Sadam, 21, 39
Husseini, Hibi, 128, 130

idealism, 36
identity, 5, 70, 145, 146–51; and conflict escalation, 168–9; and difference, 144; ethnic, 37; gendered, 144; group, 157, 170; in-group, 161; multiple, 23; national, 150, 165, 166–7; out-group, 161; shared, 161; within-group, 170
illegal aliens, 150
immigration, Third World, 134
in-groups, 157; identity, 161
India, 197
individualism, 3, 121, 23–4, 215
Indonesia, 122
inequality and race, 143
instinct, 100, 102
Institutionalists, 12–13
institutionalization, 231
instruction-rule, 229, 231
instructive-rules, 230
interests, 160
international theory, 97; classical, 90–1
intifadah, 128
involvement, differential, 219
Iraq, 40
irredentism, 37
Islam, fundamentalism, 177
Israel, 121, 125–30, 173
Italy, 18, 34; immigration, 134

Jerusalem Institute for Arbitration, 128, 130
Jospin, Lionel, 177, 178

Kant, Immanuel, 97, 102, 104
Kaptchuk, Ted, 99
Keating, Paul, 120–1, 123–5
Kelman, Herb, 131
Keohane, Robert, 13–14
Kerner Commission, 136
kinship, 157
Kissinger, Henry, 34–5
Kluckhohn, Clyde, 117

Krasner, Stephen, 209
Kung-sun Lung, 100
Kurds, 165

Lacan, Jacques, 144
laissez-faire, 105
language, 92, 117–19
Lao Tzu, 101, 108
law, international, 15
League of Nations, 77
Lebanon, 197
legal systems, 220
lexical analysis, 118
Liberia, 200
lingua franca, 120
litigation, 117, 126
Liverani, Mario, 119
Locke, John, 103, 104
logos, 100
loyalties, 23, 29

Machiavelli, Nicolò, 91
Mahathir, Mohamad, 120, 123–5
Malaysia, 120–5
Malinowski, Bronislaw, 91
Mandela, Nelson, 173, 174
markets, 67–8
Marshall Islands, 43
Martin, Lisa, 13–14
meanings, shared, 160
Mearsheimer, John, 13, 14
mediation, 6, 117, 130
mediators, 125; Arabic, 126; Jewish, 127
memory, historical, 23
meta-racism, 151
metanarratives, 91
metaphor, 160, 170, 171, 172–3
Micronesia, 44–5
migrant workers, 150
migrants, North African, 175–80
mindsets, 4
mini-nationalism, 22–3
Mitterrand, François, 176
Mo Tzu, 103, 105
modernity, 147–8
modernization, 74
Mohism, 100; and anarchy, 108
Morganthau, Hans, 91, 97, 101

mourning, 173–4
mufakat (unanimous decision), 122
multiculturalism, 15, 24
multinational corporations, 22, 206
musyawarah (consultation), 122, 123
myths, 166; national, 29

NAFTA, 22
narratives, 5
Nasser, Gamal, 187
nation-states, 27, 28
National Front (France), 176
national identity, 166–7
national myths, 29
nationalism, 27
NATO, 22
nature, 104, 108, 227; and anarchy, 108; as mirror of society, 227; state of, 103, 104
negotiation, 117; international, 37, 38
neorealism, 12, 89–106
Neumann, Ivor, 5
'new racism', 151
new world order, 188, 189
NGOs, 22
Nietzsche, F.W., 91, 95
non-state actors, 16, 206–38
norms, 162
North/South relations, 135, 150
Northern Ireland, 158, 170, 173

Onuf, Nicholas, 229–33
oppression, 29
order, global, 105; societal, 97; universal, 105
ostracism, 230
out-group identity, 161

Pakistan, 197
Palau, 40, 42–55; Americanization 45; bilateral competition, 51; *bital ma bital*, 51, 54; constitution, 47; leadership, 53–5; *Olbiil Era Kalulau*, 55; ranked hierarchy, 51; –US status negotiations, 41–2
Palestine, 125–30, 173
Parsons, Talcott, 2, 221

Index

Patrushev, Pyotr, 131
peace, 102, 107
Peace Corps volunteers, 45
peacekeeping, 187–201
Philippines, 122
philosophy, Chinese 92–109; French 91; transcendent, 94; western, 91, 97, 102
pluralism, cultural, 62
policy choices and outcomes, 210
political economy, international, 61–80
politics, domestic, 37; global, 27
polity, 26
Popper, Karl, falsification test, 101
positivism, 139
post-materialism, 4
poststructuralism, 109, 144
poverty, as cause of violence, 29
power, 35–6, 234; asymmetry, 40; balance of, 36; inequalities, 76; relationship, 234
power distance, 121–2
power politics, and diplomacy, 106; realist, 93
prisoners' dilemma, 162
privilege holders, 229–30
procedures, and intercultural disputes, 119
property ownership, 67
property rights, 72
psycho-cultural analysis, 167–74
punishment, 219, 230; acceptance/rejection of, 234

race, 4, 5, 28 134–52; categories, 144; conceptualizing, 140–5; and inequality, 143; and International Relations, 137; and regional integration, 128; and self-identification, 128; social nature of, 144
race riots, 134
racial codes, 144
racism, 134, 136, 144
Radcliff-Brown, Alfred, 91
rational choice theory, 158
realism, 12, 35, 163–4

reality, 101–2; socially constructed, 91, 93–6
reason, 100, 102, 107; and Tao, 103
reconciliation, 126
reductionism, 97
refugees, 150
representation, cultural, 64; symbolic, 118
resources allocation, 73, 219
rites of reversal, 190
ritual, 102, 126, 161, 166, 190; group, 219
ritual behaviour, 190
rituals, peacekeeping, 195–6
role access and exchange, 220
Rosenau, James, 22, 137–8, 208–9
Rothman, Jay, 131
Rousseau, Jean-Jacques, 91, 104
Ruggie, John, 146, 147
rules, 16, 213, 228–33; primacy of, 230

Sadat, Anwar, 173
Sahlins, Peter, 20, 21
sameness, 36
sample surveys, 2
Schlesinger, James, 44
Schwartz, Benjamin, 104
security dilemmas, 75, 102, 107
self-determination, 28, 71; claims, to, 164; national, 165
self-help, 61, 71, 75
self-interest, national, 163
signs, 117
slavery, 143, 149
Smith, Adam, 73
Smith, Anthony, 28
social change, 3
social construction, 63–5
social environment, 215
social justice, 102
social life, 65
social mapping, 215
social mobility, 67
social reality, 230
social relations, organization of, 4

social solidarity, 219
socialization, 6, 167
societies, differentiating, 166–7; generalizing, 166, 167
society, Christian, 69–70
Somalia, 200
Sophism, 100
South Africa, 134, 174–5
sovereign states, 15; equality of, 69
sovereignty, 15, 68, 70; racial, 148
speech-acts, 229
Spinoza, Benedict, 104
spontaneity, 100
Sri Lanka, 134, 158, 173
standardization, 220
state theory, 15
state, definition of, 164–5; reification of, 18–20; role of, 207–11; as social entity, 210
state-centrism, 30, 206
state–society boundaries, 209
state–society complex, 207, 217
Stevans, John Paul, 26
Stevenson, Adlai, 137
structural-realist theory, 95
Student Non-Violent Coordinating Committee, 225
subcultures, 3
subsidiarity, 31
Suez War, 187
symbols, 117, 118, 119, 166; peacekeeping, 191–5

taboos, 219
Taoism, 92, 100; and anarchy, 108
teleology, 100
territoriality, 146
theory-building, 101
Third World immigrants, 134
Thirty Years' War, 21
Thomas, Clarence, 26
Thucydides, 15, 91
Tilly, Charles, 71
time, nonlinear, 99
trading state, 72
translation, 119–20

transnationalism, 30
traumas, chosen, 170–1
Treaty of Versailles, 21
truth, ahistorical, 91
turbulence, 22

UN Emergency Force, 187
UN Interim Force in Lebanon, 197
UN Military Observer Group in India and Pakistan, 197
UN Peacekeeping Force in Cyprus, 197
UN Truce Supervision Organization, 192
uniformitarianism, 36
United Nations, 21, 22, 77, 136–7; Charter, 21, 28; Military Observers, 193; peacekeeping forces, 4, 187; peacekeeping missions, 187; Security Council, 78, 188
United States, 121; US-Palau relations, 42–55
United States Trust Territory of the Pacific Islands, 43
universal order, 105
utilitarianism, 102
utility maximization, 36, 100

values, 4; common, 69; shared, 230
Verba, Sydney, 2
violence, 29–30; resolution, 6; racial, 134; revolutionary, 21; state, 16–17
virtue, 108

Waltz, Kenneth, 96–9, 101–2
war, 102, 107
Washington Institute of Multitrack Diplomacy, 131
Watson, Adam, 62
wealth creation, 70, 71
wealth expansion, 73
wealth, global, 71–2
Weber, Max, 16, 100

welfare, economic, 61
Wendt, Alexander, 13, 14, 15, 96
West African Peacekeeping Force, 200
Westphalia, Peace of, 15, 16, 21, 69; model, 30
Wight, Martin, 102
Wilson, Woodrow, 21
wisdom, 100, 102

world economy, 61, 71, 72
worldviews, 160

xenophobia, 134; in France, 176–80

Yin–Yang School, 94–100

Zilberman, Ifrah, 128, 130
Zimbabwe, 199